Team Building *for* Quality

Transitions
in the
American
Community
College

George A. Baker III
and Associates

Published by the Community College Press, a division of the
American Association of Community Colleges
One Dupont Circle, N.W.
Suite 410
Washington, D.C. 20036
(202) 728-0200

ISBN 0-87117-286-0

DEDICATION

I t would be easy to dedicate this book to a person. A team wrote the book, however, and on whom could we all agree as the single person most deserving of such an honor? We could dedicate this book to a concept. Perhaps we could dedicate this collective work to the twin concepts of team building and quality. These concepts seem to be driving community colleges to provide increased access and more effective learning. We could dedicate this work to the process of change. We would focus on the forces moving us ever onward toward a future not yet fully in our vision. We will settle on the concept of forces. We choose to dedicate this book to the collective entities and their representatives that we believe move the enterprise of the community college both haltingly and expectantly forward toward the millennium:

To the American Association of Community Colleges, the leaders, components, staff, and members, and especially to the last three presidents: Edmund J. Gleazer, Jr., Dale Parnell, and David R. Pierce, and to the recently retired vice president of 15 years, Connie Odems. To our Canadian friends in the Association of Canadian Community Colleges.

To the legendary American community college presidents and chancellors who have provided leadership, structures, and paradigms for others to follow. Examples are Karen Bowyer, Dwight Burrill, Donald Cameron, Charles J. Carlsen, Richard DeCosmo, Robert DeHart, Paul Elsner, Geraldine Evans, Ronald Horvath, Helena Howe, Lee Howser, James Hudgins, Maxwell King, Paul Kreider, Albert Lorenzo, Robert H. McCabe, Richard McDowell, Judy Merritt, David Ponitz, Ruth Shaw, Lawrence Tyree, and Joyce Tsunoda. To Canadian community college leaders such as Roy Giroux and Robert Gordon.

To the new generation of American and Canadian presidents who are quickening the pace of transition to quality. Examples are Cathryn Addy, Liz Ashton, Walter Bumphus, Susan Carroll, Charles Dassance, Greg DeCinque, Allen Edwards, Deborah Lee Floyd, Lee Howser, Doug MacRae, Jan Mose, Beverly Simone, Ann Stephenson, Jerry Sue Thornton, Arnette Ward, and Belle Wheelan.

To the community college leaders who left or joined our ranks to lead from the foundations, state systems offices, and in the halls of government. These leaders include Betty Duvall, Judith Eaton, Geraldine Evans, Robert Lahti, Jan LeCroy, Michael McCall, Kay McClenney, David Mertes, James Morris, Arnold Oliver, Donald Puyear, and Robert Scott.

To the community college presidents who moved into the professoriate and who daily help us to tie theory to practice. Anne Mulder, Joshua Smith, and George Vaughan are examples.

To the prolific researchers in the community college who have shifted from the profit sector to the public sector and kept us on the cutting edge of technology and theory; people such as Richard Alfred, Frances Brawer, Burton Clark, Arthur Cohen, K. Patricia Cross, William Deegan, John Dennison, Paul L. Gallagher, B. Lamar Johnson, Dorothy Knoell, Abe Konrad, Jane Matson, Leland Medsker, Terry O'Banion, Richard Richardson, John Roueche, Dale Tillery, and James Wattenbarger provide us with grist for our mill, and we thank you.

To the hundreds of men and women who have worked to become community college chief executive officers but await their turn.

To the community college teachers, such as the Carnegie Foundation for the Advancement of Teaching 1994 Community College Awardees: Anthony P. Pitucco (Pima Community College), Maxine Sample (DeKalb College), Lynda Jerit (Oakton Community College), Carolyn Neptune (Johnson County Community College), Vashti Muse (Hinds Community College), James Banks (Cuyahoga Community College), and Ellen Kay Miller (Tulsa Junior College), we pledge our dedication and support.

Finally, to the students who are enrolled in the more than 1,200 community colleges in the east from Maine to Florida and in the west from Alaska to Hawaii and the more than 200 Canadian community colleges and postsecondary institutions from the Arctic Circle to the Northwest Territories and to Newfoundland, we dedicate this book.

North America's future workforce is preparing for the next century in our high schools and community colleges today. Many of these students will soon enter the workforce, and many are already in the workforce while involved in formal education. All that is and all that will be in the community college movement is dedicated to your success.

George A. Baker III
February 1995
Writing for the team

CONTENTS

PREFACE

his book is the fulfillment of a vision to put in the hands of community college practitioners and researchers a set of chapters to help community colleges make the transition to quality. My colleagues and I have been pursuing this vision quite deliberately since John Roueche, Dick Brownell, and I wrote *Accountability and the Community College* for the American Association of Community Colleges (then AACJC) in 1970–1972. From 1978 to 1992, while at the University of Texas, John Roueche and I conceptualized, researched, and wrote a series of books on the general theme of access and excellence. We wrote *Access and Excellence: The Open Door College* with the research team of Patricia Mullins and Nancy Omahaboy. With the research team of Rosemary Gillett-Karam, Mary Ann Roe, and Robert Rose we wrote *Shared Vision: Transformational Leadership in American Community Colleges*. We wrote *Teaching and Leading: Profiles of Excellence in the Open-Door College*, based on a massive research study of American and Canadian teachers, with Rosemary Gillett-Karam, supported by Millicent Valek, Joe Barwick, Charlotte Biggerstaff, Eli Eric Peña, Anita Janis, and John Rucker. From 1991–1992, I worked with several doctoral students to publish the results of their dissertations. Charlotte Biggerstaff, Tessa Martinez (Tagle) Pollack, Mary Ann Roe, Rosemary Gillett-Karam, Eli Peña, Michele Nelson, Phyllis Barber, and G. Allan Clark wrote chapters in *Cultural Leadership: Inside America's Community Colleges*. In 1992, I undertook the mission of organizing the first *Handbook on the Community College in America*. This volume, centering on historical and management themes, consisted of ten parts and more than fifty chapters. North American researchers and practitioners wrote the work; aided ably by Judy Dudziak and Peggy Tyler, we edited and organized this volume for the Greenwood Press for worldwide distribution.

Judy Dudziak and I started work on this book in 1994. We organized the themes around quality and team building. We asked leading practitioners in community colleges to integrate quality and team building into various structural or thematic aspects of the American community college. The titles and affiliations of the chapter writers are included with their chapters. Vaughn Upshaw and I researched and developed an overall framework for the book and subsequently provided it to the chapter writers and asked each to develop a particular chapter from our conceptual structure. Chapter 1 is titled "A Team Approach to Institutional Quality: Toward a Model." Our model consisted of seven dimensions, all surrounding the central theme of quality teams. These themes are: culture and commitment, organizational mission, systems thinking, team membership, processes, communication, and outcomes and rewards. Our research led us to conceptualize how these dimensions could be applied in functional teams, which comprise the formal structure of the college, and to cross-functional teams that are established across various roles of the college to deal with systemic problems, such as student retention or registration.

The next seven chapters follow the organizational structure from a hierarchical perspective. George Boggs, who writes "The President and the Board: A Team of Leaders," begins this chapter by stating, "No single relationship in an organization is as important as that between the board and its chief executive officer." This chapter illuminates definitions of trustees, membership of boards, institutional mission, and the relationship of the CEO and the board to this concrete vision of the college. The meat of this chapter is in the powerful descriptions of how CEOs and boards work together to understand the culture of the college and to form it while at the same time committing to it. Boggs brings great insight to CEO and board processes and communications, systems thinking, and the outcomes and rewards enjoyed by these leaders when they succeed in collectively influencing the direction of the college through teamwork and quality concepts. The reader should realize that applying the concepts of team building and quality varies with the size and complexity of the organization.

Chancellor Jeff Hockaday and Philip Silvers wrote the chapter "The Chancellor and the Multicampus Team: An Application of Life Cycle Theory," in which they apply some of the recently advanced organizational theories to the day-to-day reality of leading a large, multicampus community college from 1990 to 1994.

Hockaday and Silvers employ the concept of organizational climate to discuss the state of the district before Hockaday's arrival in 1990. The chapter tracks the projects, processes, and results of the leader-initiated change from 1990 to 1994. Mission evaluation, decentralization, leadership development, strategic planning, adjunct faculty upgrade, development of departmental chairs, program review, and the development of student outcome measures provide a framework for analysis. The second part of the chapter demonstrates how quality concepts, supported by systems thinking and team building, became the major tools by which the college culture was changed.

In Chapter 4, George Boggs takes another look at the community college structure through the lens of "The President and the Executive Leadership Team: Solving Strategic Problems." Boggs follows the framework, as developed in Chapter 1, to develop a rationale for membership on the executive leadership team and relates ways that the CEO and the team can affect the culture of the organization. He discusses how teamwork between the CEO and the board can increase commitment to the college and its mission, and he addresses organizational processes, such as the use of systems thinking, to infuse quality through teamwork. He describes how teams conduct meetings and use communication processes. Mission, goals, outcomes, and rewards are presented within the framework of quality and teamwork. The chapter concludes with insights into Boggs's coaching and leading style.

In Chapter 5, Sandra Acebo and her team present an overview and several organizational perspectives from team leaders of various functional and cross-functional teams. Kathleen Burson writes about quality and team building from the line position as dean of an academic unit. Cyril Gulassa develops his portion of the chapter from the perspective of leading the faculty association. Sharon Miller emphasizes the dean of instruction's role within general education and liberal arts, and Chris Storer applies team-building and quality concepts to the role of secretary to the academic senate.

Marguerite Culp explores the use of the team approach in transforming student services in the community college in Chapter 6. Culp develops a philosophical framework and conveys how the team created a climate for change. She describes the quality tools employed in the change process and tells how the student services team grew into a quality-oriented division. She explains how team members created partnerships and improved program outcomes. Her chapter concludes with a section on how team members became empowered through working together for change designed to improve student service.

Lester Reed, after almost thirty years' experience in resource management, presents Chapter 7, titled "The Team Approach to Managing Resources: An Open Systems Approach," in which he reports that, before the mid-1980s, the chief business officer in community colleges frequently played a solo role in the management of human and nonhuman resources. He concludes that, once resources began to be restricted, other administrators became interested in how resource allocation was determined. This chapter demonstrates how participative management ideas and the development of resource allocation teams were employed in one college in order to gain increased commitment to the collective management of resources. Reed employs several examples of new resource management techniques, such as adjunct faculty management, new construction, and registration, describing how these concepts became reengineered through the application of team and quality initiatives.

In the community college system of North Carolina, Southwestern Community College is recognized as one of the leaders in making the transition to quality through the use of participative leadership and quality concepts. Barry Russell, the president of Southwestern Community College, and Constance Haire, director of resource and community development at the college, have written Chapter 8, "Team Building, Quality Initiatives, and Strategic Planning: A Consolidated Approach, which is a case study of a small rural community college that has been moving toward quality since the early 1990s. This chapter demonstrates how short lines of communication and smaller institutions can, under participative leadership, achieve tremendous change in a short period. As the title suggests, the chapter shows how team building, quality processes, and strategic planning were neatly organized to move the institution toward total quality management ideals. This chapter concludes the section of the book written from a formal structure perspective.

Chapters 9 and 10 provide opportunities for the reader to gain insight into the operation of cross-functional teams within a community college organizational structure. Helen Burnstad and Amy Lee Fugate show how the staff and professional development area of the college can be organized into effective teams to manage the most important assets of the college, its human resources. The writers follow the outline from Chapter 1 to relate how mission, systems thinking, team membership, decision processes, communication, and outcomes and rewards can provide a framework for discussion on the operation of an area of the college that enjoys major interest of all employees.

Chapter 10 focuses us on the twin issues of gender and equity in the American community college. Rosemary Gillett-Karam, one of the most prolific community college writers on these issues, provides a rationale for ensuring that quality teams include representatives of the gender and ethnic diversity of the institution. She reviews the literature on work-team effectiveness, team building, trust development within the team, communication processes, change theory, collaboration, and conflict resolution. Her thesis is that careful consideration to balanced representation in the structuring of teams is the best evidence of the institution's highest commitment to gender and ethnicity equity.

The book concludes with a chapter that focuses on the two keys in the operating core of the community college. In the quality and team-building movement as it applies to education, the relationship between students and instructors is critical. This chapter should be read by those who administer academic programs and especially by those who are assigned to prepare today's and tomorrow's quality workforce. George Baker and Ann Doty present a collaborative learning model for teachers and students in the community college. This model includes a discussion of how the organization can support student learning and how faculty can use team-building and quality concepts to prepare students for higher education and the world of work. The idea of systems thinking as it applies to the environment, the student, the teacher, and the instruction is overlaid with the concepts of collaborative learning and quality initiatives.

Team Building for Quality: Transitions in the American Community College is an extremely timely book. Few books exist on the use of quality and team building in higher education. Most higher education practitioners must read material written for consumption in business and industry. Often, the translations from organizations designed to manufacture products and organizations that provide service for profit provide poor paradigms for practitioners in higher education. The authors of this book trust that our efforts will provide clear directions and useful organizational studies that will help community colleges make the transition to quality successfully.

If the community college is to become America's best hope for preparing a literate and competent knowledge worker as we race toward the millennium, we cannot fail in our attempts to change our institutions to be not only the best bargain in higher education but also the institution that customers, taxpayers, and employers of our graduates and former students most respect.

George A. Baker
Raleigh, North Carolina
February 1995

CHAPTER 1

A TEAM APPROACH TO INSTITUTIONAL QUALITY

Toward a Model

GEORGE A. BAKER III
VAUGHN MAMLIN UPSHAW

Introduction

Many organizations are discovering that an effective way to improve institutional performance is to establish quality teams. By employing team concepts within the existing units and designing new teams that extend across functions, organizational leaders can create and empower new working relationships. Before creating teams, however, leaders must gain their own commitment and the commitment of others to improve both outcomes and the processes by which outcomes are achieved. Juran (1992) outlines a trilogy of concepts which, when applied in conjunction with one another, constitute a framework for institutional quality: quality planning, quality control, and quality improvement. Juran further notes that planning begins with a commitment to quality and meeting customer needs. For quality planning to occur, it is essential to know who the customers are, what their needs are, and what products, services, and processes respond to these needs. After identifying and diagnosing customer needs, the organization assesses its actual performance by conducting baseline studies and then compares its success at meeting customer needs with its performance goals. The differences between the organization's actual performance and its goals become the new targets for quality improvement.

1

Quality improvement takes place when leaders develop the processes for identifying what will be improved, then establish teams that have been charged with clear goals and expected outcomes for improving service and outcomes for customers. To be effective, leaders must ensure that teams have the necessary resources, motivation, and training to diagnose problems, stimulate remedies, and establish standards.

Approaches to quality might address specific processes within an institution or extend beyond the organization to directly involve customers, suppliers, and oversight agencies. The type of quality initiative selected depends largely upon the leader's style, perspective, and level of commitment. A commitment to quality improvement goes hand-in-hand with a commitment to team development and a means for collecting and making decisions with current information (Scholtes, 1988). Any commitment to improving institutional quality should further the existing institutional mission.

Leaders must decide whether a quality initiative will be applied across the organization, within a specific division, or beyond the organization. Two ways that quality teams can be introduced into the organization are by employing team concepts within existing structural units and by creating teams that operate across the organization's existing structure. Baker (1994) provides a higher education example of a quality team working to improve student retention that involves all units of the college. This cross-functional team could be made up of stakeholders from units across the organization who are involved in recommending policy or procedures that collectively affect student retention. Baker acknowledges that cross-functional teams are harder to implement, require more time, and need greater support from institutional leaders than do functional teams. The advantage, however, is that cross-functional teams increase the leader's ability to resolve institutional problems that cut across functional areas, increase motivation of participants, and generate permanent solutions.

Establishing teams to improve quality has gained acceptance as evidence has grown demonstrating that groups often "make more accurate decisions, but are often slower than individuals" (Hampton, Summer & Webber, 1987). Quality improvements take time because quality processes typically involve complex issues. Baker's (1994) research supports the fact that groups will typically take as much as five times longer than individuals to make decisions on identical problems. The payoff is that complex problems are better resolved by groups that represent a range of expertise capable of proposing and implementing appropriate and lasting solutions. A team, according to Scholtes (1988), is "a group of people pooling skills, talents, and knowledge" (pp. 2–7). Teams typically enjoy advantages over individuals acting alone because teams take advantage of the range of skills, talents, and expertise of all their members to meet performance objectives.

Many factors account for the greater accuracy of group-developed decisions over individual decisions. Maier (1967) finds groups at an advantage over individuals because groups have a greater sum total of knowledge; a greater number of approaches to a problem; more participation in problem solving, which leads to greater acceptance; and a better understanding of the decisions when made. Yukl (1994) expands upon the advantages of teams within organizations, pointing out that teams improve commitment, quality, and efficiency and lower costs, absenteeism, and turnover. Acebo (1994a) writes, "Indeed, the most important value of the team is that it can produce results: Through the diverse talents of its members, an end product will be created that is beyond the capability of the members acting individually" (p. 583). Team building is a complicated process, and realizing the advantages of quality teamwork depends upon the interplay of many different factors. The formal leader should ensure that the team is properly constituted, charged with the right tasks, and most importantly, structured so that the team is aware of its role to make decisions or to make recommendations. Some of the most important factors to consider before implementing a team approach in institutions are presented in the discussion that follows.

Toward a Model

This chapter describes the decisions that precede a quality initiative and focuses on principles central to developing teams of various types. Spanbauer (1992) describes one type of team as "the planning group and focal point of activity for the quality process" (p. 10). Baker (1994) considers this structure to be most appropriate as the president's leadership team or the president-board leadership team.

What are the most important factors to consider in setting up a functional or cross-functional team in an institution? Five professionals experienced with total quality initiatives answered this question in June 1994: Sandy Acebo, vice president for instruction at DeAnza College, California; George A. Baker III, J.D. Moore professor, North Carolina State University; Kathy Baker-Smith, North Carolina Department of Community Colleges; Loretta Harper, assistant vice chancellor for human resources, North Carolina State University; Carole Schwinn, Jackson Community College, Michigan; and Tim Todd, director of outreach and development, Graduate School, North Carolina State University.

Interviews with these experts in universities and community colleges revealed that the following principles are important in developing quality teams: support the existing system; understand the organization's culture; develop commitment to quality and teams starting at the top; select team members carefully; clearly articulate the quality team mission, purpose, and authority; structure the quality team to develop and monitor its own work process; foster relationships and communication; and provide regular feedback on outcomes and rewards. The framework shown in Figure 1.1 provides an overview of these components as they relate to developing teams in institutions:

Figure 1.1
Framework for Establishing Quality Teams

Teams can exist in two environments within organizations. The first of these, a *functional* team, exists within a single unit, has members largely from within the unit, and focuses on improving services and processes within the unit. A *cross-functional* team occurs across several institutional units. Members of a cross-functional team may represent many organizational units and a variety of leadership levels. A cross-functional team concentrates on tasks that require coordination and cooperation among different units in the institution. Cross-functional teams expand relationships between people and divisions within the institution, and thereby increase the global perspective of activity within the institution. The seven components shown in Figure 1.1 relate to both functional and cross-functional teams, but the way these components affect functional and cross-functional teams can differ. Some possible variations are illustrated in Table 1.1.

Leadership

Leaders are almost never as much in charge as they are pictured to be, and followers almost never are as submissive as one might imagine.

Gardner, 1987
"Leaders and Followers"

Effective leadership is essential to the development of the team concept within an institution. Through vision and action, leaders establish an environment that values quality and supports teams as an approach to accomplishing quality goals and the organizational mission. Articulating a vision for the team, clarifying the team's mission, goals, and operating context, and linking the team's mission to the organizational mission, values, and principles are critical skills for successful leaders.

The leader sets the tone for the institution by ensuring that teams have both the vision and the capacity to accomplish their work. Yukl (1994) describes Bennis and Nanus's research on transformational leaders, which revealed three leadership skills: creating a vision, developing trust and commitment, and facilitating organizational learning. The leader's role in promoting successful teams depends heavily upon these three sets of skills. The leader must be able to describe a vision of the future that is compelling enough to capture other people's imaginations. Once the vision is shared, it can become a reality only when a leader demonstrates commitment to achieving the vision and gains the trust of others whose contributions help make the vision a reality. The third element of transformational leadership, organizational learning, describes the leader's perpetual role in facilitating learning about the organization's stakeholders, customers, processes, and future challenges. Leaders that embody these transformational leadership skills enjoy a head start in creating an environment in which teams can succeed.

Articulating a vision, professing a commitment to quality, and promoting learning will appear hollow unless leaders also model their beliefs. "When the perception is that leadership actions fall behind leadership promises, the credibility gap invariably widens" (Kouzes & Posner, 1993, p. 40). Before leaders initiate a quality team approach, they must be prepared to demonstrate commitment, continually reinforce the common vision, and participate in learning more about *and from* the organization. In addition, leaders must be ready to share some of their power for making decisions and creating change with the teams they establish. As Senge (1990) points out, people in leadership positions are "often unprepared to share control.... They end up participating in quality activities but only going through the motions. They graciously acknowledge [workers' suggestions] but fail to implement them" (p. 100).

5

Table 1.1
Team Matrix

FUNCTIONAL	CROSS-FUNCTIONAL
Culture and Commitment	
Commitment to team and goals usually exists within the group; members operate within existing chain of command.	Commitment to team and goals must be built within the group; members operate across the existing chain of command.
Mission	
Organization leaders and governance structure define mission and goals for team. Team typically will prioritize goals.	Organization leaders and governance structure define mission and goals for team, usually planning and cross-functional processes.
Systems Thinking	
Typically operates as a permanent team; has an obvious place within the organization structure; can possess a unique system of information or draw from a common base of information.	Usually a less permanent team; may require rethinking the structure of the organization and relationships between departments; system of information is similar to functional group.
Membership	
Formal leaders select team from within units of the existing organizational structure; team selects own leader, or leader is appointed; membership usually permanent.	Leader appoints team from across units of the organization; membership usually ad hoc, or semi-permanent; formal leader may designate leader of team.

The leader permeates all of the components for developing successful teams because the leader structures both the problem and the vision. The leader has a central role in defining the team's mission, setting parameters for the team's work, recruiting or selecting team members, and communicating the team's accomplishments. Establishing teams requires leaders to reconsider the ways that they have previously done business. Unless the leader accepts the challenge to create an environment in which teams can succeed, teams will operate superficially, members will become disillusioned, and quality efforts will suffer. The discussion that follows sets forth a paradigm for developing quality teams in which all of the components depend upon effective leadership.

Table 1.1 (continued)

FUNCTIONAL	CROSS-FUNCTIONAL
Process Team leader shares problem with group, and leader makes decision that may or may not reflect team's influence; or leader shares problem with team and leader only implements solutions that have support of the entire team (Hampton et al., 1987).	Leader shares problem with team and leader only implements solutions that have support of the team's majority (Hampton et al., 1987).
Communication The team functions within the hierarchical structure; team members have close physical proximity to one another, which facilitates regular interaction within team and with others affected by the team's decisions.	Hierarchy should not be an issue in the team and all team members are equally important; broader representation requires greater attention to communication within the team and with those affected by the team's decisions.
Outcomes and Rewards Broad outcomes that explore questions of policy and assess whether the mission is being accomplished; these measures are typically called institutional effectiveness.	Specific outcomes focus on the accomplishment of process initiatives, such as efficiency, increased cooperation between units, and the development of new procedures.

Culture and Commitment

Culture refers to the totality of socially transmitted behavior patterns, arts, beliefs, institutions, and all other products of human work and thought characteristics of a community or population.

American Heritage Dictionary, 1991, p. 348

What is the prevailing culture on the campus regarding a team concept? Deal and Kennedy (1982) list five elements of culture: the physical environment in which activity takes place; the organization's basic values, concepts, and beliefs; the people who exemplify cultural values and provide role models; the organization's rites, rituals, and ceremonies, both mundane and extravagant; and the informal network of stories and myths that tell what the organization's values are. Leaders can begin to identify their institution's attitude toward teams by asking people to explain the difference between teams and teamwork. Questions might include asking people to distinguish between personal and organizational responsibility. As leaders walk around their institutions, leaders can observe how people operate and organize themselves; do people work independently of one another or in groups to accomplish their work? Whom do people identify as the institution's leaders? Do these leaders exemplify strong, independent action, or do they reflect a collective leadership style? In what ways does the institution recognize and reward accomplishment? Are rewards allocated exclusively to individuals, to groups, or to some combination of both?

Todd (1994) observes that, upon examination, a leader may learn that people report a positive attitude toward teams but have no idea of what teams would do or how teams would affect performance. Todd asked, "Are people willing to change the way that they do business?" and answered, "If the prevailing attitude is apathetic, or negative toward establishing teams, it may be necessary to devote energy to developing a more favorable culture prior to establishing any teams." Baker and Glass (1993) describe a quantitative process for measuring the climate dimension of organizational culture on six scales: conformity, responsibility, standards, rewards, clarity, and team spirit. The survey process outlined by these authors asks respondents to indicate where the institution is, and where it should be. The discrepancy between these two scores provides an indication of where people are most satisfied, and where improvements are needed. The National Initiative for Leadership and Institutional Effectiveness (NILIE) at North Carolina State University now assists colleges with climate studies to promote institutional effectiveness and quality initiatives.

In a recent chapter, Acebo (1994a) describes the important paradigm shift necessary for institutional leaders to distinguish between committees and teams. Traditional committees bring people together to discuss a problem or program, but the group rarely has responsibility for implementing the decision. If an institution wants to implement a team approach, she suggests that the leadership identify the kind of team that can best accomplish the work and will best fit the institution's culture. Using baseball, football, and basketball team structures, Acebo illustrates the differences among various team approaches. A baseball team depends upon talented individuals who operate with a great deal of autonomy. In contrast, a football team moves the ball down the field according to the coach's directions. In basketball, the team succeeds when every member contributes to the overall team performance in an integrated manner. Picking the best approach for implementing quality teams at any institution requires careful consideration of the nature of the process to be improved and people's need for autonomy, instruction, or interdependence.

"Even more critical than policies, however, is how management uses company resources plus its own time and attention to foster team performance" (Katzenbach & Smith, 1993, p. 240). Spanbauer (1992) writes: "Commitment means much more than giving an annual speech on how important quality is to our [institution]. It requires unending enthusiasm and devotion to quality improvement. It calls for an almost fanatical promotion of and attention to new ways to do things. It requires constant review of each and every action" (p. 15). Commitment of top-level leaders to quality initiatives is essential if teams are to succeed. Teams will fail to operate effectively as long as their efforts are discounted by those who established them. Often organization members describe experiences in which the leader gives a team a problem to solve, but the team's recommendations are never implemented. The team consequently is demoralized, and team members become cynical about quality initiatives and team performance. Imagine the tremendous effort it will take to revitalize and motivate these individuals on the next iteration of team initiatives.

Commitment to the team approach must be genuine if the process is expected to achieve results. Charging teams with the responsibility for improving an institutional process must be accompanied by the means and resources to implement necessary changes. The leader and the team need to know in advance what the team is responsible for achieving. When a leader asks a team to develop a new process, but fails to ensure that the new process is carried out, the consequences can be devastating. Yukl (1994) cautions that "The initial success of self-managed teams is often discounted by people who view them as a threat to their own power and status in the organization" (p. 185).

Kovel-Jarboe (1993) describes another aspect of how commitment can be undermined. The author warns that different groups within an organization may interpret quality initiatives in different ways. Sometimes the vision of the organization is poorly defined and, therefore, people lack a common framework for their efforts. Lack of commitment and diffuse authority can also result when people agree upon an outcome but fail to establish a clear and shared definition for what will represent success in meeting the goal. For example, the board may be interested in quality as a way to increase accountability and be "inclined to view quality [as a result] that focuses on inspection rather than quality as a result of attention to customer needs, process control, and system redesign" (p. 329). It is therefore essential that people understand what they are committing themselves to, and that this commitment is clearly articulated and communicated throughout the organization.

Yukl (1994) emphasizes the role of external leaders in committing to and encouraging teamwork. He proposed that top-level leaders demonstrate their commitment through coaching, supporting, and developing team skills. For team efforts to succeed, formal leaders must serve as advocates, championing team activities with other top decision makers, and model support for shifting authority to groups within the organization. Leaders must provide the team with sufficient authority to carry out quality initiatives. Baker (1994) states that

9

successful teams "should be empowered to make recommendations that lead to ways to change the formal structure to improve productivity." Yukl reinforces this point, writing that a team's success "depends very much on having sufficient authority to carry out its responsibilities" (p. 184). Not only must the team have authority, however; it must also have cooperation and participation from the institution's leadership.

Institutional leaders have a critical role in interpreting and shaping the culture and commitment of the institution toward quality. Support from institutional leaders and decision makers benefits the work of the quality team, individual performance, and people's commitment to the institution (Baker, 1994). Baker and associates (1992) concluded that the new quality-focused paradigm will require leaders who facilitate change, catalyze quality, and are self-confident, group-oriented, and dedicated to creating a culture with renewed commitment to accomplishing a complex mission.

Mission

The delegate[s] also need to have certain agreements with the leader. Together they will define reality, establish the validity of the mission, and understand and accept the work to be done.

DePree, 1992, p. 161

A specific mission and purpose, clearly defined by the institution's leadership, will increase a team's success. The team's purpose should specifically outline the team's role in furthering the broader institutional mission, objectives, and goals; for without clear direction, a team will be fraught with disagreement about its priorities and processes for accomplishing its objectives (Yukl, 1994, p. 183). Meyer (1994) agrees with Yukl, recommending that senior leaders dictate strategic goals and ensure that the team understands how its job fits into the institution's strategy. Twombly and Amey (1994) wrote: "Building communities and effective teams requires the ability to articulate visions, goals, and ideals; to create functioning teams aligned with the pursuit of common goals; to assume team membership, which may not always mean team leadership; and to educate constituents about consensus building, teamwork, information sharing, and shared decision making" (p. 272). Quality initiatives succeed when teams within the organization know that they are directly responsible for identifying, designing, and improving a *process* that improves satisfaction among the institution's internal and external customers.

Schwinn (1994) notes that a cornerstone of successful team efforts, like any good quality initiative, is knowing the customer, the purpose of the quality initiative, and the objectives to be accomplished. Acebo (1994b) states it this way: "How do we know if we're doing a good job? What are we looking for? And how will we measure it?" When establishing a team, it is essential that the group's charter, mission, or task be clearly defined and limited to a specific time frame. Acebo used an example from her institution, which set a goal to "double the number of students in degree programs over the next four years." Such a goal articulates to the team what the organization seeks to do and by when. With such a target, every member can find a way to contribute.

In addition to spelling out the role of the leadership team in structuring and leading the institution's quality effort, the charge should clearly describe whether the team's work will be limited to the development of quality initiatives or whether it will continue to have a role in overseeing the ongoing implementation of a change process once it has been established (Harper, 1994). DePree (1992), in his discussion of delegation, writes that both delegates and leaders must work to refine the validity of the mission to the institution. Both the leader and delegates, he explained, must understand and be committed to the work. The terms of performance, evaluation, and mechanisms to discuss failure also must be clearly defined.

Baker-Smith (1994) articulates the importance of accountability and follow-through. She finds the most successful teams are those with members and leaders who ensure that the work actually gets done, have a clear mandate for what is to be accomplished, and are in general agreement about the problem and how to address it. Defining a team's mission, therefore, goes beyond just describing the final outcome. The mission also includes parameters for the work, who will be held accountable, and who will be responsible for maintaining and improving the process once it has been established.

Leaders must strike a balance between giving general guidelines and specific requirements. Yukl (1994) cautions, "The effectiveness of teams is reduced with restrictions on decisions about work assignments, procedures, and strategies for problem solving" (p. 184). One way for a leader to monitor team performance without limiting the team's creativity and autonomy is for leaders and teams to establish rules and criteria for team performance and measurement review.

Systems Thinking

Senge (1990) defines systems thinking as "a discipline for seeing wholes . . . a framework for seeing interrelationships rather than things, for seeing patterns of change rather than static 'snapshots' " (p. 68).

Creating an environment in which teams can operate can enhance an organization's ability to accomplish its objectives by involving people in the process of tackling and solving problems. Before establishing teams, it is essential to consider the system within which they will operate. Developing a plan for implementing quality or establishing teams with quality improvements as outcomes requires an examination of the total institution.

Successful quality initiatives will augment, not undermine, the formal organizational structure. Acebo (1994b) says: "How you proceed with planned change depends upon whether you are a poet or a scientist." In essence, leaders must know their own styles and proceed accordingly. A leader that sees things broadly and thrives on large-scale change may elect to integrate quality techniques throughout the institution. On the other hand, a more calculating leader may prefer to test quality initiatives in a targeted area and then expand the effort as people gain experience. Tackling a broad-scale quality program ensures that everyone is involved in the quality process but presents simultaneous challenges and introduces risks that people will be overwhelmed. In contrast, a focused effort provides an opportunity for some people to test and learn about quality processes yet can alienate people in the organization who do not participate.

Developing a successful approach to quality requires that it fit into the institution's formal leadership and decision-making structures. Baker (1994) says that "A quality team that supports the existing decision-making structure will succeed, whereas one that is at cross purposes with the formal structure will not." Harper (1994) agrees that effective quality teams are those that exist within institutions that have an interest in quality and a structure for implementing quality initiatives. Harper suggests placing the ultimate responsibility for the quality team with the chief decision makers. By making top-level decision makers responsible for activities of the quality team, quality initiatives can be more quickly integrated into existing strategic and operational plans. Schwinn (1994) emphasizes this point: "A critical first step is that the leadership team, or quality team, be integrated into the general management structure of the institution. When a team is created apart from the understood mechanics of decision making and administration, the effort is doomed from the start."

Leaders must consider the systems thinking that the institution could use for decision making and make the quality team a part of the existing framework for policy and procedure development. In this arrangement, team members would reflect on and support existing policies and procedures. In a collective bargaining environment, bargaining leaders should be included in the team from the outset. Similarly, faculty, administration, support staff, students, and board members who typically participate in the work of the team should be represented on both functional and cross-functional teams.

Regardless of whether quality principles and team approaches are introduced throughout the organization or within a single unit, it is important to introduce changes in an orderly and patient manner. Acebo (1994b) cautions that moving to a team environment could backfire if people consider the change to be superficial. "When some people hear the word 'quality,' " she remarks, "their eyes glaze over and they wait for this new phase to pass." Instead of forcing skeptics to participate in a new structure, Acebo recommends using existing committees to incrementally introduce quality approaches. A faculty curriculum committee, for example, might have a trainer come in and assist them with a systems analysis of the curriculum development process. The trainer might ask the committee members to allow a few administrators and support staff to participate in the process, thereby changing the membership of the committee to encourage new thinking and improve the quality of decision making.

Reviewing the formal structure to determine how quality initiatives fit in often means looking beyond what currently exists to what could exist through improved planning, problem solving, and decision making. Quality initiatives can unite disparate units within the organization under an integrated goal. Schwinn (1994) states that "A leadership team for quality does not exist apart from budgeting, curriculum, and administration, but operates as an umbrella under which all other functions join together." For example, the quality team should be able to link recommendations for changing resource allocations and curriculums with the ultimate goal of enhancing student recruitment efforts.

Depending upon the structure of the organization, quality initiatives might take many forms. Providing the flexibility for teams to work requires an understanding that, within any institution, leadership is nested, with layers of leaders throughout the hierarchy. In addition, some leaders will have more power and influence than others. For these reasons, a team approach might more quickly be accepted in some parts of the organization than in others. In an academic unit, where faculty are accustomed to acting independently, it may be difficult to gain support for a team approach because the accepted practice has been to operate autonomously. Alternatively, a unit that is accustomed to significant coordinated effort may quickly integrate principles of quality and team decision making because the advantages of shared responsibility for outcomes have been learned by all of the participants. The critical element in successfully integrating any quality initiative is to ensure that the quality principles support and supplement, rather than compete with, the existing structure.

Membership

Delegation is one of the ways leaders connect voice and touch. It is a precious way of enabling people to participate, to grow, to reach toward their potential.

DePree, 1992, p. 154

We've noted that teams have the advantage of more ideas, more insights, and more productivity over individuals acting alone. For this reason, it is important that teams include members committed to working with others and who are experienced in quality initiatives. Team members also should represent a mix of people from throughout the organization. The problem to be solved should dictate the membership of the team. Teams are often given the responsibility for finding solutions or making recommendations or decisions that have repercussions well beyond the group itself (Doyle & Strauss, 1976). Therefore, when considering people to serve on the quality team, it is important to look

13

beyond those who have the authority and information necessary to solve the immediate problem and include people who play formal and informal roles in carrying out the decisions within the system.

Acebo (1994b) points out that quality can begin as a campuswide initiative or as a single issue. Depending upon the prevailing campus culture, it may be effective to model small successes with quality principles before expanding to other areas, or it may be preferable to gain broad commitment to a set of institutionwide initiatives. Regardless of scale, it is important that the team represent a broad spectrum of people from the institution. Faculty, professional and classified staff, the board of trustees, and students can get involved in quality initiatives. Students, a crucial customer group in an educational institution, should be considered as members of appropriate teams, "although," Harper (1994) admits, "student representatives often don't participate as fully as other team members because of schedules and other priorities." To facilitate student participation on teams, some institutions have scheduled an open period during lunch so that students have time to attend team meetings.

Specific guidelines for establishing teams depend upon the nature of the work to be accomplished; however, some general rules-of-thumb can improve the function and success of teams. Hampton et al. (1987) write that in cross-functional teams membership should be voluntary. Baker (1994) recommends that in these circumstances, the initial volunteers be people who are committed to and trained to deal with quality principles, and these members should focus on areas that lend themselves to reengineering and have a high need for quality solutions. Harper (1994) says that team members should include people closest to the process of making quality initiatives work and include key players within critical institutional units. Harper agrees that faculty and administrators who demonstrate an interest in initiatives that improve services to students should serve on the steering team. "But," she cautions, "just because individuals have clout within a department does not guarantee that they will be committed to the development of quality initiatives." In addition to those groups listed above, Harper recommends that someone linked with professional and staff development be involved in the team effort to provide the training necessary for the team to successfully accomplish its mission.

Identifying volunteers committed to quality and selecting people with skills appropriate to the task are important elements of successful cross-functional team membership. Equally important, however, are the characteristics and the number of people appointed to the team. Quality teams that operate most effectively are those that balance similarities and differences among group members. Teams with too much homogeneity are vulnerable to groupthink—going along with the group—and lack of creativity (Yukl, 1994). Harper (1994) says it is more important for the quality team to have participants who represent the institution's demographic, gender, racial, and professional mix than it is to have people representing specific institutional functions. Yukl recommends that a team have the smallest number of people necessary to complete the task, ideally six to twelve members (p. 183). In Harper's experience, ten or fewer is a manageable group. However, because the size of the group is limited, and the scope of the work is broad, it is important to recognize that all units, divisions, and departments may not be represented on the team. "Bear in mind," Harper continues, "that the work of the team will encompass issues outside any individual's expertise; therefore, the specific duties of individuals on the team are less important than their interest in developing a quality institution for everyone."

By its very nature, the repercussions of a cross-functional team's work will extend beyond any unit leader's authority. It is therefore essential that these teams be organized and staffed to allow for independence, responsibility, and authority to accomplish their missions. Thus, teams that will work across the major units of the organization should, under most circumstances, report to the CEO, or his or her immediate staff. Quality team members should have diverse skills, resources, a stake in the chosen process, authority to make changes in the system under study, clout to make things happen, and courage to do what is necessary (Scholtes, 1988).

Process

Before beginning work, a group can negotiate a set of responsibilities and working relationships. Task, environment, time, skills and individual needs are all important factors in designing a structure that will work.

Bolman & Deal, 1991, p. 112

"The process used to structure and solve the problem within the cross-functional team is critical to effective functioning," says Baker (1994). It should be the task of the group, unless appointed by the formal leader, to select a team leader and adopt a technique to reflect upon its own performance as a team. Initially, it may be necessary for a trained facilitator to help develop team processes and keep the group on track. As team members gain experience, they can monitor their own processes by agreeing to principles of group behavior and monitoring their collective performance. Regardless of how this monitoring is accomplished, teams need to be responsible for developing a work plan and agreeing upon a process for accomplishing their assigned work.

Teams need to diagnose their environment, their objectives, and their individual needs so they can design a process for how they will collectively accomplish their work. Keidel (1984) proposed that teams answer the following questions when designing an appropriate structure: "(1) What are the nature and degree of task-related interaction among unit members? (2) What is the geographical distribution of unit members? (3) Given a group's objectives and constraints, where does authority reside? (4) How is coordination achieved? (5)

What words best describe the required structure—conglomerate, mechanistic, or organic? (6) What sports expression metaphorically captures the task of management—filling out the lineup card, preparing the game plan, or influencing the game's flow?" (p. 110). Critical skills include the team's degree of openness and trust, as well as the team's ability to develop strategy, plan, foster shared leadership, provide feedback, make decisions, and allocate resources as necessary to accomplish the tasks. The processes the team uses to accomplish its objectives are as important as the end result. For a team to develop, each member must be able to assess his or her own and other's performance and ensure that all members of the team are participating in the work.

Teams have leadership responsibilities at individual and group levels. Schwinn (1994) feels that the team should model the behaviors that it wants others to adopt. She emphasizes that the quality team's relationship to other groups within the institution should be built collaboratively and that teamwork, not individual achievement, should be the group's goal. Harper (1994) suggests that although the team will have a leader assigned or will elect one, the leader should not always lead the group. Instead, this individual takes leadership responsibilities for coordinating meetings, developing a process for decision making, and ensuring that reports are completed on time. In fact, other team members should periodically act as the team leader in order to improve their skills and increase their motivation.

Teams may be configured in a variety of ways. Depending on the task assigned, size of the team, and the nature of the work, team members may work in subgroups to accomplish tasks outside the team meetings, or work individually with other technology resources external to the team. Harper (1994) and Schwinn (1994) agree that once work has been assigned to a subgroup or an individual, it is critical that the individual or subgroup be held accountable for completing the assigned work effectively and efficiently. Structuring a team so that all individuals and subgroups contribute is an important element in team success. Yukl (1994) describes effective teams as those in which members have meaningful tasks and are held personally responsible for contributing their knowledge and skills to completing the task on schedule and meeting desired outcomes (p. 183). Maximizing creative thinking should be required of each team member, and the task should require the expertise of all members to find a solution. "Teamwork assignments should be based upon skill, not position," write Katzenbach and Smith (1993, p. 231). In addition, every member should contribute equally to doing actual work, and every member's job should consist of more than delegation and oversight. Each person on the team must participate in interviewing, researching, writing, and reviewing. For a team to flourish, it must work to build team collaboration and to assign all team members positions of responsibility where they may be required to interact with people both internal and external to the organization.

One of the most challenging aspects of teamwork is group dynamics, but a failure to attend to group process, or an inability to identify, confront, and solve process problems, can derail even the best of intentions. Team members who are suspicious of one another's position and status or who have disagreeable personalities can diminish the team's effectiveness. "As with most teams, membership was more a personal than personnel matter" (Katzenbach & Smith, 1993, p. 33). Maier (1967) writes that group liabilities include behaviors such as applying social pressure, exerting individual dominance, or trying to win support instead of selecting the best option. Team members with hidden agendas, or those who seek to control and manipulate others, can quickly undermine a team's efforts. A synthesis of problems appears in Table 1.2.

Sometimes problems have less to do with personalities and more to do with unclear or unrealistic expectations for the team to produce a solution. To ensure a successful team process, Katzenbach and Smith (1993) recommend that the team work on specific, rather than general, problems. To identify areas suited to quality initiatives, Scholtes (1988) suggests that teams select work that affects customers directly; produces visible results quickly (the entire process should repeat at least once a day); is not already in transition; is simple to implement; is clearly defined and time constrained; and is substantial and relevant to managers, company, and customers.

Using data to make decisions is critical to an effective team process. Scholtes (1988) refers to this data use as the scientific approach, which means that the team agrees to look at the process that produces results and to examine the roots of problems rather than react to the problem's symptoms. Focusing on the causes of problems usually follows the Pareto Principle, or 80/20 rule: 80 percent of the difficulties in an organization can be traced back to 20 percent of its problems. Further, systemic causes account for 80 percent of organiza-

Table 1.2
Ten Common Group Problems

- Floundering
- Overbearing participants
- Dominating participants
- Reluctant participants
- Unquestioned acceptance of opinion as fact
- Rush to accomplishment
- Attribution
- Discounting member contributions
- Digression and tangents
- Feuding members

(Scholtes, 1988, pp. 6–37)

tional problems, while people cause the remaining 20 percent (Scholtes, 1988). An effective team process will include an examination of underlying complexities that result in mistakes, delays, inefficiencies, and variations. Tools such as flow charts, work-flow diagrams, deployment charts, Pareto charts, cause and effect diagrams, matrices, time plots, stem and leaf diagrams, and scatter diagrams may be used to assist teams in scientifically analyzing the processes that need improvement. Once the data have been presented in a visually helpful format, teams can use brainstorming, nominal group techniques, and Delphi processes to reach consensus (see Appendix 1 in Chapter 11).

Communication

> *Creation of empowered employees depends on providing them with the information necessary to make good decisions and to see the results of their actions.*
>
> Gore, 1993, p. 359

As we've seen, the team needs support from administrators and others to ensure that it operates effectively. Equally important is that leaders communicate with the team openly and frequently, ensuring that the team receives the information it needs to solve its problems and make decisions. Yukl (1994) observes that the "success of a team is dependent on its access to information necessary to regulate the team's activities and monitor its performance" (p. 184). Leaders play an important role in ensuring that information gathered within the organization's framework and beyond is made available to the team. Rather than waiting for information requests to pass through channels, leaders should anticipate the value of information to the team and guarantee that team members receive information they need to accomplish their tasks.

Once information is available, the team should organize it so that it is useful for decision making. Baker (1994) stresses that the team should be responsible for receiving, collecting, formatting, and distributing information within and outside the team, as well as for developing visual aids. Information needs to be organized efficiently so that it is accessible and meaningful. Spanbauer (1992) emphasizes the valuable role of current technology to enhance quality and excellence and advocates that teams take advantage of computer reports, audio-visual instructional aids, and computer networks—all of which expand the use of information and enhance people's technological literacy.

Good communication occurs on a variety of levels, observes Harper (1994). She indicates that first, team members must communicate well among themselves; and second, the team has an obligation to regularly communicate about its activities with decision makers, with the broader organization, and with peers who are developing quality initiatives in similar organizations. Gore (1993) echoes the importance of the transfer of learning about quality initiatives between institutions, writing, "Communication among institutions, highlighting successes with the identification, definition, ownership, and improvement of key processes, should become a valuable and widespread activity" (p. 361).

Communicating with outsiders about team activities is essential, but it can be treacherous. Baker-Smith (1994) points out that information can provide strength to supporters and, at the same time, give ammunition to foes. During a team brainstorming session, for example, many ideas may be generated and a variety of possibilities considered. Individuals or subgroups who do not agree with some aspect of the process can select a single item from such a list and use it to accuse, to misinform, or to accomplish hidden agendas. The team needs adept team leadership and information management skills to guarantee the regular flow of internal and external communications and to ensure that intermediate issues do not threaten the larger goals.

Outcomes and Rewards

One benefit of having a team create its own measurement system is that members who hail from different functions end up creating a common language, which they need in order to work as an effective team. Until a group creates a common language, it can't reach a common definition of goals or problems. Instead of acting like a team, the group will act like a collection of functions.

Meyer, 1994, p. 102

If Meyer's (1994) observation is correct, a team must have a common understanding of its goals and functions. The major way to facilitate a team's collective performance is to guarantee that team members receive feedback about how team efforts affect larger organizational activity (Hampton et al., 1987, p. 333). The most effective measurements help teams understand how well processes work; they do not necessarily provide management with a way to gauge progress. With input from leaders, a team should design its own measurement system that tracks cross-functions, time spent on activities, and types of work performed. Because the nature of work is complex, the team should keep its measures to "no more than fifteen," according to Meyer, because "what gets measured gets done" (p. 96).

When teams and leaders fail to develop measurement criteria and provide regular feedback, teams flounder. Baker-Smith (1994) observes that team members without responsibility or accountability will allow external work to take priority over teamwork, eventually causing the team's responsibility to be pushed out of the organization or to another group within the organization. Thus, a lack of accountability often results in teams with poor morale, a lack of focus, and uncertain outcomes.

The team concept works when its efforts result in enhanced productivity within the institution's formal structure. Baker (1994) points out that the team concept applied to functional and cross-functional areas can improve individual, group, and organizational productivity. The key is enhanced performance through motivation and perseverance. Through their participation on teams, individuals learn new skills that enable them to work more efficiently and effectively within the formal structure. Team approaches provide a way for innovators to change formal structure, for scientists to test and incubate new approaches within formal structure, and for leaders to model new initiatives within the larger formal structure. "The products of a leadership team might include developing a strategic plan, identifying system needs, prioritizing financial resources, monitoring progress or improving team relationships, and learning about quality and collaborative decision making," says Schwinn (1994). Krueger and Evans (1993) suggest that teams concentrate on outcomes that provide indications of institutional effectiveness such as student-faculty contact, increased cooperation among students, active learning, prompt feedback, time on task, high expectations, respect for diverse talents and ways of learning.

"Many institutions never think beyond rewarding individual accomplishment," says Baker (1994), noting that, "Instead, we need to rethink reward systems so that we recognize and reward the team's contribution to the organization's essence. To reward the team, we must link rewards to specific performance criteria and reward individuals for both personal and team contributions. In addition, we must design performance criteria to recognize the contribution of the team." Appropriate recognition should go to the team's good work, and as Yukl writes, "reward individuals for their contribution to the overall performance of the team" (1994, p. 184). Any financial or tangible rewards should be clearly linked to skills and performance relevant to the team's work. While praise from leadership provides teams with important recognition, the greatest reward for teams comes from seeing their work produce results within the institution. When the team's effort visibly improves customer satisfaction, increases student retention, raises enrollment, or results in a new delivery system, then team members gain genuine satisfaction from seeing how their efforts contributed to improving their institution's quality.

"Ultimately," Schwinn (1994) points out, "leaders do it themselves—they model and practice principles of quality." As a tool for quality decision making, Jackson Community College developed and distributed "Blue Cards" to decision makers. This single tool has improved quality at Jackson Community College perhaps more than any other initiative, Schwinn reports, because the card communicated the quality team's priorities to others. At Jackson Community College, people carry their Blue Cards to meetings and use the checklist when proposing or passing new programs. The content of the Blue Card appears in Table 1.3.

Table 1.3
The "Blue Card" from Jackson Community College

Questions to ask when considering a proposal for a new or improved college program:

Who are the customers? What do they need?
How do you know? (i.e., show me the data!)
What is the purpose of the initiative?
How is it consistent with our institution's mission?
What are the products/services to be provided to achieve the purpose?
What are the resources (physical, financial, human, knowledge) required to produce the products/services?
How will they be acquired/allocated?
What is the process or system by which this initiative will be implemented? Who "owns" the system? What impact will it have on other systems (counseling, marketing, finance, etc.)? How will people in other systems be involved in planning, doing, studying, acting?
How will you know the new initiative is any good (measures, variability, re: function, cost, safety, delivery, employee satisfaction)? How will these data be gathered and analyzed? Who will improve the process/system?

The other side of the card reads:

Considerations when developing a proposal for a new initiative or program.
See other side.

Summary and Conclusion

Creating teams within an organization starts with a commitment to improving institutional quality. Single-unit or cross-functional teams may be assigned to address specific or comprehensive quality issues within the organization. Regardless of the team's scope, however, the leader must clearly articulate the team's improvement goals, the team's duties, and the institution's commitment to the process. In addition, the leader must ensure that the team has the resources necessary to accomplish its work and should participate with the team in analyzing the processes that will be used to achieve quality outcomes.

The model outlined in this chapter describes key components for developing functional and cross-functional teams within an organization. As a first step, the model integrated the team concept into the existing organizational system,

21

illustrating how successful teams are developed with an understanding and vision of the organization as a whole. With an understanding of and appreciation for the whole, teams become a tool for enhancing the operations and functions of the system. Teams, when used appropriately, enable an organization to further its mission, improve specific work processes, and enhance quality in services and products.

Although the structure of the organization serves as a framework for developing ad hoc and permanent teams, designing teams that augment the organizational chart alone will not ensure a successful team approach. Success depends heavily upon the support and dedication of the organization's leadership. Commitment from top-level decision makers is essential because leaders provide teams with critical resources, guidance, motivation, and support that enables them to diagnose problems and implement solutions. Leaders who embrace quality principles will foster an environment within which teams can work to address quality goals and instill commitment to institutional quality and service throughout the organization.

Quality teams that complement the organization's structure and operate with top-level commitment also need team members who are committed to accomplishing the team's objectives. Team membership should reflect the purpose of the team. If the team is responsible for proposing a specific curriculum within a given department, then team members should include faculty, registrars, students, and staff affected by curriculum decisions. When the team's purpose is to increase student enrollment, a broader group of administrators, faculty, students, and staff would be required. The scope of the team's responsibilities is important in selecting team members who will be committed to the goals, supportive of quality principles, and influential in implementing change both formally and informally throughout the institution.

Clearly articulating the team's mission, purpose, and authority is essential to team success. By providing explicit directions and expectations, the leader focuses the team's energy on its priorities, thus reducing the time team members spend arguing over the purpose of their work. A leader can facilitate the team's work by articulating how the team's mission fits into the institution's strategic priorities and how the team's efforts will be integrated into the ongoing work of the organization. A successful team operates with the authority to make and implement the decisions to accomplish its purposes but knows that the leader will hold the team accountable for its actions.

Another essential component of successful quality team initiatives guarantees that teams develop and monitor their own work processes, including the tools the team will use to diagnose and analyze problems, the principles that will guide their behaviors, and the mechanisms they will use to monitor and evaluate their performance. Once the leader has provided the team with clear direction and structure, the team should be responsible for determining how its objectives will be met. With the leader, the team should agree upon boundaries and establish a structure for monitoring progress and providing feedback, but the processes for accomplishing work should be delegated to the team.

Successful organizational teams foster strong relationships with leaders and others within the organization, and frequently communicate their progress toward meeting their objectives. Written progress reports, flow charts, weekly meetings, and site visits are just a few of the ways that teams can facilitate communication with administrators and others within the organization. Similarly, the organization's leaders have a responsibility to keep team members informed of issues that affect the work of the team.

To ensure that functional and cross-functional teams accomplish and receive recognition for meeting their objectives, a system for providing feedback is essential. Leaders have a responsibility for providing teams with feedback, but it should always include information that helps the team assess its processes. This feedback system is different from monitoring the team's progress toward meeting its assigned objectives. For example, in addition to seeing how much enrollment had increased, a team's evaluation might examine how well team members communicated with one another, whether they diagnosed the problem appropriately, or whether the time budgeted to accomplish a task met or exceeded the actual time required. The team's work should be recognized and rewarded, but the reward system should appropriately recognize how the team, as a group, improved institutional quality.

Figure 1.2
Relationship of Key Components to Quality Teams

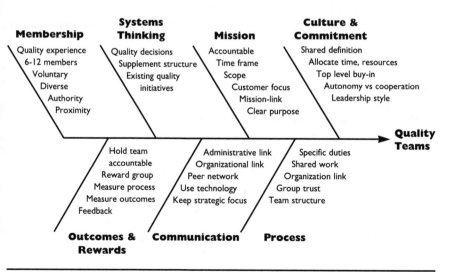

In conclusion, organizational quality can be improved through teams, but the success of a team approach requires an understanding of, and early attention to, a complex system of interrelated components. Strong, committed leadership sets the groundwork for effective team performance. Ensuring that teams operate with clear direction, authority, and limits is an expansion of the leader's responsibility. Once charged, the team is responsible for accomplishing assigned objectives through the application of team-building principles. The combination of good leadership and good team guidelines results in improved service quality and performance for the institution (see Figure 1.2). Above all of these principles is the fact that team building permeates all aspects of our democratic society. For writers of the chapters that follow, teams and teaming are central to their philosophy of how to deliver on promises. Perhaps, like Peter Senge, these writers can capture the excitement of being a part of something greater than ourselves. "When people genuinely care, they are naturally committed. They are doing what they truly want to do. They are full of energy and enthusiasm. They persevere, even in the face of frustration and setbacks, because what they are doing is what they must do. It is *their work*" (1990, p. 148).

References

Acebo, S.C. "A Paradigm Shift to Team Leadership in the Community College." In G.A. Baker III (Ed.), *A Handbook on the Community College in America*. Westport, Conn.: Greenwood Press, 1994a.

Acebo, S.C. Interview with V. Upshaw, June 22, 1994b.

American Heritage Dictionary. Boston: Houghton Mifflin Co., 1991.

Baker, G.A., III. Interview with V. Upshaw, June 8, 1994.

Baker, G.A., III, and Glass, C. "The McClelland-Atkinson Model of Motivation." In *Leadership in Higher and Community College Education Course Pack*. Raleigh, N.C.: North Carolina State University, 1993.

Baker, G.A., III, and Associates. *Cultural Leadership: Inside America's Community Colleges*. Washington, D.C.: The Community College Press, 1992.

Baker-Smith, K. Interview with V. Upshaw, June 9, 1994.

Bolman, L.G., and Deal, T.E. *Reframing Organizations: Artistry, Choice and Leadership*. San Francisco: Jossey-Bass, Inc. Publishers, 1991.

Burns, J.M. *Leadership*. New York: Harper & Row, 1978.

Deal, T.E., and Kennedy, A.A. *Corporate Cultures: The Rites and Rituals of Corporate Life*. Reading, Mass.: Addison-Wesley Publishing Company, 1982.

DePree, M. *Leadership Jazz*. New York: Dell Publishing, 1992.

Doyle, M., and Strauss, D. *How to Make Meetings Work: The New Interaction Method*. New York: Jove Books, 1976.

Gore, E.W. "Total Quality Management in Education." In D. Hubbard (Ed.), *Continuous Quality Improvement: Making the Transition to Education*. Maryville, Mo.: Prescott Publishing Co., 1993.

Hampton, D.R., Summer, C.E., and Webber, R.A. *Organizational Behavior and the Practice of Management.* New York: Harper Collins Publishers, 1987.

Harper, L. Interview with V. Upshaw, June 8, 1994.

Juran, J.M. *Juran on Quality by Design: The New Steps for Planning Quality into Goods and Services.* New York: The Free Press, 1992.

Katzenbach, J., and Smith, D. *The Wisdom of Teams.* New York: McKinsey and Company, Inc., 1993.

Keidel (1984) in Bolman, L.G., and Deal T.E. *Reframing Organizations: Artistry, Choice and Leadership.* San Francisco: Jossey-Bass, 1991.

Kouzes, J., and Posner, B. *Credibility.* San Francisco: Jossey-Bass, 1993.

Kovel-Jarboe, P. "Implementing TQM in a Research University." In D. Hubbard (Ed.), *Continuous Quality Improvement: Making the Transition to Education.* Maryville, Mo.: Prescott Publishing Co., 1993.

Krueger, D., and Evans, G. "Total Quality Management in Education." In D. Hubbard (Ed.), *Continuous Quality Improvement: Making the Transition to Education.* Maryville, Mo.: Prescott Publishing Co., 1993.

Maier, N. "Assets and Liabilities in Group Problem Solving: The Need for an Integrative Function." In L. Bradford (Ed.), *Group Development.* San Diego: University Associates, 1967.

Meyer, C. "How the Right Measures Help Teams Excel." *Harvard Business Review,* May-June, 1994, 95–103.

Scholtes, P. *The Team Handbook.* Madison, Wisc.: Joiner Associates, Inc., 1988.

Schwinn, C. Interview with V. Upshaw, June 23, 1994.

Senge, P.M. *The Fifth Discipline: The Art and Practice of the Learning Organization.* New York: Doubleday, 1990.

Spanbauer, S.A., *Quality System for Education.* Milwaukee, Wisc.: Quality Press, 1992.

Todd, T. Interview with V. Upshaw, June 7, 1994.

Twombly, S. and Amey, M. "Leadership Skills for Participative Governance." In G. A. Baker III (Ed.), *A Handbook on the Community College in America.* Westport, Conn.: Greenwood Press, 1994.

Yukl, G. *Leadership in Organizations.* Englewood Cliffs, N.J.: Prentice-Hall, 1994.

CHAPTER **2**

THE PRESIDENT AND THE BOARD

A Team of Leaders

GEORGE R. BOGGS

Introduction

No single relationship in an organization is as important as that between the board and its chief executive officer (Carver, 1990). That relationship, well conceived, can set the stage for effective governance and management. Clearly, the college president and the board of trustees need to develop and maintain a well-defined, trusting, and effective relationship for the college to be successful. Kauffman, former president of Rhode Island College, notes that nothing is more important for a college president (Popcock, 1989).

Nonetheless, stories of problems between presidents and their boards abound. Sometimes presidents come to view their boards as a necessary evil rather than as a valuable group that brings an external perspective to the leadership of the college. These presidents look for ways to survive their boards rather than seeing themselves and their boards as a team that provides direction to a complex enterprise. If the board and president are to be effective as a team, they must have a clear idea of the roles they are expected to play, and they must work to make the relationship a productive one.

A trustee, by definition, is one to whom property is entrusted for management (Community College League of California, 1995). College boards of

27

trustees or governing boards act on behalf of the owners of the college to be sure it is operating effectively and efficiently in agreement with its mission. For public community colleges, the owners are the citizens of the geographic district that the college serves. The tradition of governance by qualified lay people unencumbered by special interests is basic to the philosophy of higher education in America (Axelrod, 1989).

The selection of a president is one of the most important responsibilities of a board. As the chief executive officer of the college, the president will be expected to see that the policies and directives of the board are carried out. The day-to-day operations of the college are in the hands of the staff members that report to the president. Moreover, the president will be expected to advise the board in the adoption of college policies and in planning for the future of the college.

Carver (1990) goes so far as to say that a board should think of itself as having only one employee, the CEO. While this view may seem extreme, in practice it is the president whom the board must hold accountable for the operation of the college and for the performance of the other employees. None of the other employees of the college should report to or be evaluated by the board (Nason, 1982). The board must act through the president, making the president as important to the success of the board as the board is to the success of the president.

Kerr writes that the chief responsibility for a board is to have a presidency that is effective and thus potentially attractive to highly qualified persons (Nason, 1989). A college president is faced with conflicting demands, insufficient resources, hectic schedules, and long hours (Stecklow, 1994). It is the board's responsibility to structure the job so it can be accomplished and to provide the needed support. The greatest test of the board in the long run is the quality of the presidents it is able to attract and retain (Ingram, 1988).

Ideally, the board and the president should be viewed as a team of leaders who share common philosophies and objectives. The effectiveness of one depends upon the effectiveness of the other. Each has an important and complementary role to play, and each role must be respected.

Membership

Many factors determine the composition and term of office of a college board of trustees. Private colleges have different requirements from public colleges for membership on their boards. Even among American public community colleges, boards differ by state and even by district. In some states, boards are appointed by other elected officials or bodies. In others, they are elected by the public. Terms of office vary greatly, with an average term of office for community college boards of six years (Ingram, 1988). Colleges in some states are governed by a state board rather than a board for each college. Others have boards at both the state and college level.

Arguments could be made that an appointed board is less politically motivated than an elected one. However, Lee and Bowen point out that a governor or other appointing official can no more ignore political considerations in the selection of trustees than deny the reality of the next election (Nason, 1982).

Governing boards range in size from five to eighty members (Nason, 1982). Private institutions have larger boards, usually between twenty and forty members. The great majority of public colleges have boards of seven to ten members; the actual number is normally set by statute.

Nason (1982) compares some of the characteristics of small and large boards. Creating an environment that allows large boards to deliberate on the issues and to feel personally involved is difficult. Meetings are usually infrequent because they are more difficult to schedule. One danger is that the executive committee of a large board will take over the responsibilities of the board. On the other hand, critics say that small boards fail to reflect a sufficient variety of points of view and therefore lack the depth necessary to deal wisely with the issues confronting the college. The danger is that smaller boards and standing committees of larger boards will drift away from policy issues into administrative decisions.

Although college presidents and board chairs usually cannot determine the size of the board, they can mitigate some of the potential problems with boards that are either very large or very small. An appropriate committee structure usually makes it possible to divide large boards into smaller groups in which the members are actively involved and able to deliberate appropriately. Small boards of nine members or fewer often do not need to divide into committees (Ingram, 1988). However, the smaller boards may have advisory committees or shared governance committees study recommendations as a way of including more points of view before the board is required to act. The president and the board chair will have to steer the board away from the actual administration of the college.

When boards are appointed, the appointing agency may consult with the college president or with current board members to seek suggestions for potential candidates. It would not be politically wise for the president, as an employee of the board, to lobby for the appointment of one of its members. The president would be astute, however, to encourage the interest of people who would make good board members.

Like other teams, the effectiveness of a board is enhanced by a diversity of backgrounds and interests in its members. Governing boards should be balanced by gender and reflect the ethnic makeup of the community. Historically, college boards have been male-dominated and mostly white (Nason, 1982). Female and minority trustees can bring important perspectives and sensitivities to the board table (Ingram, 1988). They can, for example, help to assess whether the campus provides appropriate support services to female and minority students and employees, whether marketing strategies are effective, and whether the institution's affirmative action program is well conceived.

Qualified people who would add to the depth and balance of the board should be exposed to the college and its programs. Affiliation with the college through service on an advisory committee or on a foundation board would provide excellent experience for a future member of the college's board of trustees.

In the case of an elected board, a college president must never endorse or support one of the candidates. The president can conduct an orientation session for the candidates, answer their questions, and supply information to them as long as all candidates receive equal opportunity. Board candidate forums are best organized and held without the direct involvement of the president, although it is probably a good idea for the president to attend.

Some states have passed laws that add a student to the membership of the college board of trustees. Nason (1982) criticizes the concept of a student trustee, noting that students serve too short a time to master all they need to know, and they will not be around to live with the consequences of their decisions. The idea behind these laws, however, is that the presence of the student at the board table will ensure that the board listens to the views of students while deliberating.

The student trustees are usually elected by the students and have the obligation to represent student perspectives to the board and to report and perhaps explain board action to the student government. Student trustees usually do not have the same rights and responsibilities as publicly elected or politically appointed board members. Sometimes they have an advisory vote, but they usually cannot make or second motions, and they usually are not allowed to join the board in closed or executive sessions.

A disturbing trend in recent years has been the election of people who have special interests to school and college boards, including those who have a specific agenda other than the best interests of the overall institution in mind. Board members who advocate personal religious beliefs or who bring nonrelated controversial issues to the board table damage the very institution they are charged with protecting. Sometimes people run for boards for vindictive reasons or even to start a political career. These members can present a challenge to a college president.

Another troubling trend is the success that employee unions are having in getting candidates elected to college governing boards. According to Ingram (1988), all trustees have an obligation to be and to remain independent of special interests or groups. Trustees who feel an obligation to a particular internal group can hardly be unbiased in their decisions. In some cases, employees of one college are being elected to serve as trustees in another. Trustees sometimes have spouses in the employ of the college they govern. Laws in some states even permit trustees to teach a class at the college for pay. Each of these situations presents opportunities for conflict of interest. The college president and the other board members will have to be aware of this potential and to advise the particular board member of the appearance of such a conflict.

Mission

The mission of a board of trustees, according to Nason (1982), is to act as guardians of the college mission. They must ensure that the institution's programs conform to its stated purpose and that the college funds are spent in support of this mission and the shared vision for the future of the college. The college mission statement describes the direction of the institution; it defines a clear purpose for existence. The vision is a picture of what the institution will be at some point in the future, which should emerge from an understanding of the needs of the communities served by the college and of the internal strengths and abilities of the institution (Boggs, 1993a). The mission and vision statements themselves should be periodically reviewed and updated by the board as indicated by careful research.

Boards set the policies of the college. These policies must be in alignment with the college mission and its vision for the future. Although conventional wisdom is that policy is the business of the board, and administration is the business of the president and the staff (Nelson, 1989), in practice, the board usually expects the president to recommend policies for board approval. In colleges that have strong traditions of shared governance, internal committees and constituencies thoroughly study recommendations for changes in policy before the revisions are brought to the board. In any case, the president should be prepared to recommend proposed policy changes.

Boards are obligated to ensure that the institution is well managed (Nason, 1982). That is not to say that the board should manage the college; they cannot. Instead, they select and appoint a president to lead the administration of the college. Of course, representatives of the internal college community will be involved in the selection of the president as members of the search committee and an external consultant may provide assistance, but the board should reserve the right to interview the finalists and to appoint the president. Then board members must be observant, ask the right questions, and offer advice and counsel to the president as needed. They need to evaluate both the president and themselves at regular intervals. They must also attend to the professional development and personal well-being of the president.

Colleges will not thrive unless the board has confidence in its president (Nason, 1982). Faculty and staff members and sometimes students will, on the occasion of some decision of which they disapprove, take a dim view of the president. Boards must insist, however, that presidents be motivated by doing what is right and not necessarily what is popular. The confidence and trust between a board and the college president must be based upon a long-term relationship and not wax and wane with immediate concerns of the campus community. Boards can do a great deal to support, both privately and publicly, a president under fire for making an unpopular but correct decision. If the board does not have the confidence that the president is willing or able to carry out its policies and to lead the institution, it must act to change presidents.

Trustees and presidents are obligated to ensure the fiscal health of the college. When the budget becomes unbalanced, the response must be some combination of increasing income and decreasing expenditures (Nason, 1982). Unfortunately, laws in many states have greatly restricted the flexibility of local colleges in adjusting either expenditures or income. Authority to set student tuition charges and property tax rates or to adjust the size of the contract faculty and staff differs by state. Nonetheless, local boards and their presidents are held accountable for the proper fiscal management of the college.

Trustees and presidents should also be sure that college funds are invested wisely. Unfortunately, occasional reports surface of colleges and other public agencies that have lost large percentages of their financial reserves or endowments because of risky investments. The college funds must be protected, and investment strategies must be conservative.

Fund raising, long the purview of private colleges, has now become common in public colleges. In response to funding constraints, college boards and presidents are making private fund raising a priority. College development or advancement offices are staffed by professionals who are skilled in all aspects of fund raising, including capital campaigns and annual, deferred, and planned giving (Legon, 1989). Public relations, governmental affairs, alumni affairs, and grant writing activities are often coordinated under the office of college advancement. In private colleges, board members are expected to make substantial financial contributions and to solicit donations from others. In the public colleges, a foundation board often serves this purpose.

Nonetheless, board members and presidents need to support the private fund-raising efforts of the college. They should contribute financially to the extent of their abilities. One hundred percent giving by board members and the president demonstrates the commitment necessary to convince others to give. The board and the president must recognize their responsibility to see that the college's fund-raising efforts are consistent with the mission and priorities of the institution (Legon, 1989). Their attendance at special fund-raising events is important to demonstrate their support. Involved and well-informed board members, willing to help the president by speaking to their colleagues and to groups about the college's goals, priorities, and accomplishments, provide a spirit and enthusiasm that lead to greater involvement in the college and support for its mission.

Some creative college presidents and trustees have found ways to stretch the resources of the college through partnerships with other agencies. For example, Palomar College in Southern California constructed a new Wellness and Fitness Center on the college campus, using funds provided by the city and equipment purchased from funds provided by a local hospital district. The building doubles as a community fitness center and a classroom for students, two compatible functions.

The board and the president have important roles to play in legislative advocacy. For public colleges, state and local appropriations are essential. Both public and private institutions depend in part on federal funds (Nason, 1982). In the competition for limited funds, presidents and trustees should be spokespersons for their institutions. Boards and presidents also need to be vigilant of the efforts of special interest groups that might propose legislation that could hurt the college or its students.

Legislative advocacy does not begin with a need to lobby for or against a bill. Instead, boards and presidents should develop a relationship with legislators and their staffs over a period of time. Board members who are either publicly elected or politically appointed should have an advantage in gaining access to legislators.

It is also important for legislators to see the college president and the board members as people who can sway public opinion. That means that the president and the board members must be visible in the community, and they must support community activities. Writing opinion pieces for the editorial pages of local newspapers or participating in radio or television interviews are other ways that presidents and trustees can gain an image as influential people.

Although college presidents should never financially support candidates for their own board of trustees, they and their board members can support the campaigns of candidates for other public offices. Nothing prevents them from supporting candidates from both political parties. Board members and presidents can provide candidates with information about education to help them build their campaign platforms. Presidents can also moderate candidate debates or forums. This kind of support and visibility often makes a difference in gaining access to busy legislators after the election.

Presidents should invite legislators and their staff members to campus to learn about the college, its programs, and its needs; the lawmakers can go on a short tour of the campus and take that opportunity to visit with students and faculty members. Presidents should ensure that legislators and their staff members see the areas of the campus that need improvement.

In some instances, it will be necessary to mobilize the campus community and college supporters to advocate for needed legislation. Trustees, foundation board members, and college advisory committee members can help by sending letters on business letterhead. The president can improve the response rate of these college supporters by enclosing a sample letter with the request for assistance.

Presidents must take the lead both in communicating frequently with legislators at the local, state, and federal levels and in keeping the board members aware of important legislative issues. Communications with legislators should appeal to any interests they might have that are related to the college mission. As they write letters to legislators, presidents should be sure that all board members receive copies. When legislators help, they should receive thank-you notes from the president.

Boards must also ensure that the college has adequate physical facilities (Nason, 1982). This requirement necessitates planning for future needs as well as maintaining existing facilities. Board members, in particular, must be sure that a facilities master plan for the college is developed and that it is consistent with the educational master plan. In the absence of board attention, faculty and staff members, including the president, may be too deeply concerned with the current problems of operating the college to plan adequately for its future. Because colleges are human service institutions, they tend to focus on the problems of its people and can lose sight of facility needs.

Boards have a special responsibility for future generations of students. While the college community, including the president, may be focused on short-term problems, trustees have an obligation to insist on long-term planning. Here again, it is not the responsibility of the board to draw up the long-range plans, but to insist that the administration and faculty do so in terms that the board can approve. Long-range or strategic plans are defined as plans that embody the institution's key decisions about its mission, its agenda for the next three to fifteen years to fulfill that mission, and its overall goals and objectives (Park, 1989). Long-range plans should implement the college's shared vision statement. All planning should be driven by the college's educational master plan, with adequate attention to instructional, facilities, staff, and student services plans.

Another important mission for boards is to act as both bridge and buffer between the college and the community (Nason, 1982). As lay people involved with the issues and concerns of the community, board members are in a position to interpret the educational needs of the community to the college. According to Nason (1982), trustees ought to be the antennae of the college, relaying what the surrounding world is like and initiating constructive change. The board voice can also be most persuasive in informing community members about the programs and needs of the institution.

Colleges, by their very nature, are seats of controversy (Nason, 1982). Actions of students and faculty members frequently seem at odds with the expectations of at least part of the community. Yet academic freedom, freedom of thought and expression, and exploration are essential to the operation of a quality learning institution. Board members can act as buffers between the college and the community to protect these freedoms and processes and to explain why they are necessary. Institutional autonomy must be preserved.

Trustees also serve as the lay court of last appeal (Nason, 1989). Students, employees, community members, and applicants who are unhappy with administrative decisions can appeal to the board. Even though the board has confidence in the president and the administration, the appeal should be an honest one, with the board basing its decision on the facts at hand. A complainant who is not satisfied with the board's decision has the option of litigating through the courts or filing a complaint with a federal or state agency. Boards must be sure that their decisions are both just and legally defensible.

According to state and local laws, college boards have to take certain other actions. They usually have to approve budgets, financial transactions, property acquisition, curriculum changes, and contracts. They ratify the employment of faculty and staff and approve employee salary schedules. Serious employee or student discipline decisions, termination of employment, and suspension of students may require board ratification. While some of these actions are routine, others are emotional and time-consuming.

The job of a trustee is an important one for a college, and it can be a tough assignment, requiring a commitment of time and hard work. Together with the college president, board members provide visible leadership. Their actions and those of the president set the tone for what happens throughout the institution.

Culture and Commitment

Although trustees may have backgrounds in private business, they will soon realize that colleges cannot be run like private business enterprises (Nason, 1982). The shared authority with faculty and staff, the individualism of the academic departments, the principle of academic freedom, the authority of accreditation commissions, the potential for intrusion by state boards and legislatures, and the limitations on presidential power need to be understood by lay board members. State and federal laws restrict the freedom of judgment of both the president and the board. In addition, the operations of the board, in most states, are governed by strict open-meeting laws. Actions, which in private business might be confidential, are open to public view in a tax-supported college.

To prepare new board members to serve in this complex environment, the wise president schedules at least one orientation workshop and allots sufficient time to provide information about the college—its mission and vision, and its structure and operations—and about trusteeship, ethics, and expectations for trustees. Members of the president's executive leadership team can help the president by presenting information about the operation of the major divisions of the college. The president should discuss the college mission, vision for the future, long-range plans, and the college's shared governance system. The president also can schedule a walking tour, along with opportunities to talk with faculty, staff, and students, for board members not familiar with the campus.

Ingram (1989) suggests that an outside consultant or trustee from another institution, rather than the president, should lead the discussion about trusteeship, ethics, and expectations, thus allowing the president to participate instead of facilitate. The president also avoids having to lead the discussion on the relationship between the board and the president.

A facilitator can use the college's own code of ethics for trustees, which is now required for community colleges by most accreditation commissions (Boggs, 1993b). Codes of ethics and written expectations should constantly guide the behavior of the board in its important work, not just at an orientation workshop.

In particular, trustees must pledge to devote sufficient time, thought, and study to their duties as board members so they can render effective and creditable service. They should attend board meetings on time, reading agenda materials, and preparing adequately for board meetings. It is also helpful, however, for trustees to attend campus events and functions, especially commencement exercises and program graduation ceremonies. Although they cannot speak for the board without authorization, individual board members should also plan to attend community events as representatives of the college.

Board members must understand the importance of working with their peers on the board and the president in a spirit of harmony and cooperation, in spite of differences of opinion that may arise during vigorous debates of points at issue. Some boards and presidents emphasize the importance of board consensus or unanimous decisions. Divided board votes do not have to be a problem as long as a divided board does not emerge. Individual decisions must be based upon all available facts about the issues. Minority opinions should be respected, but the majority decision of the board must be supported. Abiding by these principles sets an example for the rest of the college to follow.

In cases in which a college president has to work with a split board, it is important that the president not become politically aligned with one faction over the other. Political winds change, and a majority faction may find itself in the minority after the next election. A president can get trapped by these political shifts. Political turmoil between board members or between the president and board members is not healthy for the college. Constant turnover of personnel in the position of president is a sign of poor leadership by the board, and this instability affects the whole college.

Some college presidents would view it as a personal defeat if the board did not support one of their recommendations. Surely, the board must seriously consider the recommendation of the college president. The president has studied the options and brings years of professional experience and personal knowledge of the college to bear in making a recommendation. Board members, however, must always make their decisions on the merits of the recommendation rather than who is making it. To do otherwise would indicate a weak board acting as nothing more than a rubber stamp for the president's wishes. Popcock (1989) indicates that presidents must supply solid recommendations, but they must accept the fact that boards will, on occasion, reject them. Consistent disregard of a president's recommendations signals that the board and president do not share common philosophies, and both should be looking for a change.

Board members need to know that, as individuals, they have no legal authority outside the meetings of the board. Comments by individual board members to the president, for example, are taken as suggestions, whereas actions by the majority of the board in a board meeting are directives for the president to implement. In talking with the press, an individual board member does not represent the board unless the majority of the board so directed in a board meeting.

The president and the board members must resist every temptation and outside pressure to use their positions to benefit themselves or any other person or agency apart from the total welfare of the college. Even the appearance of a conflict of interest can create negative publicity and perhaps legal problems for the college as well as for the person involved.

In issues of principle, it is important for the board and the president to convey clearly their commitment to particular philosophies. Student access to an affordable and quality higher education is an almost universal value of the community college movement. Trustees and presidents should also express their commitment to student equity efforts that measure and support the success of students regardless of gender and ethnicity. Strong support of the college's affirmative action efforts by the college president and the board is important if the college community is to take these efforts seriously.

Trustees should pledge to learn continually about their responsibilities and to avail themselves of opportunities to enhance their potentials through participation in educational conferences, workshops, and training sessions offered by local, state, and national associations. They should strive to be informed about the actions and positions of state and national trustee associations.

In the course of working together as a team, the college president will, no doubt, develop friendships with some board members. Both the president and the board member, however, must be sure that personal friendship does not interfere with professional responsibilities. Presidents must ensure that all board members receive the information and support they need to perform their duties. Presidents should never become involved in intimate relationships with members of their board. The unfortunate presidents who have done so usually have paid for this mistake with loss of their jobs and damage to their career.

Process and Communications

The business of the board is, for the most part, conducted in open and publicly announced meetings. Meetings are not designed to be entertaining, but neither should they be boring. Reports can be scheduled to inform the board about college programs and to give them needed background on items that will eventually be on board agendas. These reports, however, should be concise and to the point.

The frequency and length of board meetings varies by type of college and by state. Many community college boards meet once or twice a month for two to three hours. Meetings that are more infrequent or considerably shorter may indicate a board that is not meeting its responsibilities. Meetings that are more frequent or considerably longer may indicate a board that is either unprepared for the meetings or too involved in the administration of the college.

Preparing the agenda for board meetings is an important responsibility for the college president. In colleges with strong board chairs, the chair may also be involved in the development of the agenda. Members of the president's executive leadership team perform most of the work of preparing the agenda and gathering the backup materials, while the president's staff coordinates the work. Materials should be assembled and distributed in time to meet the requirements of public notification and to allow the board members time to review and study the issues.

If the board is small, presidents may want to call board members after they have had time to review the agenda and the backup materials. This telephone call gives the president a chance to answer quick questions and prepare the staff to answer more involved questions at the meeting. Members of larger boards should be encouraged to call the president with their questions in advance of the meeting. Without this advance notice, staff members may be caught unaware and not be able to respond appropriately at the board meeting. The president should not use the telephone call to advocate for a particular position. Arguments about the issues should be reserved for the boardroom.

Trustees and the president should welcome and encourage the active involvement of students, employees, and citizens of the district when changing college policies. Their views should be considered by the board in its deliberations. Some boards provide seats at the board table for representatives of the faculty, staff, and students. Opportunities should be provided in meetings for members of the audience to address the board briefly to provide information about agenda items.

The board should set aside time for public comment during the meeting. Comments regarding agenda items may be heard as these items are taken up by the board. Some board policies require attendees to submit written requests to the president before addressing the board. Policies may also limit the time that speakers have to make their statements. Presidents and boards can use these policies to control the meetings, but they must be careful not to restrict public comment. Board members should not engage in lengthy discussions about items not on the agenda so they can avoid violating open meeting laws.

Board members and the president must recognize that deliberations and discussions of the board, staff, and legal counsel in closed or executive session are not to be released or discussed in public without the prior approval of the board by majority vote. Open meeting laws in most states restrict closed-session topics to such items as personnel matters, student discipline, pending litigation, salary negotiations, and land acquisition.

The board members and the president must bear in mind under all circumstances that the board is legally responsible for the effective operation of the college. The president will be held accountable to the board for the administration of the educational program and the conduct of college business in accordance with board policies. Actions of the president and the board must always be in the best interests of the college, its programs, and its people.

In some colleges, the tradition of a strong board chair changes the relationship that presidents have with board members. Agreements between the board chair and the president may require presidential communications to board members to be channeled through the board chair. The board chair, rather than the president, may be the person designated by the board to speak on its behalf (Popcock, 1989), in which case, it is important for the president and the board chair to establish a relationship characterized by mutual respect and trust. In a survey of board chairs and presidents, Cleary found the personal interaction between the president and chair to be the single most important factor in the trustee-president relationship (Popcock, 1988).

In many cases, college presidents will find that the most influential member of the board may not be the chair. Strong board chairs are less likely to be found in instances in which the board chair position rotates, either by policy or by practice. Presidents would be wise to remain uninvolved in the board's selection of officers, especially the board chair, except to answer questions and to explain the requirements of the positions.

A president will find a strong board chair to be most helpful when problems arise with a board member. Popcock (1989) points out that no president should be expected to discipline a board member. A board chair or another influential board member can help by discussing concerns with the particular trustee in private. Occasions may emerge in which the whole board has to deal with a disruptive trustee or with one who is not living up to expectations or ethical standards. Unfortunately, open-meeting laws in some states do not permit a board to address these issues in closed or executive sessions.

The president's office should be the main point of contact between the board and the college. Having a separate board office on the campus or hiring a separate staff for the board threatens the effectiveness of the president and invites the board to cross the line between policy and implementation.

Some presidents want all communications from board members to pass through them. The president can then contact appropriate staff members to gather information before answering the board member's questions. Other presidents are comfortable with board members contacting other members of the executive leadership team directly as long as the president knows about the contacts and their nature. It is important in such a case for both the board members and the members of the executive leadership team to keep the president in the information loop.

A president cannot control contacts to the board members from students, faculty, staff, and community members. Board members, however, should learn how to deal with information relayed in these contacts. If the communication reveals a potential administrative problem, the board member should refer the issue to the president to address through appropriate administrative channels. If the person is trying to influence a board decision on policy, the board member may choose to listen but should reserve judgment for the boardroom, which is the appropriate venue for airing recommendations from shared governance committees and the president. Popcock (1988) cautions board chairs to resist the temptation to respond to queries from faculty, students, administrators, and the news media until they are confident of the facts and have the president's agreement on the response. Board members should never commit to any course of action based upon what they hear from people outside of a board meeting.

Board members may choose to visit the campus occasionally to become better informed by talking with students and employees and sitting in on some classes and shared governance committee meetings. In these cases, the college president should always be informed. The president's office can help to facilitate the visit. A trustee who does not inform the president about campus visits can, by this action, convey a lack of trust in the president. Meetings between a union and a board member during a collective bargaining impasse can damage the negotiations process. A board member who consistently attends a shared governance committee runs the risk of inhibiting discussion and interfering with a process that is intended to bring informed recommendations to the board.

Board members and the college president are highly visible people that the public almost always identifies with the college. News stories usually link these college leaders to the college even though the story may be completely unrelated to the institution. Thus, the president and the trustees must be particularly careful that what they do does not damage the reputation of the college.

Systems Thinking

A board of trustees is more than just the sum of its individual members. Interactions among members and between the president and the members make the board a dynamic and complex group. The group can spend its time on individual board interests and disruptive issues—or it can act to ensure the effective leadership of the college and to plan for the institution's future. The board must ultimately act as a board and not just as a collection of individual members.

Board agenda items may seem to provide an opportunity to take isolated and unrelated actions. It is vital, however, for the actions of the board to fit into overall college systems. Where board committees are a part of the structure of the board, board members should work to avoid getting too specialized and concerned about one aspect of the college at the expense of the entire institution. If board committees exist, they should advise the board, not college staff members.

Board members and the president must recognize the complexity of the college and its operations. Board members must take the long-range view, especially when to do so is difficult for the president and the college community. They must insist on periodic review of the college mission and vision statements. They must be sure that the college community engages in planning and develops a useful educational master plan in agreement with the college mission and vision statements. The facility, staff, instruction, and student services plans must be integral parts of the educational master plan for the college.

It is often helpful to the board and the president to schedule occasional retreats or workshops. At these meetings, away from the demands of a regular board meeting, trustees and the president can set goals for themselves and evaluate their progress in meeting those goals and assess the progress of the college toward its vision of the future. An outside facilitator may help to make a retreat more productive. A side benefit of these more informal meetings is a better understanding of roles and a better working relationship among members.

We've seen that boards approve the policies of the college. Implementation of the board policies is the business of the president and the staff. Policies that the faculty and administration adopt must be consistent with or subordinate to policies that the board adopts (Nelson, 1989). Through its authority to set policies and its attention to the long-range interests of the college, the board is in control of the systems that operate to define the college and its character.

Outcomes and Rewards

Community college presidents and board members do not often think of themselves as researchers. The label does not seem to fit people whose jobs are to inspire, lead, and set policy. In many ways, however, college presidents and board members should be among the most knowledgeable researchers on their campuses. They must be in touch with the realities of their campuses. They should expect staff members to be able to perform and recognize quality research and evaluation and to use those findings to improve the quality of college programs and services (Boggs, 1988).

Board members set policy based upon the information they receive in board agendas and meetings. They need to be sure the information is accurate and reliable. After they approve the policies, they need to be sure they are implemented as intended. The tool that board members have to accomplish these tasks is the ability to ask the right questions. A common board folly, according to Carver (1990), is for boards to want to "know everything that is going on" (p. 119).

Carver (1990) suggests that boards receive only three types of information: Decision information is that information that a board receives to make decisions. This information is not judgmental. It is prospective in that it looks to the future, and boards use it to evaluate some aspect of the future.

Monitoring information is used to gauge whether previous board directions have been satisfied. This type of information is judgmental in that it intentionally measures performance. It is retrospective in that it looks to the past. Good monitoring information is a systematic survey of performance against criteria.

Carver defines information that is not decision information or monitoring information as incidental. Most of the information presented at board meetings, he notes, is incidental information. Carver warns that incidental information often masquerades as monitoring information, and he implies that it is less valuable. It does, however, serve to educate boards about the college and its programs.

Monitoring information is important for boards to be sure that the college is fulfilling its mission. The reports of outside auditing firms provide valuable information about the college's financial operations, investment strategies, and fiscal solvency. A board should be aware, however, that every request it makes, including requests for information and reports, entails a cost to the college. Boards should not burden the staff with requests for unnecessary information.

Boards should periodically evaluate their own performance. The purposes of board evaluation are to clarify roles, to enhance harmony and understanding among board members, and to improve the efficiency and effectiveness of board meetings. The goal is to improve college operations and policies for the benefit of the community, the students, and the employees. The self-evaluation process is often best scheduled at a special meeting or retreat. An outside facilitator might help to keep the discussions productive. Board members should complete a short self-assessment before the meeting to provide a basis for discussion. Palomar College, California, uses a self-assessment form that asks the board members to rate themselves and their fellow board members in a variety of areas.

Evaluation of the president is one of the most important responsibilities of a college board. Many opportunities arise for informal evaluative comments during the course of interactions between the president and the board, but an annually scheduled formal evaluation of the president works especially well. The purpose is to clarify the expectations placed on this position by the board of trustees and to assess performance based upon these expectations. Improvement of performance, a clearer sense of direction, and reinforcing recognition should be the primary goals of the evaluation. The process and criteria used should be understood by and mutually acceptable to the board and the president. The formal evaluation should result in a written record of performance upon which the board bases its annual review of the president's contract.

To assist the board in its annual evaluation of the president, the president should prepare an end-of-year report, which can serve as a self-evaluation. These reports can document the activities of the president in maintaining positive community and college relationships, in administering the college, and in providing educational leadership. A section of the report should be devoted to the degree to which the goals set by the president and the board have been accomplished. According to Carver (1990), organizational performance and CEO performance are the same.

The president's contract should clearly state the terms of employment for the president, including duties, salary, benefits, expense allowances, travel allowances, important working conditions, and the term of office. Presidents and boards should never agree to any benefit for the president that is not included in writing in the contract. The contract serves as a written record and can be used to prevent misunderstandings that otherwise could prove embarrassing to the president and the board.

When the majority of the board find it necessary to make a change in presidential leadership, the board should communicate this to the president in a closed-session board meeting. It would be unusual for a president to be surprised by an action like this because of the informal and formal feedback provided by the evaluation process. Nonetheless, it is important for the board to make its decision known to the president clearly and in enough time for the president to plan for the future.

Similarly, it is important for the president to communicate plans to leave the presidency in a timely enough manner for the board to plan for the future of the college. The board will need time to decide whether to employ a search consultant, what characteristics would be desirable in a new president, and what the involvement of the college community will be in the search process.

All too often, changes in college leadership are accompanied by controversy. Newspaper articles and contentious lawsuits focus negative attention on the college, the board, and the president. Barring evidence of a president's unethical behavior, the board's responsibility to protect the president does not end until the president leaves. If the board were to help with the transition of the president, it should be possible to avoid these problems.

When colleges have effective presidents, boards should do what they can, within reason, to retain them. The best match between the skills and abilities of the president and the needs for leadership of the college is not always easy to find. Moreover, a presidential search is costly in time and money.

The rewards for service on a college board are, for the most part, individually derived. In some states, board members receive a small stipend for their service on a college board. Board members can often receive insurance coverage or other benefits from the college. Sometimes they receive a plaque when they retire from the board or when they complete a term as board chair. These benefits, however, are not compensation enough for the hard work and long hours necessary to do a good job as a board member.

Some board members and presidents enjoy the visibility and prestige that come with college leadership. Presidents should always try to ensure that their board members are recognized publicly and that they are given credit for their leadership. The most significant reward for presidents and board members, however, is the knowledge that they are contributing to the successful operation of a college and thereby improving both the community and the lives of students. A sense of satisfaction should result from this most important civic contribution.

References

Axelrod, Nancy R. *A Guide For New Trustees*. Washington, D.C.: Association of Governing Boards, 1989.

Boggs, George R. "Institutional Distinctiveness." In Steven W. Jones (Ed.), *Shaping the Community College Image*. Greeley, Colo.: National Council for Marketing and Public Relations, 1993a.

Boggs, George R. "Making An Ethical Statement." In *Trustee Quarterly*. Washington, D.C.: Association of Community College Trustees, 1993b.

Boggs, George R. "The Research Function Of Community Colleges." In *Leadership Abstracts*, 1988, *1* (13).

Carver, John. *Boards That Make A Difference*. San Francisco: Jossey-Bass, 1990.

Community College League of California. *Community College Trustees: Powers and Responsibilities*. Reference Information Guide for California Community College Trustees. Sacramento, Calif.: Community College League of California, January 1995.

Ingram, Richard T. "Organizing The Board." In R.T. Ingram & Associates (Eds.), *Making Trusteeship Work*. Washington, D.C.: Association of Governing Boards, 1988.

Ingram, Richard T. *Trustee Orientation and Development Programs*. Washington, D.C.: Association of Governing Boards, 1989.

Legon, Richard D. *The Fund Raising Role*. Washington, D.C.: Association of Governing Boards, 1989.

Nason, John W. *The Nature of Trusteeship*. Washington D.C.: Association of Governing Boards, 1982.

Nason, John W. *Trustee Responsibilities*. Washington, D.C.: Association of Governing Boards, 1989.

Nelson, Charles A. *Distinguishing Between Policy and Administration*. Washington, D.C.: Association of Governing Boards, 1989.

Park, Dabney. *The Board's Role In Planning*. Washington, D.C.: Association of Governing Boards, 1989.

Popcock, John W. "Maintaining Effective Chair-CEO Relationships." In R.T. Ingram & Associates (Eds.), *Making Trusteeship Work*. Washington, D.C.: Association of Governing Boards, 1988.

Popcock, John W. *The Board Chair-President Relationship*. Washington, D.C.: Association of Governing Boards, 1989.

Stecklow, Steve. "Chief Prerequisite for College President's Job: Stamina." *Wall Street Journal*, December 1, 1994, pp. B1, B6.

CHAPTER 3

THE CHANCELLOR AND THE MULTICAMPUS TEAM

An Application of Life Cycle Theory

JEFF HOCKADAY
PHILIP J. SILVERS

D uring the early 1990s, management literature has seen a surge of changes in recommended practices and paradigms. The age of information networks, increasingly global, turbulent environments, and continuing pressures for quality improvement and accountability have sent managers and theorists scrambling for success strategies.

This chapter applies some of the recently advanced organizational theories to the day-to-day reality of leading a large, multicampus community college from 1990 to 1994. After a brief description of Pima Community College (PCC), Arizona, in its historical setting, the chapter will review the key quality initiatives undertaken at the college, the use of multicampus teams, and lessons learned from our experience.

Some Observations on the Organizational Climate: 1990

As the college approached its twentieth anniversary, it was emerging from several years of governance turmoil. The new chancellor found a college characterized by major enrollment growth, the successive establishment of new campuses, and a history of faculty attempts to influence governing board composition and actions. Over the years, the college had moved through two phases of the organizational life cycle described by Cameron and Whetten (1984): First, an *entrepreneurial* phase in which the faculty led a surge of innovation and creativity and then a *collectivity* phase—a period of high cohesion and commitment. When the new chancellor arrived, the college was struggling through the third phase of *formalization and control*. The college sought stability and institutionalization during a period when it had added four new campuses and experienced a growth trajectory from 3,000 to 28,000 students. The challenge facing the new chancellor was to move beyond the formalization and control phase into the fourth life-cycle phase of *structure elaboration and adaptation*. At the same time, he needed to change certain patterns of behavior internally while responding to the external requirements of the state board and the regional accrediting authority. Two prerequisites suggested by Lorsch (1976) were present: The "psychological contract" between the college and its employees must be maintained and the college and the community must support necessary change. Although community leaders had rallied around the college and assisted in recruiting a new class of governing board members to replace those who had resigned or who had been removed, major challenges lay ahead.

Projects, Processes, and Results: 1990–1994

Before taking office, the chancellor tapped several information sources necessary to understand the history, organization, and culture of the college. He reviewed a vision statement recently developed by the new board and college representatives, as well as findings and recommendations from a visit by a North Central Association accrediting team. He held a series of open forums for faculty at each of the campuses and met with administrative staff and community members. The forums aimed to shape the existing culture and gain commitment of the faculty to the mission that each professional would be expected to support.

The first priority was to evaluate the college mission and establish mission-related goals (*Indicators of Success*). Decentralization of responsibility for services and functions followed the mission review, along with initiatives in leadership development and strategic planning, creation of new policies on the use of part-time faculty, and a reduction in the number of departments and new roles for department chairs. Other initiatives on information services and student outcomes assessment are still under way. Table 3.1 summarizes these initiatives, the team processes used, and the results.

Key Initiatives Undertaken

To move toward increased collectivity as suggested by Cameron and Whetten (1984), the college undertook six tasks. They were: the development of a new

46

Table 3.1
Effecting Change at Pima Community College

Task	Team Process	Outcome
Mission Evaluation and Goals (indicators of success)	Two community charrettes, followed by a task force to operationalize the indicators.	Highly successful both internally and in the external community. Process has been adopted by units of the college and by other institutions.
Decentralization of Services and Functions	Task forces, followed by cabinet review. Provosts serving as a team.	Moderately successful. Uneven assumption of responsibility at campuses. Some lower priority issues did not get adressed or fell through the cracks.
Leadership Development For provosts	Retreats, meetings to assess and modify the process. Team-building assignments; e.g., here is the problem: You go solve it.	Provosts, who had been centralized on their campuses, came together as a team.
For the college in general	Week-long seminar teams, "Investment in Excellence" teams, administrative and staff development workshops.	Knowledge about the college and about leadership was empowering; attention paid to employees increased their willingness to participate in projects.
Strategic Planning	Community and college surveys and charrettes. Issue-oriented task forces. Reciprocal activities between campuses and district.	Highly successful. Termed *exemplary* by NCA team. Survey showed employees have positive attitude toward the planning process.

(continued on next page)

Table 3.1 (continued)

Task	Team Process	Outcome
Adjunct Faculty	Survey, followed by a task force chaired by the chancellor.	Successful. Five-year plan agreeable to full-time and part-time faculty. Adjunct faculty now have highest pay level among adjunct faculty in statewide system.
Department Chairs	First attempt: Decentralized approach—delegated to provosts to handle at the campus level.	First attempt: Failure—found it was a district rather than a campus issue.
	Second attempt: Task force of affected department chairs chaired by the chancellor.	Second attempt: Successful. Reduced departments from 79 to 36.
Program and Services Review	Task force of campus faculty and administrators.	Moderately successful. Adversely affected by process of shifting to a decentralized environment. Evolved from a complex to a simplified format.
Student Outcomes Assessment	Task forces of campus faculty and administrators.	Minimal progress. Stymied until the department chair issue was resolved.

mission statement, decentralization of college functions and responsibilities, leadership development, strategic planning, development of adjunct faculty, and development of department chairs.

Development of a New Mission Statement
The first major project was the 1990 update of the college mission statement. The college used a charrette process, a fast-moving, interactive assembly of a

cross-section of stakeholders as the key vehicle. The group of 100 community citizens and college employees represented a variety of roles, occupations, ages, ethnicities, and geographical areas. The 100 participants became ten teams; each team with a designated facilitator and an assigned aspect of the college mission, e.g., student development, general education, and bilingual/multicultural education. Expertise in the subject area and leadership skills were the basis for selecting facilitators. For example, the facilitator for the team dealing with *access* was hearing impaired.

Before the charrette, team members received the results of a community goals and values survey about the college, articles on college missions, and the results of the new chancellor's "Call for Papers" from every employee of the college. Employees were asked to write on any aspect of the college mission, and thirty responded. These papers provided a foundation for the charrettes that followed.

The charrette facilitator, Dale Parnell, held a luncheon meeting with team leaders and recorders before the charrette started. Once in motion, the charrette moved quickly to a conclusion after two half-days (one afternoon and the next morning). The ten groups each drafted pieces of a mission statement, related to their assigned topic. A jury of two faculty, a student, a business leader, and an administrator heard presentations of results. Prompted by the jury's comments, the teams reconvened and reworked their statements. This process occurred several times until the jury and each of the committees was satisfied with the statements. After a concluding luncheon celebration, the results were turned over to an editorial committee, which integrated the statements into a unified document. Within two weeks the draft mission statement was approved by the chancellor's cabinet and the governing board and published in the local papers, along with the names of charrette participants.

The college used a similar charrette with the same participants five months later to develop measurable *Indicators of Success* for each aspect of the new mission statement. Each year, the chancellor issues a "Report to the Community," which documents the outcomes for the indicators. This double-team process resulted in increased commitment and support of the college mission by college faculty, staff, and administration and by the community. Other institutions and the statewide system emulated the charrette process that had so benefited Pima Community College. The next task was to decentralize power by applying the mission concepts to college functions and reassigning responsibilities to college units, teams, and individuals.

Decentralization of College Functions and Responsibilities
Working in teams, key administrators, staff, and faculty identified the appropriate level of decentralization for every task or function within the college. For example, one team dealing with student financial aid identified the service functions most appropriately performed at the campus level, inter-campus level, or the district level. The cabinet, along with faculty and staff councils, reviewed the team recommendations.

Resulting sentiment was overwhelmingly positive about the move to decentralize. It took months of evolution, however, to devise appropriate decision-making mechanisms to deal with inter-campus and district decisions. Uneven assumptions of responsibility occurred at the various campuses, and lower priority issues often were not properly addressed or delegated.

Leadership Development

Several leadership development initiatives relied on team processes as well. To foster leadership among the provosts, the chancellor provided general guidance, principles, and feedback within the cabinet setting. Most important, however, was the challenge to the provosts to come to an agreement *on their own* about rational resource allocation among the campuses and greater efficiencies in the financial management of the college. Meeting before the cabinet meetings for several months, the provosts developed a consensus on resource allocation and program coordination. The resulting agreements broke long-standing antipathies among campuses over resources. Still under way, however, is the fostering of strategic decision making within the group, i.e., analyzing external events and trends to effect strategic positioning of the campuses and the college within higher-education resources for the community.

Leadership development initiatives also were extended to faculty, administrators, and staff. In the *Leadership Seminar*, all college employees were eligible for nomination by peers and supervisors. The twice-a-year series of week-long seminars for twenty participants focused on such aspects of leadership as financial management, disability access, media relations, law and liability, and the future of higher education—each taught by distinguished local or national experts. Alumni of this program not only grew in knowledge, but experienced increased bonding to the institution. This bonding occurred among the provosts and with the chancellor and cabinet members who were invited to attend.

All employees were similarly eligible to apply to participate in *Investment in Excellence in the 1990s,* a six-week series of training and group interactions that focused on goal setting through visualization and the development of leadership traits and skills. These leadership development opportunities resulted in some of the participants' emergence as leaders when they were called upon to accept new challenges.

Strategic Planning

The college's approach to strategic planning orchestrated a *reciprocating* process between campus and district planning. That is, the processes were interdependent with each level influencing the other. On both levels, planning teams were representative and cross-functional and comprised individuals who had distinguished themselves by their vision and competence. While the planning teams were limited to ten to twelve persons, *all* employees had some opportunity to contribute to the process—through surveys, written input, or charrettes.

The chancellor provided the basic structure for coordination of the process but allowed the planning teams the freedom to pursue alternative methods and sources. While planning was ongoing, the process required strong leadership in order to become ingrained into the college fabric. The college scheduled major planning charrettes, surveys, meetings, and reports carefully so as not to disrupt the operational business of the institution. The institution implemented planning in two phases: a *strategic phase*, which set a direction for the college based on changing environmental conditions, and a *master-planning phase*, which provided detailed action plans, timelines, and required resources. The cabinet and the faculty, staff, and student councils reviewed and approved the draft plans that the teams had produced before the plans were sent through the chancellor to the board of governors for approval.

The planning process produced superb results: It provided to the college a vision of the future, and for the first time, employees knew that planning truly influenced the budgeting process. A North Central Association accrediting team called the PCC planning process "exemplary."

Adjunct Faculty

When the new chancellor arrived in 1990, a major pressure issue from both inside and outside the college was the use of part-time faculty as instructors. Some questioned the high proportion of part-time faculty; others questioned the quality of instruction, and still others complained about compensation and support for the part-time instructors.

As an initial step, all department chairs and all 1,300 part-time faculty were surveyed on a variety of topics. In response to the chancellor's request in the cover letter, 80 percent of the adjunct faculty and 89 percent of the department chairs responded to the survey in a timely manner.

The chancellor also commissioned a survey of part-time faculty compensation at PCC's peer institutions nationwide and at all colleges within the state. He then assembled a team of twenty department chairs, administrators, and part-time faculty to develop a set of recommendations regarding part-time faculty. At the initial meeting, the chancellor distributed the research results, charged the task force, and assigned six two-person teams to develop their thoughts on topics believed to be key issues. The issues included recruitment and screening, compensation, professional development, and support for part-time faculty. In a series of semi-weekly meetings, the chancellor led discussions and debate on each of the papers, culminating with a series of recommendations on each issue. Upon hearing the ensuing recommendations, the cabinet agreed to implement scheduling cost-efficiencies to offset the recommended increases in part-time faculty compensation. The governing board thereupon approved the recommendations to be phased in over a three-year period. Pima Community College adjunct faculty now are highly competent and enjoy the highest compensation rate in the state, and almost all of the recommendations are fully implemented to the satisfaction of both department chairs and adjunct faculty.

Department Chairs
Consolidation of the number of departments was a thorny issue, with faculty and department chairs openly resistant to change. As the college grew to five campuses over a twenty-year period, departments proliferated. An effort to coordinate programs across campuses was floundering. College administrators knew that seventy-nine departments were unwieldy and unworkable.

The chancellor first assigned the project to the team of provosts. Meeting as a team, the provosts devised a plan for down-sizing departments from seventy-nine to forty-five. The plan accommodated different departmental configurations for each of the five campuses. The plan used little input from those most affected—department chairs—and it ignored the recommendations of a faculty task force, which had visited other colleges to study the issue. A furor erupted when the plan was announced. At that point, explanations and rationales did little to resolve the matter. The faculty were unhappy about any process that would change the status quo.

Realizing that the issue was a district one and not a campus-level issue, the chancellor asked the provosts to withdraw their plan. He then assembled a blue-ribbon task force of the most concerned department chairs, which he himself chaired. The task force moved slowly, meeting over lunch for several weeks before any directions began to emerge. The chairs first came to realize that the proliferation of departments was indeed debilitating to the academic enterprise. They also realized that solutions would not be simple. Over the ensuing weeks of meeting, the department chairs reconfigured the department structures and formulated a set of recommendations for departmental chair responsibilities. While the emerging consensus required some major accommodations by every participant, the plan was deemed workable. To the surprise of nearly everyone, the department chairs had reduced the number of departments to thirty-nine—six fewer than the provosts had recommended. The major lesson learned was that when problems are resolved at the level where the participants are most vested, teamwork and effective decision making can produce surprising results.

Theory Playing Out in Reality: The Use of Multicampus Teams

The first part of this chapter was designed to illustrate how organizational concepts were used to reengineer Pima Community College during the period 1990–1994. The second part will demonstrate how quality concepts supported by systems thinking resulted in a changed culture at Pima Community College during the same period.

The following section illustrates how principles in literature relevant to organizational processes and leadership were applied at one multicampus community college in the early 1990s to create positive change. We will attempt to identify instances where theory was proven true in reality, as well as note initiatives that were successful and those that faltered.

Quality improvement relies on approaches that recognize and effectively utilize systems thinking. This chapter focuses on the major components of a multicampus college system as they played out at PCC from 1990–1994: organizational culture, the external environment, organizational structure, leadership and stakeholder relations, and teams as a systems component. We will explore some of the salient literature related to each component and, later, draw some implications for multicampus leadership of teams.

Organizational Culture

Over the past decade, scores of authors have written on the influences of organizational culture on college processes and outcomes. For Bolman and Deal (1985), *organizational culture* consists of the values, beliefs, and meanings that organizational members subscribe to in institutional life. These qualities are identified in organizational structures and through patterns of interactions between individuals and in images and themes explored in the analysis of conversations. Peterson and Spencer (1990) expand this view by describing *deeply embedded* patterns of behavior, values, and beliefs that actually guide members' daily activities. At Pima Community College, campus personnel tended to fault the central administration for controlling information, for the autocratic development of policies/procedures, and the allocation of funds and other resources. Another prominent pattern was the practice of faculty members contacting governing board members so as to gain power in influencing administrative decisions.

This concept is addressed by Trice and Beyer (1993), who believe that subcultures—often based on function, geographic location, and occupation—can engender the attitude that one race or group is superior within the organization. This belief leads invariably to competition and conflict. The major manifestation of this concept within the subcultures at PCC was the inter-campus competition for programs and resources.

At PCC, it was important for the chancellor to understand these deeply embedded patterns as they surfaced in faculty-board interactions, inter-campus relations, and other organizational processes. Once understood, the challenge was to rechannel some of these patterns and to defuse dysfunctional patterns through the use of new symbols, structures, and team processes. In effect, many instances arose in which the college approached the *learning organization* coined by Peter Senge (1990) in which "new and expansive patterns of thinking are nurtured, where collective aspiration is set free, and where people learn how to learn together" (p. 3). While the culture of the college has evolved since its founding, the institution has experienced major shifts in the culture and subcultures through team-based approaches initiated during the past four years. Decentralization has given campuses more control over resources and decisions. Given major responsibility for district resource allocations, the campus provosts team now works together in deciding how to share programs and resources.

The External Environment

Alfred and Smydra (1985) observe that the nature and degree of influence carried by individual groups will vary with changing environmental conditions facing the college. In the vacuum of public apathy toward college governance in the late 1980s, small groups of faculty gained influence with elements of the governing board. When board indiscretions and administrative snafus at PCC triggered probation by the regional accrediting authority, public indignation led to the formation of a "citizens" support group. Suddenly, the community began seeing the college as a key part of the larger socioeconomic system (Lorenzo & LeCroy, 1994). The community was poised to support responsible and effective leadership. Similarly, the vast majority of college employees were looking to the new chancellor to lead the college out of its dysfunctional behavior patterns.

Although the perception of PCC in the *external environment* in 1990 was characterized by lack of public confidence in college governance, local economic downturn, diminished state funding, 4 to 6 percent enrollment growth, and a lapse in community leadership, the chancellor collaborated with employees and community leaders in using a team approach to organizational change. As discussed in the first part of this chapter, two community charrettes effectively brought college employees together with community leaders to create a new mission statement and a set of indicators by which the mission would be annually evaluated (Hockaday & Silvers, 1994).

Organizational Structure

Richardson and Simmons (1989) have observed that community college organizations established in the early 1970s have undergone very little organizational change. While this stability may be true for colleges that remained primarily one-campus organizations or that operated in relatively placid external environments, PCC experienced continuing change as it added four new campuses from 1974 to 1993. As PCC grew, the college faced the classic challenges reported by Lawrence and Lorsch (1986). These are: differentiation, integration, and adaptation to the external environment. The external environment was volatile. A roller coaster economy, declining state funding, a burgeoning population with increasingly minority representation, and citizen apathy toward the governance process were explosive issues. Simple rational and mechanical means did not spur integration and collaboration once the college was split into multiple campuses. Nor did administrative *fiat* bring about change. Teams became the primary means of integrating and reengineering college processes. Those teams consisted of task forces, community charrettes, standing committees, and the chancellor's cabinet.

To develop an organizational strategy, the chancellor focused his attention on the first two of five organizational levels described by Mintzberg (1979) as *the operating core* (faculty) and *the strategic apex* (the cabinet). Through the decentralization initiative, the chancellor also shifted the college from a heavily hierarchical structure to a more lateral structure (Galbraith & Lawler, 1993). Hierarchies are thought to impede the flow of information, cooperation, and decision making. To create a flatter structure, as Bess (1988) suggests, the chancellor needed to make it worthwhile for the campuses to collaborate. The payoffs for the campus provosts included increased resources and increased responsibility in district decision making.

The use of project teams at PCC validated Kanter's (1983) point that, in modern organizations, specialization is not as important as coordination. As each project team completed its work, the college found itself being transformed through reengineering processes (Hammer & Champy, 1993). The earmarks of these new processes were:

- Some jobs were combined into one (e.g., coordination of academic affairs and student development);
- Work was performed where it made the most sense (e.g., the job-placement function was decentralized; department chairs resolved the issue of a proliferation of departments);
- Checks and controls were reduced (e.g., simplified and less frequent evaluation of faculty by students);
- Hybrid centralized/decentralized operations (e.g., strategic planning, human resources services, student financial aid);
- Work units changed from functional departments to process teams (e.g., Program and Services Review);
- People's roles changed—from controlled to empowered (e.g., provosts and deans); and
- Focus on performance shifted from activity to results (e.g., mission indicators of success).

These changes, however, were not simply the result of logical planning. As James Champy (1994) notes, the best designed reengineering efforts fail unless managers can organize, inspire, deploy, enable, measure, and reward the value-adding operational work. In other words, *effective leadership* is essential.

Leadership

Bensimon (1994) reports that the bureaucratic leadership style is most common among community college CEOs. She also notes that, unlike university presidents, leaders in community colleges usually employ only one style rather than multiple styles. Richardson (1984) observes that faculty prefer an organizational structure in which they can exercise considerable influence over those things that affect their jobs. When PCC was founded in 1970, the culture of the college allowed faculty considerable power. When community leaders began to question the effectiveness of governance through consensus, the board of governors selected a new chancellor who brought with him a more effective leadership style. The culture created by two successive presidents was eventually challenged by small groups of faculty until a new faculty-sponsored majority on the board of governors ousted the president, thus creating an environment that was almost impossible to govern.

Enter the new chancellor in 1990 with a style that was more situational and participative (Bolman & Deal, 1984). In the terminology of Birnbaum (1988) and Bensimon (1994), the chancellor employed a more *contingent style*, which, as described by Segiovanni and Carver (1980), responds to particulars found in the environment at large, to the unique work or technology of the organization, and to the needs of members of the organization. The key concept is to find the best fit in an open-systems environment between the situation and the style. These contingent styles embrace several different strategies based on the situation. The early initiatives—decentralizing services and functions, reorganizing information services, and in modifying the faculty role in governance—employed a more bureaucratic style. Mission development, strategic planning, leadership development, and student outcomes assessment used a political style. Initiatives dealing with part-time faculty and department reorganization were primarily collegial. The symbolic style was evident in mission evaluation, leadership development, and decentralization.

Teams as a Systems Component

Katz and Kahn (1980) recommend assessing an organization at the *systems level* first—which accounts for the greatest amount of internal variance or dysfunction. Senge (1990) advises consideration of the whole and creation of a framework for understanding interrelationships. At PCC, the key role of the chancellor was to complete the requisite initial analysis before establishing teams. He needed to know what parts of the system were ineffective, dysfunctional, ignored, or alienated. Once these critical areas of need were identified, project priorities and the nature of the responses could be identified. The priority-response plan would then dictate which projects should be tackled first and which individuals and groups should be involved.

For March and Simon (1993), conflict in an organization reflects an imbalance because of a lack of integration among members and units in the organization. Lawrence and Lorsch (1986) see teams as a primary means of achieving integration. Cross-functional teams, according to Katzenbach and Smith (1993), differ from other working groups in that they offer a set of complementary skills, and they are committed to a common purpose for which they hold themselves responsible. Similarly, Kanter (1983) suggests that project teams (functional or cross-functional) provide multiple links, more relationships, and increased sources of information and their existence acknowledges the interdependencies required by complex situations and innovations.

According to Thompson (1967), interdependencies can be addressed in a *pooling* fashion, or *sequentially*, or in a *reciprocal* fashion. At PCC, a reciprocal movement of plans back and forth (e.g., from campus to district and back to campus) was particularly effective in establishing integration and consensus.

The accomplishment of each of the major college initiatives came about through project teams and task forces. In each instance, the chancellor's cabinet reviewed and approved the task force's work. The cabinet illustrates Bensimon and Neumann's (1993) leadership team as an example of the development of culture—a way of overcoming a web of factors integrating one with another through norms, beliefs, rituals, and values.

Lessons Learned from Using Teams in a Multicampus Setting
The size and complexity of a multicampus organization typically defeats attempts at top-down, hierarchical approaches to leadership. Thus, the role of the leader becomes one of identifying dysfunctions or gaps in the system, identifying the key stakeholders affecting and affected by a given issue, and commissioning a team to recommend or effect integrated solutions. It is then the role of the cabinet (i.e., the chancellor's team) to review the results of the team process and ensure that the solutions have integrity, meet preestablished goals, and are likely to achieve the intended results. The chancellor's cabinet frequently will request that the respective campus cabinets or interest groups review the results before they are finalized. This two-way review is the reciprocating *process* described earlier (Thompson, 1967). Figure 3.1 shows the relationships between task forces, campus cabinets, the chancellor's cabinet, and the college governing board. The schema has four levels of decision-making activity: the project team, the campus, the college district (chancellor's cabinet), and the governing board.

In the four years of using multicampus project teams at PCC, the college has learned the following about their effectiveness:

- A systems view of the college is a necessary first step: to determine which projects must come first—either by their nature (e.g., mission evaluation) or by the urgency (e.g., faculty role in governance). Similarly, the chancellor must determine whether the issue is a district issue or one that pertains to the campuses.
- Reengineering of a college seems to work best when accomplished from a cross-functional approach. Solutions that will serve the system as a whole require multiple information sources and perspectives. Reengineering will also involve different groups for different projects.
- Generally, multiple task forces are more effective than multiple committees. At PCC, districtwide committees were reduced in favor of project teams. In the final analysis, the leader should attempt to undertake only one major project at a time.
- Project teams have to be given tight, but practical, timelines. The tight timeline helps keep the team focused and enables the college to move on to other pressing issues.
- Membership of project teams should comprise those who have the greatest interest in the project. Thus, the problem to be solved helps dictate the membership of the team.

Figure 3.1
Multiple Team Utilization at Pima Community College

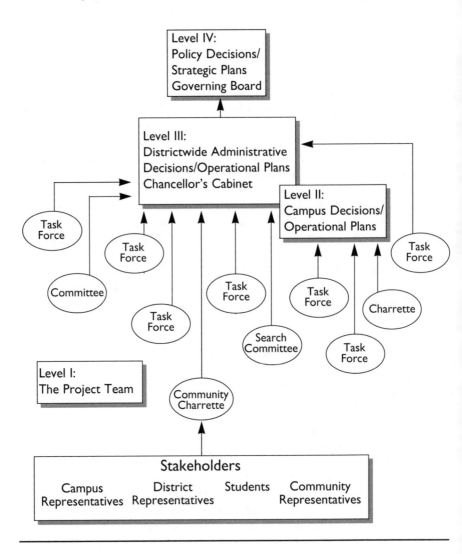

- Teams need to have a sense not only of the importance of the project but of the authority vested in the team. When the college community recognizes this sincere vesting in the first project, a sense of confidence gradually builds that the system can, and will, be responsive.
- Generally, the leader should work from within a contingency model. That is, sometimes the leadership will provide symbolic influence; sometimes

the leader will provide political influence; and sometimes the leader will approach the team in a collegial manner. And, like the captain docking a ship in stormy conditions, sometimes the leader needs to take the helm in a more controlling fashion. Although the foregoing principles are readily identifiable and the leader does the right things, the effort will not always succeed. Often, we learn from failure how to succeed in the subsequent attempt to lead from the contingent approach.

Summary and Conclusion

As a college moves from a single-campus model to multiple campuses, leadership requirements become qualitatively different. Additionally, shifting management paradigms of reengineered processes, customer satisfaction, and global perspectives have created new demands on leaders. The time-staged orchestration of cross-functional project teams has become a primary, and most useful, leadership strategy for the multicampus community college president or chancellor.

This chapter has described how one multicampus community college and its leaders successfully changed the major system components of the organization—the organizational culture, the external environment, the organizational structure, and the use of teams as a systems component. The quality of these initiatives lay in the motivation of the key stakeholders to become fully involved in problem solving through participation and shared responsibility. The emerging consensus from these stakeholders is that, while the college has found some key steps to success, it has room for considerable progress in its quest to become a learning organization.

References

Alfred, R., and Smydra, D. "Reforming Governance: Resolving Challenges to Institutional Authority." In W. Deegan, D. Tillery, and Associates (Eds.), *Renewing the American Community College: Priorities and Strategies for Effective Leadership.* San Francisco: Jossey-Bass, 1995.

Bensimon, E. "Understanding Administrative Work." In A. Cohen and F. Brawer (Eds.), *Managing Community College.* San Francisco: Jossey-Bass, 1994.

Bensimon, E., and Neumann, A. *Redesigning Collegiate Leadership: Teams and Teamwork in Higher Education.* Baltimore: The Johns Hopkins University Press, 1993.

Bess, J. *Collegiality and Bureaucracy in the Modern University.* New York: Teachers College Press, Columbia University, 1988.

Birnbaum, R. *How Colleges Work: The Cybernetics of Academic Organization and Leadership.* San Francisco: Jossey-Bass, 1988.

Bolman, L., and Deal, T. *Modern Approaches to Understanding and Managing Organizations.* San Francisco: Jossey-Bass, 1984.

Cameron, K., and Whetten, D. "Models of the Organizational Life Cycle: Applications to Higher Education." In L. Bess (Ed.), *College and University Organization: Insights for the Behavioral Sciences.* New York: New York University Press, 1984.

Champy, J. *Reengineering Management: The Mandate for New Leadership.* New York: Harper Collins, 1994.

Galbraith, J., and Lawler, E., III. "Effective Organizations: Using the New Logic of Organizing." In J. Galbraith and E. Lawler III (Eds.), *Organizing for the Future: The New Logic for Managing Complex Organizations.* San Francisco: Jossey-Bass, 1993.

Hammer, M., and Champy, J. *Reengineering the Corporation: A Manifesto for Business Revolution.* New York: Harper Collins, 1993.

Hockaday, J., and Silvers, P. "Indicators of Success: Evaluating the College Mission Through Assessing Institutional Outcomes." In North Central Association of Colleges and Schools, Commission on Institutions of Higher Education, *A Collection of Papers on Self-Study and Institutional Improvement.* Chicago: North Central Association of Colleges and Schools, 1994.

Kanter, R. *The Change Masters: Innovation and Entrepreneurship in the American Corporation.* New York: Simon and Schuster, 1983.

Katz, D., and Kahn, R. "Organizations as Social Systems." In E. Lawler III, D. Nadler, and C. Cammann (Eds.), *Organizational Assessment: Perspectives on the Measurement of Organizational Behavior and the Quality of Work Life.* New York: Wiley, 1980.

Katzenbach, J., and Smith, D. "The Discipline of Teams." *Harvard Business Review,* 1993, *71* (2), 111–120.

Lawrence, P., and Lorsch, J. *Organization and Environment: Managing Differentiation and Integration.* Boston: Harvard Business School Press, 1986.

Lorenzo, A., and Le Croy, N. "A Framework for Fundamental Change in the Community College." *Community College Journal,* 1994, *64* (4), 14–19.

Lorsch, J. "Managing Change." In P. Lawrence, L. Barnes, and J. Lorsch (Eds.), *Organizational Behavior and Administration: Cases and Readings* (3rd ed.). Homewood, Ill.: Richard D. Irwin, 1976.

March, J., and Simon, H. *Organizations* (2nd ed.). Cambridge, Mass.: Blackwell Publishers, 1993.

Mintzberg, H. *The Structure of Organizations.* Englewood Cliffs, N.J.: Prentice-Hall, 1979.

Peterson, M., and Spencer M. "Assessing Academic Climates and Culture." *New Directions for Institutional Research,* 1990, *68,* 3–18.

Richardson, R. "Management Challenges, Principles, and Strategies for the 1980s." *Emerging Roles for Community College Leaders: New Directions for Community Colleges,* 1984, *46,* 21–31.

Richardson, R., and Simmons, H. "Is it Time for a New Look at Academic Organizations in Community Colleges?" *Community College Review,* 1989, *17* (1), 34–39.

Senge, P. *The Fifth Discipline: The Art and Practice of the Learning Organization.* New York: Doubleday, 1990.

Sergiovanni, T., and Carver, F. *The New School Executive: A Theory of Administration* (2nd ed.). New York: Harper and Row, 1980.

Thompson, J. *Organization in Action.* New York: McGraw Hill, 1967.

Trice, H., and Beyer, J. *The Cultures of Work Organizations.* Englewood Cliffs, N.J.: Prentice-Hall, 1993.

Chapter 4

The President and the Executive Leadership Team

Solving Strategic Problems

George R. Boggs

Introduction

It is all too easy for a college president to take for granted an effective administrative team. (Here we refer to the leader as president. The same concepts would apply to chancellor, superintendent, provost, or similar titles of the CEO of a college or college district.) After all, the president must try to satisfy many constituencies: board members, faculty, staff, students, community members, and sometimes alumni. It is often assumed that the administrators should work to satisfy the president and not the reverse. It can be a significant mistake, however, for a president to ignore the needs and development of administrators, especially those who form the executive leadership team.

College presidents are in vulnerable positions. They are dependent upon the members of their administrative teams to give them advice and to represent them accurately to faculty, staff, and students. Moreover, presidents cannot successfully lead institutions single-handedly. They must depend upon teams of competent and dedicated executive administrators. The effectiveness of an executive leadership team will determine the degree of success of a president.

Bennis (1976) indicates that any leader's first and foremost priority should be to create an executive team. The team members, according to Bennis, should not be carbon copies of the leader or of one another. Instead, they should be compatible, able to work as a team, knowledgeable within their areas of specialization, and very serious about working as a team.

A leader, according to Smith (1989), should rarely be a problem solver. Rather, a team leader should facilitate the problem-solving work of the team members. The psychic reward that team members get from problem-solving is important. It builds self-esteem and enhances the team members' ability to do still better in subsequent situations. By being the problem solver of last resort, the president can help both the executive leadership team and the college to grow and thrive.

Many teams, of course, operate on a college campus. Campus personnel are likely to find that they are members of many teams simultaneously, some functional and some cross-functional. Some may even overlap or be teams within teams. A person may be a team member in one setting and a team leader in another. Teams may be formed for a specific task or time frame and then dissolved when they complete their work or after a certain date.

The executive leadership team, however, is an ongoing team whose purpose is to ensure the efficient and effective operation of a college. Its work is never completed. It is an unusual team in that its members have a high level of individual responsibility, and they must be trusted to make decisions without a great deal of supervision. The appropriate sports team analogy, according to Acebo (1992), is the basketball team. Unlike football or baseball, a basketball team must be able to function quickly as a unit without precise direction by its coach. Because of the speed and flexibility required in basketball, coordination has to come from the players themselves, as a group.

The decisions needed to operate a college require similar flexibility and timeliness and cannot all be made by a team sitting together around a table. For that reason, executive leadership team members must share a common vision for the institution and a common set of values. Communications between team members have to occur frequently, not just in meetings. One of the college president's most important responsibilities is to ensure the proper functioning of the executive leadership team.

Membership, Culture, and Commitment

Many authorities advise leaders to build their teams based upon the skills, talents, and expertise of the members rather than to select members based upon position in the organization. The executive leadership team is again an exception. Its members are the leaders of the major divisions of the college. Membership is defined by position. Members are expected to perform the duties outlined in their job descriptions in much the same way that athletic team members are expected to play their positions.

Executive leadership team members are expected to be committed to the college and to meeting their responsibilities, and they should be committed to quality and improvement. Membership by position does not mean, however, that the president has no say over who the team members are or how they operate.

Often the executive leadership team comprises the college president and the vice presidents in charge of instruction, student services, business services, and human resource services. Sometimes a president may choose to expand the leadership team to include a broader group of administrators, including deans or directors. Even in the presence of shared governance committees, which usually include representatives of the students and employee groups, the president will need to rely on an executive leadership team, sometimes called the president's cabinet or president's council. The size of this team should be decided by the president and depends upon both the philosophy of the president and the culture of the campus.

The most vital teams are made up of members who bring diverse skills, abilities, and talents to their assignments. Another sign of good health for a team is for its members to have different leadership styles or orientations. Bolman and Deal (1991) describe four frames of leadership and argue that leaders are usually inclined toward one or two of these orientations and less inclined toward the others. Structural leaders, according to Bolman and Deal, emphasize rationality, analysis, logic, facts, and data. They are likely to believe in the importance of clear structure and well-developed management systems. Human resource leaders emphasize the institution's people. They believe in the importance of coaching, participation, teamwork, motivation, and good interpersonal skills. Political leaders believe that managers live in a world of conflict and scarce resources. They emphasize the importance of building alliances, networks, and coalitions. Symbolic leaders believe in the importance of vision and inspiration. They make use of symbols and stories in ways that give people hope and meaning.

Although finding one leader who is well balanced in these four frames may seem unlikely, it is possible to achieve balance and depth of styles and skills in a team if its members are chosen wisely. These complementary skills and leadership orientations will help the team to view situations and challenges from a variety of perspectives. The quality of team decisions should be better, and advice to the president should be more complete.

Among the most critical decisions that a college president makes is the employment of new executive leadership team members. Most presidents welcome the chance to "hire their own" team members, even though a selection committee often does most of the applicant screening and a board of trustees actually does the hiring. Still, the president must be able either to make the final decision or to make a recommendation to the board.

Even before the selection process starts, the president should meet with the screening committee, which should include representatives from the executive leadership team, to discuss the qualities sought in the new administrator. The time is right to think about the skills, talents, and expertise needed, not only to do the job but also to add depth and balance to the team. Teams can be made more effective by hiring leaders who have diverse and complementary sets of styles and talents. The executive leadership team should also be diverse in gender and ethnicity. It is important for the administration of a college to reflect the diversity of the student body and the community. If the need arises to balance the team, hiring decisions provide the opportunity.

What is most important in selecting new team members is that the skills and talents of the prospective new member must match the needs of the team and the college. The successful candidate must have values that are compatible with those of the team and the team leader. The philosophy of the candidate must agree with the culture of the college. A president should use all available means to determine whether a good fit exists before recommending the employment of a new executive leadership team member. The cost of making a bad hiring decision is high.

The president should develop interview questions that not only measure knowledge and experience, but also probe beliefs, philosophy, style, and values. Reference checks are important, but it is usually most instructive to interview the references face-to-face during a site visit at the candidate's current institution. The president can specify that particular people be scheduled for reference interviews. For example, it is usually helpful to talk both to the candidate's supervisor and to employees that the candidate supervises. Colleagues of the candidate can provide valuable information. Employee union and faculty senate representatives provide a valuable perspective of the candidate's style and human relations skills.

When the president makes a recommendation for employment of a new executive team member, it should be done with the confidence that can come only from a thorough evaluation of the finalists. The president must be convinced that the recommended candidate is the best available person to meet the needs of the college and to add needed diversity, depth, and balance to the team. Without the necessary match, the best solution is to extend or to reopen the search.

Once the team members are in place, the president must clearly define the expectations for behavior of the members, evaluate the performance of both the team and the individual members, and provide opportunities for professional development and team building. Team members should be complimented for their contributions toward effectiveness of the team. Corrections should be made in private between the individual team member and supervisor.

Occasionally, it may be necessary to remove someone from the team and reassign the administrator to other responsibilities. Ousting a team member is one of the most difficult decisions for a president to make and should not be considered lightly. Only when a team member behaves unethically, is unable or unwilling to perform job responsibilities, is disruptive to the operation of the team, or does not respond adequately to recommendations for improvement should such a change be contemplated. Even then, legal and political consequences usually must be considered. It is important for the president to check with legal counsel to be sure that individual rights are protected and that the college will not incur unnecessary legal expenses.

The president must be sure that the board of trustees will support the decision and prepare for a period of unrest on the campus, especially if the reassigned administrator is popular with faculty and staff members or with students. The person affected by the reassignment may very well remain with the institution for some time, so the president should show whatever consideration is necessary to ease the transition and to avoid embarrassing the employee.

The membership of the executive leadership team, even though it is usually defined by position, is not necessarily static. The president may expand the membership to include other levels of administrators. Members will leave for new positions or to retire, and new members will join the team to replace them. Over time, a college president will have ample opportunity to shape the team by determining its membership.

Process and Systems Thinking

Effective team members are expected to know the rules and to play by them. The president, as the leader and coach of the executive leadership team, must communicate the expectations for team members clearly. These expectations must be reinforced and even repeated frequently. New administrators, in particular, may not fully understand that, as their role in an organization changes, so does their level of responsibility and their relationship with those people for whom they are now responsible (Boggs, 1993a). They also have a new obligation to assist and support their supervisor and to be an effective member of a leadership team. Executive leadership team members may have to behave in a much different manner than they did in their former positions (Boggs, 1993b).

Executive leadership team members must be models of integrity, honesty, and high ethical standards. Codes of ethics should clearly state a commitment to make judgments that are fair, dispassionate, consistent, and equitable. Team members need to exhibit openness and reliability in all they say and do. They must confront issues and people without prejudice. In particular, they must ensure that students are respected as individual learners and protected from disparagement, embarrassment, or capricious behavior (Boggs, 1993c). They must realize that retaining their popularity is not as important as doing what is right.

Team members are not required to become good friends with all of their colleagues, but they do need to develop good working relationships with people. They will need to cooperate with other team members in attaining mutual goals. To maintain confidence in the college administration, team members should visibly support each other.

Team members must come to realize their interdependence. A college cannot succeed unless each division succeeds and unless the divisions coordinate their processes and activities. Successful teams think and make decisions based on systems that are likely to cross divisional lines. Systems thinking that emphasizes interrelationships of divisions and departments is a skill that will need to be developed. Executive team members must be institutional rather than just narrow constituency advocates.

To be successful in today's environment, executive leadership team members must find ways to involve people in their decisions. They should be catalysts in finding ways to make things happen for the college and its people. They should encourage and support innovation and discovery.

Just as the president communicates high expectations to the members of the executive leadership team, team members must communicate high expectations to the faculty and staff members with whom they work and to the members of the teams they may lead. Executive leadership team members must also care about their people and let them know they care. They need to seek out and reward good behavior, and, just as importantly, they must confront unacceptable behavior.

Members of the executive leadership team should be visible on the campus, in the community, and at the state or national level. On the campus, it is important for leaders to attend student and faculty events and performances. Faculty and students spend long hours preparing for performances and athletic events. Their leaders' attendance sends an important positive message. In the community, administrators are seen as representatives of the college and the president. Their presence at community events provides a link between the college and the community it serves. At state and national meetings, administrators represent the college, learn new ways of doing things, develop support networks, and grow professionally.

The president, as leader of the executive leadership team, should model the behaviors expected from other team members. People pay more attention to action than to rhetoric. No inconsistency should exist between what is expected of team members and the team leader's own behavior.

Team Meetings

Most of the work of the executive leadership team will occur outside of its team meetings; however, meetings serve some valuable purposes. They provide the opportunity for group discussion, problem solving, and planning. Meetings can also coordinate the activities of the team. Meeting together, the executive leadership team is a powerful advisory body for a college president.

Some ground rules are important for using meeting time productively and for enhancing the creative abilities of the team. The president should never call the team together merely to share information. Information sharing can be accomplished through much less time-consuming methods such as memoranda, voice mail, and electronic mail. Time is quite valuable for this important group.

Since the executive leadership team is made up of members with demanding schedules, a regular time should be established for meetings. Meetings can always be canceled if no reason exists to conduct them. Meeting agendas with appropriate back-up materials should be distributed enough in advance to allow the members to prepare their thoughts.

The president has some important functions to play in discussing critical issues or engaging in problem solving. First, the team should be clearly told whether the final course of action will be decided by the team as a whole or determined by the president after listening to the discussion at the meeting. Occasions should be available for both kinds of decisions. Recommendations and decisions must be motivated by doing what is best for the college in light of its vision statement, mission, goals, and needs.

If the decision is to be made by the team, the leader should indicate whether the decision will be made by consensus of the group or by vote after the case has been presented and discussed. Voting may be more efficient, but consensus usually yields more team support for the decision.

Second, the president should try to create an environment in which it is permissible for members to react to the leader's preliminary decisions without risk as long as members support the final decision of the team or its leader. Even so, it is usually wise for the president to stay neutral, at least until a decision is about to be made. An early indication of judgment by the leader may inhibit the critical discussion that is necessary for the most informed decisions.

Third, the president should keep the group on schedule, on task, and focused on the problem at hand. Participation should be encouraged by all members of the group, even those who might seem most removed from the problem. No one should be permitted to dominate the discussion. Personal criticism cannot be tolerated, and no attempt should be made to fix blame on any team member.

For the executive team to function appropriately, it is essential that its members respect their colleagues and behave courteously to each other. That is not to say that conflict or disagreement should not exist. In fact, disagreement is important for the proper functioning of a well-balanced team. Kiernan (1989) points out that conflict can strengthen a team. When it is openly recognized, conflict can serve to test the merit of ideas against direct challenges from others. Conflict can stimulate other points of view as long as all members feel free to participate. In an effective team, divergent views are respected, disagreement is expected and encouraged, and criticism is open, constructive, and functional (Bacon, 1983). An atmosphere that encourages divergent opinions but still maintains the integrity of the team is the most desirable.

The president should encourage members to try to influence the outcome of decisions as long as they are professional in doing so. Strongly held positions and heated discussions are acceptable as long as the members can support, explain, and defend the final decision of the team or the team leader. Lee (1994) states this requirement somewhat more directly: Team members cannot "bad-mouth the team, the players, or the process to outsiders."

Finally, the president should bring the meeting to an effective close. Conclusions should be reviewed, assignments to specific team members might have to be made, and timelines may have to be established. In subsequent meetings, teams should spend some time in self-evaluation. The team should view failures and mistakes as learning opportunities. Successes should be acknowledged and celebrated.

Communication

It is difficult to imagine how an athletic team could be successful without nearly constant communication between coaches and players and among the players. Huddles around the quarterback during football games, elaborate signals between coaches and players and between catchers and pitchers during baseball games, and the directions given by basketball coaches during time-outs are but a few examples of the many forms of communication needed to execute plans and to coordinate play. Although communication between members of the college executive leadership team is not usually as intense as it is for an athletic team during a contest, it is nonetheless as important for success.

The executive team members are, among other things, the eyes and ears of the president. The president should know, at least in general terms, what the issues, problems, and concerns of the campus community are. The president should never be sheltered from the truth even though it may be unpleasant. Similarly, the president is obligated to pass along information to team members and ensure that they communicate so that they can do their jobs as effectively as possible.

Communication at a college takes many forms: oral communication in meetings or one-to-one, telephone calls, written communication by letter or memorandum, and, more recently, voice mail and electronic mail. Each of these forms of communication has its advantage. Given the high degree of individual responsibility of the team members and the many demands on their time, however, electronic and voice mail have taken on greater importance. Electronic mail, in particular, has many advantages in keeping communications flowing quickly and efficiently. The message is sent immediately and can be read at the convenience of the recipient, eliminating the problems associated with "telephone tag" or with trying to find the time in a busy day for a meeting. Messages can be sent to one or more team members at the same time. Team members can take lap-top computers with them when they travel and connect to a telephone line to read and respond to their mail.

The president must always be aware of the type of communication coming from team members. If team members seem to be constantly seeking detailed directions, perhaps they are afraid of what might happen if they take a risk and fail. If they constantly bring problems to the leader for solutions, they are inviting the president to do their jobs. The president, of course, cannot afford to accept such an invitation. Instead, the president should ask the team members to communicate their own ideas for solving problems. The president can make suggestions or guide a team member, but, if the president makes all of the decisions, the team will not function. The president must create an environment in which team members are encouraged to take calculated risks in the process of decision making.

Team members should also be encouraged to communicate regularly with people outside the executive leadership team. An effective college functions on the flow of accurate information. The executive leadership team is not in competition with other teams at the college. Rather, it is the duty of the executive leadership team to be sure that the various teams and individuals at the college function at their best, and the sharing of information is essential to that purpose. Communications from team members in the form of handwritten notes are often effective in recognizing the contributions of the college's people.

In the course of their administrative duties, executive team members will have access to information that they otherwise would not have. While it is the responsibility of administrators to promote open communications, some items must be held in confidence. Team members must develop a good sense of which issues can be communicated and which must be held in confidence. If any uncertainty arises, team members should check with their supervisor before sharing information. When administrative team members communicate, they must be sure that what they say is accurate.

Mission, Goals, Outcomes, and Rewards

Perhaps the most basic of the expectations for members of the executive leadership team is to understand and support the college mission. Team members must also share a common vision for the future of the institution. Colleges that are the most successful are those that have developed a well-defined mission and a shared vision of the future.

The college mission is a statement of the direction of the institution; it defines a clear purpose for being. The vision is a picture of what the institution will be at some point in the future. This picture should emerge from an understanding of the needs of the communities served by the college and of the internal strengths and abilities of the institution (Boggs, 1993d). The vision statement should clearly state strategic goals that everyone at the institution is committed to achieving (Boggs, 1991). Decisions and actions of the executive leadership team need to align with both the mission of the institution and its shared vision.

We've seen that the executive leadership team is an unusual team in that its work is ongoing with no specific goal to accomplish. A team cannot succeed, however, without a shared purpose or mission (Katzenbach & Smith, 1993). The mission of the team is to ensure the effective and efficient operation of the college, guided by the college's mission and the shared vision for the future and the expectations defined by the college president. However, that does not mean that the team should operate without more specific goals.

Both the team and its individual members should develop goals each academic year. To develop the team goals, an extended meeting for the executive leadership team off-campus and away from telephones and other distractions is helpful. A goal-setting retreat can also include some other team-building activities. Sometimes having an experienced outside facilitator conduct the activities is helpful; the president can then freely participate and observe the functioning of the team without having to be concerned about keeping the group on task.

According to Bacon (1983), the process of goal setting and attaining some consensus on identified goals is important. Team members become committed to achieving goals when they can see the value of the goals that are selected, when they regard them as attainable, and when they clearly view themselves as having a part in refining the goals in the group process.

Team goals, of course, must align with the college's mission and vision for the future. They should be realistic and still challenging. Most importantly, they should be measurable. At the end of the year, they can be used to evaluate progress in what otherwise is an unending series of challenges that find their way to the executive leadership team. The exercises of developing team goals and evaluating progress also reinforce the value of the team and the interdependency of its members.

Individual team member goals should be developed by the team member with the agreement of his or her supervisor. The goals will likely include important objectives for the area of responsibility of the administrator. Goals should also include areas for development or improvement for the individual team member. Again, the goals must be measurable and they should be used in the personnel evaluation process.

A team leader should reward and recognize members for their contributions to the success of the team. Team goal accomplishments can provide an opportunity for the entire team to celebrate together. The team can recognize individual goal achievement publicly within or outside the team. Personnel evaluations should mention the team member's goal achievements.

Bacon (1983) points out that group members need a sense of progress. Members work hard to achieve goals. The team should systematically review progress toward reaching those goals so that the members can feel a sense of accomplishment.

Holten (1993) notes that teamwork also brings intrinsic rewards. She has seen that when people work as a team with a common focus and goal, the experiences themselves are gratifying and memorable. Even after the passage of several years, she still maintains contact with past team colleagues who remember fondly and with great satisfaction their work together, their comradeship, and the respect they had for one another.

Coaching and Leading

Like the head coach of a college football team, the college president is held accountable for the success of the team. Head coaches can lose their jobs if they cannot develop winning teams, and so can college presidents. The success of the executive leadership team is not measured in wins or losses, but in institutional effectiveness outcomes and goal achievement. The way the team operates is extremely important in establishing a climate for excellence throughout the college.

A successful coach empowers team members to perform well. Team members must be given opportunities for professional growth and development. They need to be recognized publicly for their achievements and for their contributions to the success of the team and the college. Leaders should eliminate barriers to their success whenever possible and encourage team members to be professionally active by attending conferences, making presentations, or writing articles.

Although retaining their individual autonomy, team members need to feel a sense of belonging (Bacon, 1983). The president must communicate to all members of the team that they are valued members. According to Bacon, team members will thus experience a sense of security in the importance of their presence and their contribution to the team.

The president must guard against the excessive development of rules and regulations if the executive leadership team is to be a creative one. Carl Larson, a professor of communications at the University of Denver who has conducted extensive research on why teams are successful, has found that creativity requires leaders to "shake the shackles of institutional bureaucracy." One requirement for a creative team, according to Larson, is insulation from bureaucracy (Legg, 1994).

College presidents should be ideal role models and mentors for the members of their executive leadership teams. The president is likely to be the most experienced leader on the team and can draw on a variety of past experiences to help and advise team members. Presidents can help team members plan their careers and help provide them with the experience to move into higher levels of leadership. One of the most rewarding experiences of the presidency is the development of future college presidents. Presidents usually speak with pride about their colleagues who formerly worked for them as members of their executive leadership teams and are now leading their own teams.

Colleges can sometimes be hostile places. The president must support team members when they are unfairly criticized. Doing the right thing can sometimes be unpopular. On the other hand, when a team member needs correction, the conversation should be held in private. The president can often help by offering advice to team members, clearly distinguishing between advice and directives.

Presidents must let team members do their jobs without detailed supervision or direction. Even when the task is done in a different way than the president would have done it, or if the decision is not exactly the same one the president would have made, team members need this latitude. As long as the actions and decisions do not place the college in financial or legal jeopardy and are not in disagreement with the institutional mission or the team goals, and as long as the team member is meeting the expectations for behavior set by the president, the team member should be allowed to do the assigned job without unnecessary interference. This confidence in the team members is essential for the successful operation of the executive leadership team. Of course, the president should be informed and ready to step in if necessary to protect the college and its people, but this intervention should happen rarely.

In addition to responsibilities as coach, the president is also the leader of the team and the chief executive officer of the college. As team leader, the president must create an environment in which team members feel free to offer the president advice and even to disagree respectfully within the confines of a meeting. Once a decision is made, however, it is important for each administrative team member to support the president and the decision. This dual responsibility of being both coach and team leader can be difficult, requiring continuous effort by the president to be sure members know whether the president is acting as coach or as team leader. Executive leadership teams are most successful if the members know each other and their president well enough to interpret actions and statements accurately.

The president must be aware of any behavior that undermines the effectiveness of the team. The American Management Association, in its November 1993 newsletter, *Supervisory Management*, discusses some of these damaging behaviors. Some team members have been trained by prior experience to try to fix the blame for a problem rather than trying to solve the problem or determining how to prevent the problem from recurring. Teams that focus on placing blame on a team member will destroy the trust and morale of the team.

Warding off unfavorable information is another behavior that will destroy the effectiveness of a team. No one likes bad news, but team members cannot isolate themselves from unpleasant information or they will find it impossible to solve problems before it is too late.

Shying away from change is another way to make a team ineffective. Change is difficult for many people, but being open to change is a prerequisite to effective teamwork. It is healthy to have some team members question suggestions for change so they can be sure that the team has fully considered the consequences to the organization. We must not fall into the trap of always favoring the familiar, however.

Sidestepping performance problems is another way of rendering a team ineffective. Team members know who is performing and who isn't. The president must take the initiative and confront any team member who is not living up to expectations before lagging individual performance affects the effectiveness of the team.

Kiernan (1989) points out that teams may suffer if the teams place too much emphasis on interpersonal relationships among the members. In particular, he warns against cooperation at the expense of achieving substance. The team can sometimes misdirect its attention to social relations and organizational politics rather than substantive goal achievement. The leader must keep the team on task.

Summary and Conclusion

According to Katzenbach and Smith (1993), teams at the top are the most difficult; the complexities of long-term challenges, heavy demands on executive time, and the ingrained individualism of senior people conspire against teams at the top. In addition, the authors write that the way executives are expected to act often conflicts with effective team performance. A strong case can be made for teams at the top, however, especially for organizations as complex as community colleges.

Acting alone, college presidents simply cannot operate a college and plan for its future. Even strong presidents cannot have lasting influences on their colleges unless they can change the values and vision of the institution's people. Extending the college leadership to an effective executive leadership team can make the difference between success and failure for the president and between excellence and mediocrity for the institution. It is worth the time and effort to overcome the difficulties and to develop and nurture an effective leadership team.

The president sets both the membership and the expectations for operation of the executive leadership team, taking into account the culture of the college. Membership should include, as a minimum, the executive administrators who report to the president. Complementary styles, skills, and talents improve the health and vitality of the team. Hiring decisions provide an opportunity to bring balance and diversity to the team.

Effective teams must know their purpose, and they must know and use the college mission and vision statements in performing their jobs. They must be able to think and act within systems that will likely cross divisional boundaries. Teams should be committed to the college and to meeting their responsibilities. Team members need to operate within the culture of the institution. Teams have to know the expectations of the president and use processes that are consistent with these expectations. Members need to set both individual and team goals and should be evaluated based upon the outcomes. Leaders should recognize team members for their achievements and for their contributions to the team's success. They must communicate continually with the team leader and with other members of the team. Communications to people outside the team must be guided by knowledge of what information must be held in confidence and what should be shared.

Executive leadership team members are in very visible positions. What they do and how they do it will be closely observed by members of the campus community. Members will be expected to be honest in their dealings with people. They should find ways to make things happen within the boundaries of high ethical standards. Teams should care about people, let people know they care, and involve others in their decision making. Members should encourage and support innovation, while seeking out and rewarding good behavior. They need to be able to confront unacceptable behavior. They must cooperate with other team members in attaining mutual goals and respect and be courteous to one another. Teams must be visible. Members must tell the team leader what they know and not only what they think the team leader wants to hear. They should bring the team leader ideas and not just problems. Finally, teams must communicate their high expectations to faculty and staff members in their areas and to the teams they lead.

College presidents have the responsibility to coach and to lead the executive leadership team. The proper functioning of the team and the development of its individual members should be primary concerns for a college president. In fact, maintaining and developing the team and creating the structure and environment for its successful operation may prove to be the most important and rewarding jobs the president does.

References

Acebo, S.C. "The Team As Hero: A Paradigm Shift In College Leadership," *Leadership Abstracts*, 1992, 5 (4).

Bacon, Mary M. *Team-Building in Quality Circles*. A report prepared for the Educational Quality Circles Consortium. Redwood City, Calif.: San Mateo County Office of Education, 1983.

Bennis, Warren. *The Unconscious Conspiracy*. New York: Amacon, 1976.

Boggs, George R. "Letter to Colleagues and Friends." In *Palomar College 2005: A Shared Vision*. San Marcos, Calif.: Palomar Community College District, 1991.

Boggs, George R. "Expectations for New Administrators." In Martha Kanter (Ed.), *New Administrators Handbook: A Resource Guide*. Sacramento, Calif.: Association of Community College Administrators, 1993a.

Boggs, George R. "An Open Letter to New Administrators." In *Network*. Sacramento, Calif.: Association of Community College Administrators, 1993b.

Boggs, George R. "Making An Ethical Statement." In *Trustee Quarterly*. Washington, D.C.: Association of Community College Trustees, 1993c.

Boggs, George R. "Institutional Distinctiveness." In Steven W. Jones (Ed.), *Shaping the Community College Image*. Greeley, Colo.: National Council for Marketing and Public Relations, 1993d.

Bolman, Lee G., and Deal, Terrence E. *Reframing Organizations: Artistry, Choice, and Leadership*. San Francisco: Jossey-Bass, 1991.

Holten, Virginia "Teamwork: Pitfalls and Rewards of Working Together." In *Network*. Sacramento, Calif.: Association of Community College Administrators, 1993.

Katzenbach, Jon R., and Smith, Douglas K. *The Wisdom of Teams: Creating the High-Performance Organization*. Boston, MA: Harvard Business School Press, 1993.

Kiernan, Henry "Team building: Connecting Substance to Educational Leadership." Paper presented at the Annual Meeting of the National Council of States on Inservice Education, 1989.

Lee, Billi. "A glossary of unwritten rules for team play." *The San Diego Business Journal*, April 25, 1994, p. 30.

Legg, Charlotte M. "Walking The Dragon." In *CASE Currents*. Washington, D.C.: Council for the Advancement and Support of Education, 1994.

Smith, Perry M. "Twenty Guidelines For Leadership." *Nation's Business*, September 1989, pp. 60–61.

Supervisory Management, November 1993.

CHAPTER 5

THE ACADEMIC TEAM

A Case Study of Shared Governance

SANDRA ACEBO
WITH CONTRIBUTIONS BY KATHLEEN BURSON,
CYRIL GULASSA, SHARON MILLER, AND CHRIS STORER

Introduction

Members of the academic team at DeAnza College may disagree about which sports analogy fits them best—football, baseball, or basketball—but they would all agree that their running game is outstanding. Regardless of the work group, its task or its composition, momentum and constant improvement are the expectations. Long before the onset of quality initiatives, founding president A. Robert DeHart extolled the virtues of "constant, purposeful innovation." "If it ain't broke," he would say at every opportunity, "you just haven't looked hard enough."

Today, under the energetic leadership of President Martha Kanter, the college maintains its strong collective will to excel. DeAnza attracts more than half its students from areas outside its district, providing job training in thirty different occupational programs, and transferring more students to upper division colleges and universities than any other community college in California. The academic team has a big job. The college enrolls more than 25,000 students each quarter and employs some 300 full-time faculty, 600 part-time faculty, and 400 classified staff members at any one time.

The complexity of the institution and its culture of entrepreneurialism create an ideal environment for teams of all sorts, and in fact, a continuing challenge of college leadership is to manage the proliferation of teams and reduce the overlap of working groups. While the administrative line for the academic team consists of a vice president and three high-level deans, who in turn supervise a layer of division deans, who supervise the department heads, faculty, and staff, the reality of true team leadership creates a much more interesting structural arrangement. Within and across these lines of responsibility are critical relationships with student services, with the academic and classified senates, with the student-body leadership, and with our bargaining units, both faculty and classified.

In California, joint leadership is not only an ideal or a quality improvement concept—it is the law, inspired in part by the success of shared governance in the Foothill-DeAnza Community College District. In the early 1980s, collective bargaining conflicts in our district led to the birth of a district Budget and Policy Development Group (BPDG), an effort that people statewide saw as a radical experiment in shared governance. This group brought together administration, faculty, student, and classified leadership in a consensus-driven working committee. The accomplishments of the BPDG and its philosophically satisfying foundation became a model in the 1988 California community college reform legislation, Assembly Bill (AB) 1725, which requires, for example, that local boards of trustees "consult collegially" with academic senates in specific areas of faculty interest. While implementation of the law has been a struggle in many districts over the process of decision making and the locus of accountability, and while our own district has certainly had its moments of weakened resolve, we continue to move forward confident that the improved results of shared governance are, in the long run, well worth the effort.

Shared governance is a hallmark of the academic team at DeAnza. The best illustration of how the academic team works, and how its leaders move the agenda of improving quality at DeAnza College, is a detailed view of various cross-sections and associated team activities within what is traditionally called "Instruction." These "cuts" of the larger academic enterprise reflect stable, ongoing groups. Their efforts to manage change and focus on institutional priorities are the backbone of our existence. Without them and the high degree of professionalism the various members bring to their team task, our college could not continue to survive, much less improve. The teams, chosen for their diverse functions and representative activities, are the vice president's top administrative team, the enrollment management team, the academic senate, the faculty association, and the instructional division, as modeled here by the division of child development and education.

The Vice President's Administrative Team

BY SANDY ACEBO

The vice president's administrative team is the top of the traditional hierarchy, but the team operates in a rather nontraditional manner. The team consists of the vice president for instruction and her three leading administrators: the dean of instruction for general education and liberal arts, the dean of instruction for vocational education, and the dean of learning resources. Coordination among these four is vital, and although their lines are distinct on the organizational chart and each member takes individual responsibility for managing his or her areas, a larger collective is at work. The group meets biweekly in a gathering loosely known as "the gang of four." The business of "the gang of four" is the business of a quality team: shared focus on institutional goals, assessment of progress in meeting them, agreement on adjustments, and strategies to carry out those adjustments. "Plan, do, check, act" is the modus operandi of the team, with the vice president assuming overall responsibility for the team's agenda.

Beyond the business of the meetings is another considerably important relationship: an opportunity for the foursome to share concerns, frustrations, expectations, conflicts with one another, and all manner of emotional baggage, which can become heavy in our line of work. High-level managers, like other humans, need a safe place to take off the mantle of self-assurance, to lay their burdens down, to fight, to get a second opinion on a difficult decision, to admit failure, to complain occasionally, to warn one another of impending difficulties, and to encourage one another in an unabashed circle of support. These kinds of group maintenance activities may seem "unleaderlike" but, once learned, can mitigate the burnout, workaholism, and loneliness that top managers often experience. Further, being a trusted member of a team can inspire managers to establish a healthier emotional tone in their own work groups.

Permission to "be real" also allows for much more creative problem solving, which is often unorthodox. Game plans can be developed that jump across lines of authority, resources can be shared to take advantage of unforeseen opportunities, risks can be taken, and ad hoc tasks redistributed to even out the load. In reality, without these strong bonds and the flexibility they permit, it is not feasible to handle the "crisis du jour," the ups and downs of state funding, enrollment patterns, legislative dictates, board interests, and personnel needs, while simultaneously maintaining a steady focus on long-term quality improvement in service to students.

Each of the deans reporting immediately to the vice president for instruction provides administrative leadership in tandem with faculty and staff for at least one essential team. The dean of learning resources, for example, is responsible for the technology group, a cross-functional team responsible for development of a collegewide technology plan, including staffing, training, and equipment planning. The dean of instruction for vocational education is responsible for the program review group, with co-chair and members appointed by the academic senate. The program review group establishes quality assessment guidelines and criteria for evaluating instructional programs, assists programs in completing their reviews, and assigns a grade regarding the health of each program. This group recommends full-time faculty additions or replacements, as well as the probation or elimination of programs. The dean of

81

instruction for general education and liberal arts is responsible for the enrollment management team as well as the curriculum committee, chaired by the
academic senate. Because enrollment management is usually under the purview
of administrators, it is presented here as a model of faculty and staff involvement in a disciplined team, making critical, politically sensitive decisions vital to
instructional quality.

The Enrollment Management Team

BY SHARON MILLER

Enrollment management is defined by the Enrollment Growth Management
Task Group, a subgroup of the Community College League of California
(1992), as "strategies used to address the problems created by the enrollment
or potential enrollment of too many students to be served by the available
resources" (p. 1). With more than sixty-five of California's community college
districts exceeding their enrollment caps in 1991–92, identifying ways to
address enrollment priorities while maintaining quality and access has been an
important topic. The state legislature's decision in 1991 to raise community
college enrollment fees for all students and to triple fees for students already
holding the bachelor's degree has had an uneven effect across and within the
colleges. At DeAnza, where the student population included a good 25 percent
of students who already had a bachelor's degree, enrollments declined in physical education, creative arts, business/computer systems, and foreign language.
Waiting lists for some programs and courses grew even larger, however, particularly in core general education courses, developmental programs, and some
occupational programs.

In the past, colleges could adjust to enrollment shifts by adding part-time
faculty, program by program, according to need. The more students we got,
the more money we got. The imposition of enrollment caps combined with the
uncertainty of state funding has made these adjustments difficult indeed.
Financially strapped districts cannot afford to offer more classes than their cap
limitation will provide in the way of revenue. Real revenue to the districts cannot be ascertained until late in the summer, shortly before the academic year
begins and long after schedules have been built. In California, shortfalls in sales
and property tax revenue have created "take-backs" from district budgets well
into the academic year. As a result, enrollment management has become what
one instructional officer dubbed "a crap shoot on a heaving deck."

The need for timely and well-informed decisions, and the need for buy-in
from faculty and staff in accepting decisions with serious implications for program offerings, led to the creation of DeAnza's enrollment management team.
The team is composed of faculty, staff, administrators from services and instruction, and students. Its task is to determine program mix and recommend the

resources to achieve that mix in accordance with the finances, mission, and priorities of the college. Members are selected based on their ability to assume a collegewide perspective, communicate well, give honest input and avoid political pressure, as well as on their interest in the broad and diverse needs of students and knowledge of how students matriculate through the college. An important activity of the team is to establish annual allocations of part-time faculty positions by instructional division, and make quarterly adjustments based on our comprehensive mission, enrollment trends, and quality improvements for student flow. Its decisions are reported to the instructional divisions through the division deans council, chaired by the vice president for instruction, and the division deans are charged with the responsibility to build their schedules within the limits provided.

To accomplish this work, the enrollment management team undergoes continual training in trend analysis, including demographics, efficiency ratios, wait lists, matriculation data, and facility use. While core program stability is maintained and enhanced by the full-time faculty, and major adjustments such as program deletion and full-time faculty additions or reassignments are determined in program review, the enrollment management team performs a vital role in continuous improvement. Matching a $7 million part-time faculty budget to enrollment trends, meeting but not exceeding an enrollment cap, and maximizing efficiency—all the while staying grounded in our mission—takes an all-star team. The team's decisions are not always liked but are seldom second-guessed.

Communication is an important part of what the team does. As their expertise improves, so are they able to translate key quality indicators to their colleagues in the divisions and departments. Sometimes this means bearing up under criticism, another leadership skill! When the budget is fixed, an increase in one program to accommodate student demand means a decrease in another. When the budget is cut, it must be cut strategically—not cut across-the-board, which may be politically expedient but does nothing to improve quality. This economic climate is a different reality from the go-go, grow-grow seventies and eighties. The team approach does not reduce the responsibility for difficult decisions, which ultimately lies with administration, but it does improve the decisions themselves, shared accountability for meeting student needs, and acceptance of hard choices across the organization.

The Academic Senate

BY CHRIS STORER

The academic senate's role in California community college governance was codified by law in 1988 reform legislation, which, among other things, attempted to strengthen the senates. The law fortified the senates' role by specifying "eleven points of academic and professional matters" and by requiring that local boards of trustees, for each point, decide whether they would "rely primarily on the advice and judgment of the senate" or "provide for a process of joint development and agreement between the senate and its representatives" (Assembly Bill 1725, 1988).

The eleven points are as follows: curriculum; degree and certificate requirements; grading policies; educational program development; standards or policies regarding student preparation and success; district and college governance structures, as related to faculty roles; faculty roles and involvement in accreditation processes; policies for faculty professional development activities; processes for program review; processes for institutional planning and budget development; and other academic and professional matters as mutually agreed upon between the governing board and the academic senate. The Foothill-DeAnza board of trustees determined that the "primary reliance" on the senate, as mandated by law, would apply in our district to curriculum, degree and certificate requirements, grading policies, student preparation and success standards, and policies for faculty development activities. These choices fit well with long-established patterns of faculty leadership and joint planning with administration.

The DeAnza academic senate has taken on its now formalized responsibilities with enthusiasm and commitment. The sharing of tasks by the outgoing president, the president elect (chosen annually), and the current president assures continuity of its leadership from year to year. All three meet weekly with the vice president for instruction to discuss concerns, new initiatives, and progress on institutional goals. Again, the tone of these meetings is one of candor, respect, support, and mutual focus on quality improvement in the organization.

The whole academic senate, including senators representing faculty from every discipline across the campus, meets weekly to conduct its business. Recent accomplishments include development of a process for faculty exchange between Foothill College and DeAnza College, establishment of benchmarks to improve student equity, as evidenced by the progress of various student groups through their course sequences, and creation of a plan to implement consistent course prerequisites, corequisites, and advisories according to new state guidelines. A popular newsletter prepared by the senate's executive secretary communicates to the college the group's decisions and issues under discussion. Ongoing dialogue among faculty about important issues such as distance learning and management reorganization is also encouraged via electronic bulletin board. While the bulletin board was initiated by and is maintained by the senate, all members of the college community are encouraged to express themselves via this electronic town hall.

Because the most essential role of the senators is in the classroom as teaching faculty, and because their participation in shared governance cannot often take place with all the players on the field at the same time, various structures have evolved to maintain "primary reliance" and "joint development" without the creation of more committees. This type of organizational shorthand is best illustrated by example. When the statewide academic senate and the state chancellor's office agreed on model guidelines for instituting course prerequisites and corequisites, such as reading and writing skill levels, they were responding to a statewide issue of access and quality, which had been handled unevenly among the colleges. The task then remained for each college to determine how to implement the guidelines. Since standards regarding student preparation and success were a "primary reliance" item in our district, this task fell to the academic senate.

While the senate accepted this responsibility, a clear need emerged to embed the implementation process within the governance structure of the college to ensure compliance with the law and facilitate mandatory reporting to the state. The college's curriculum committee (a faculty committee with administration assistance) would continue to have authority over such matters as setting prerequisites; the academic senate would need to maintain oversight of implementing the guidelines; the offices of matriculation, articulation, institutional research, and registration would be involved from the administration side; and the college council, as the dominant shared governance group on campus, would need to establish the final policy recommendation from the college to the district board of trustees. This situation was clearly ripe for major shared governance gridlock.

Because of the complexity of the problem and the number of different groups affected to various degrees, an ad hoc task group seemed unworkable. It was decided that the dean of matriculation would take the lead, working from the model developed by the statewide academic senate, while attempting to tailor it to the specific circumstances at DeAnza. As the proposal took shape, drafts of relevant parts were discussed with and within the various groups involved, and reworked to accommodate concerns and insights of all parties to the final implementation process. As each group signed off on the work, the proposal became integrated into a new chapter on prerequisites, corequisites, and advisories in the curriculum handbook.

As a "team" effort, this project was especially interesting in that it broke the mold of "teams" as face-to-face working groups. Rather, a facilitator was given the task of integrating and unifying the work, insights, experience, and understanding of team members and subgroups who never worked together directly on the issues requiring resolution. The various groups were members of a team in the same sense as offense, defense, kickoff, and punt return form a single football team. Each subgroup had special concerns and responsibilities, but all were united by more general overarching goals.

The traditional complaint from faculty is that administrators develop their own culture, separated from the educational mission of the college by the nature of their job descriptions, distance from the classroom, and authoritative management styles. The faculty's lack of time for in-depth analysis of and research into complex issues often causes shared governance gridlock. These tasks are carried out by administrators who are paid for such work, but even when a project is clearly "joint development," administrative interests can dominate the work, slanting solution proposals. This administrative dominance can result in criticism and rejection by faculty, often without positive alternatives. In the face of such commonplace conflicts, the success of DeAnza's experience in this case can be attributed to several factors.

The initial work of the statewide senate and state chancellor's office had clearly and unambiguously defined the problem in relation to law and the mission of the California community college system, avoiding hidden agendas or any slant that emphasized particular interests. Had the problem not been so well defined, the team would have needed to take on this task at the outset.

Other internal factors relate to cultural values and mutual trust among college leaders, whether faculty or management, that the eleven points will be honored to the greatest degree possible for the benefit of students. To improve quality in a shared governance environment, certain operating assumptions must be consistently present. The team must avoid hidden agendas, and conflicting interests must be balanced, based on shared higher interests. Despite the mandated "primary reliance" on the faculty to recommend policies and procedures, the team must identify an administrator or reassign a faculty member to facilitate the team's interaction because faculty seldom have the time to analyze and research a proposal. The cultural climate of the institution must be one that rewards people who can avoid the narrow perceptions and interests of their particular assignments. The facilitator must have a very clear sense of the specific goals of the project and a strong commitment to the success of the mission of the institution. In this case, the matriculation officer took on this role, both because her assignment already required close working relationships with various faculty groups and because stakeholders strongly supported her in avoiding a narrow bias.

The Faculty Association: Union Relations With Management in the Foothill-DeAnza Community College District

By Cyril Gulassa

The faculty union in the Foothill-DeAnza District is an important part of the academic team. Its role in the development of shared governance has been pivotal, including the development of the landmark California community college reform legislation, AB 1725, which was grounded in our district's experience with consensus-driven leadership. The union has a strong ethic of service to the greater good, and its members are welcome additions to essential work groups such as the chancellor's council and, at DeAnza, the president's cabinet and the enrollment management team (Assembly Bill 1725, 1988).

In the strictest sense, relations between a faculty union and management are governed by an agreement, which is a legally binding record of all the articles agreed to between the union and the governing board of the district. It is a grave mistake for either managers or faculty to refer to this document as a "faculty contract." These shared covenants, always more appropriately called agreements, are owned by both management and faculty. Contrary to the view held by some managers, agreements enhance institutional governance and decision making because they provide an organized list of the rules that govern the terms and conditions of employment. They facilitate rather than hinder good management by reducing arbitrary decision making and the tendency to make special deals that reward or punish.

These agreements are also important because they spell out how differences in interpretation and application of contract language may be resolved. If the grievance can't be resolved internally, the agreements also provide for external remedies such as mediation, fact finding, arbitration, and hearings before public employee relations boards.

Agreements tend to "reel in" both autocratic managers with mandates from "God" and free-spirited faculty who believe tenure entitles irresponsibility. Agreements, however, are not always perfect instruments. Problems stem from several sources: poorly informed faculty and managers who do not understand the particulars of the articles or who prefer to do as they wish until "caught"; inadequate provisions for resolving ambiguities, oversights, and, in general, administering the contract; and flawed provisions for grievances over alleged violations of the contract.

The Foothill-DeAnza Community College District (FDCCD) Agreement was written and rewritten to avoid these problem areas. Let's look at each in turn:

Foothill-DeAnza emphasizes information and training as antidotes to ignorance and scofflaws. Union leaders are required to attend annual retreats which, among other provisions, analyze the agreement and focus on problem areas. Membership is kept informed through "Know Your Contract" articles in newsletters and bulletins. With increasing frequency, managers conduct workshops on contract issues to reduce litigation and improve efficiency and morale. In districts with adversarial relations, managers who accumulate grievances acquire status as warriors who maintain order and discipline in the ranks. In recent years at Foothill-DeAnza, however, an accumulation of grievances signals a problem area and both sides work to fix it.

New situations constantly arise that challenge the agreement. Sometimes the debate is over a definition of words, sentences, or an entire article, or about items not expressly covered. To prevent collision over such imprecision, managers and faculty meet regularly at agreed times to work out mutually acceptable solutions. Since the agreement itself can't be modified except during the negotiations process, such "mini" modifications are generally enshrined as memorandums of understanding (MOU), and have the same legal status as the agreement.

When a vice chancellor left the district a few years ago he was asked what he regarded as his greatest achievement during his term as the board's chief negotiator. Without hesitation, he pointed to the conciliation-grievance procedure. The union concurs. Many agreements fail to provide for informal resolution of problems; consequently, venial issues quickly escalate into serious grievances that consume resources, time, and morale. Article 5 of the FDCCD Agreement, however, has resolved thousands of problems in a quick, effective, and mutually satisfactory way.

The FDCCD grievance process consists of three stages: conciliation, formal grievance, and binding arbitration. We consider the conciliation phase the most important of the three. The faculty association trains a specialist on each campus, grants these specialists one third reassigned time, and makes them the first line of defense in trying to keep problems from escalating. Conciliators begin with fact finding to confirm a contract violation; if present, they assess remedies available in the agreement. If the grievant wishes to pursue the matter, the conciliator makes an appointment with the lowest level manager who has the authority to rectify the problem. This meeting is cordial, confidential, and designed to hear the manager's view of the problem and, if possible, to work out a solution. The conciliators are trained not to be adversarial or even to act as advocates. As their title suggests, their mission is to define the problem and achieve a mutually acceptable solution that is manifestly fair and preserves good will. They derive satisfaction from mediating rather than winning disputes.

Disputes that cannot be conciliated move to the grievance level and may go on to arbitration, although the vast majority of cases are resolved at the conciliation level. In a given year, only four or five out of more than 100 conciliation cases move to the grievance level. In the 18 years since the introduction of collective bargaining, fewer than a dozen cases have reached the arbitration level. The cost savings are enormous. A typical arbitration costs the union $30,000 and the district two to five times that amount.

The success of FDCCD in resolving contractual violations is remarkable. In addition to the conciliation-grievance procedure, other factors account for this record. For one, the district from the very beginning recognized the importance of granting the union reassigned time to conduct its business, enabling the union to keep an office, enlist and train staff, and to be timely and professional in executing its responsibilities. Another factor contributing to success is that the union is independent, i.e., it is not affiliated directly with a state or national organization that requires huge transfer of dues collections from the union central offices. Thus, the dues are available locally to fund a district office, hire attorneys and a full-time office manager, and pay faculty for their services or buy them reassigned time from their regular duties. Of course, faculty are encouraged on their own to belong to and pay dues individually to state and national organizations, and more than 60 percent of faculty are members of the Faculty Association of California Community Colleges (FACCC), a state lobbying organization.

Among other factors that contribute to success, the management and faculty have diligently pursued some form of "win-win" or mutual gains type of bargaining and problem solving for years, most recently hiring a consultant to train the board, management, and faculty in conflict resolution. This constant attention to reducing conflict has created a culture sensitive to people, open to ideas, and committed to the collective good of the institution.

The FDCCD agreement does not make a perfect world by any means. Ongoing issues that cannot be resolved easily in the boardroom or at the negotiations table are omnipresent. Shared governance proposes technical and legal questions that have yet to be answered to the satisfaction of everyone. How authority, responsibility, and accountability work in decision making, and what happens when consensus cannot be reached is not clear. If a decision has a disproportionate impact on one group, for example, the academic senates, should other groups with only a marginal stake be allowed to vote or even play a significant role in consensus building? If an issue appears to be in the exclusive realm of management, does that mean other groups need not be informed until after the decision is made? How do you define "exclusive domain," and further, does collaborative decision making mean proposals must be recycled through the governance system with every modification, preventing timely action?

In addition to these governance issues, negotiations over salary and benefits and other items can produce fierce debate over how resources should be distributed. These negotiations have no impact, however, on the union's commitment to conciliate grievances and to meet regularly with management in "Contract Review" to fix contract glitches.

To summarize, the Foothill-DeAnza agreement contains language that enables union officers and management to groom provisions and a conciliation process that mediates disputes efficiently and fairly, thereby reducing grievances and arbitrations to a remarkable minimum. These, together with a long history of interest in win-win problem solving and collaborative decision making, have contributed greatly to good union management relations.

The Instructional Division—Child Development and Education

By Kathleen Burson

An instructional division is a landscape experienced by its inhabitants as vast, intimate, barren, provident, open or restrictive, depending on how they are positioned within it. Of greatest significance in this positioning is the relation of the parts. Key players can construct a division that brings everyone into relation with everyone else and equidistant from reservoirs of power, or the stakeholders can create wildernesses and backwaters without meaning to, based on familiar hierarchical models. Ray Bacchetti (1988), former member of the board of trustees of our district, wrote in a leadership abstract for the League for Innovation that he held the concept of "a proper ecology"—a way of relating between and among colleagues in our institution—that could create "an environment in which good and talented people do their best work." Within the following example of a division at DeAnza College, the creation of clusters of working teams throughout the division grows out of that ecological perspective.

The role of an excellent child development and education program on a community college campus is so pervasive and complex that, like an intricate background, its significance may be felt but unregistered. The study of the foundation years of human development informs innumerable other disciplines including anthropology, sociology, psychology, education, family studies, and biology. The division's programs are diverse, combining instruction and service, transfer and certificate programs, as well as both pre-service and in-service vocational coursework. Personnel within the division include certified, classified, teaching, nonteaching, administrative, and, uniquely, the highly specialized educators of young children and their student families. In creating an organizational structure, the temptation to divide these programs neatly into noninteractive compartments seemed not unlike the temptation to substitute a frozen dinner in its tripartite plastic tray for a home-cooked meal—expedient but perhaps not so likely to contribute to long-term health and well-being. We attempted, instead, to design a structure that is the result of careful observation. We have reflected on emerging patterns, and as a result, we feel we have found a way to create a feeling of relative intimacy and access to information. We have formed clusters of work units with an overlay of a communication system that connects all the parts.

Before a group imposes any structure on an existing landscape, the members seek every advantage in the positioning. Within our diverse group of division personnel, we needed first to observe where the natural affinities were—which people tended to seek each other out and why. Far from being superfluous, this observation assisted us in building on existing strengths. Where communication was already strong, we made it stronger. We gave these natural teams a name and a task and watched the projects flourish. Secondly, we noted who worked together out of necessity. Sometimes these teams experienced even more interaction than the affinity-based teams, and yet the communication and synergy weren't always present. We also recognized these teams and supported them in breaking down communication barriers to which they may have become resigned to an unhealthy degree. Lastly, we tried to identify the instances in which disparate perspectives needed to be brought together to serve the broadest constituency. We created teams where none had existed before and thereby began the process of cross-fertilization that makes new ideas possible.

Our reflection resulted in the formation of multiple small groups with each division member participating simultaneously in at least three. The interrelationship of three types of these groups constitutes the organizational structure of the division as a whole:

Administrative team—composed of the division dean, the child development center coordinator, and the staff assistant.

Task groups—composed of one member from each instructional and service team and one member from administration.

Instruction and service teams—composed of working partners in a non-hierarchical relationship teaching in either the adult or children's classrooms.

Each team designs its own schedule and format for meeting, discussing, planning, and contributing back to the division as a whole. Periodic reports are made to the administrative team for distribution to the whole. Divisionwide retreats are held annually. The structure works because it solves several endemic problems: it forces communication where none previously existed; it puts everyone in at least one group with a member of the administrative team; and it evenly distributes the division workload. This organizational structure has resulted in a true partnership between instruction and service. The framework has resulted in the acquisition and implementation of numerous grants and the constant generation of fresh ideas that make each year constructively different from the last.

We are a division that constantly reinvents itself. Every year new teams are created; every spring new tasks are delegated to new work groups. As a result, like the residents of any busy neighborhood, each division member knows a little of every other. Through their outreach to other divisions and committees, similar healthy familiarities develop throughout the campus. Through these efforts, we hope to continue growing succeeding generations in this environment for many years to come.

Conclusion

Clearly, the academic team is a coat of many colors. Those described here illustrate the diversity of groups but are by no means inclusive of the many essential teams that comprise "The Academic Team" at DeAnza College. A certain essence, however, characterizes the fabric of them all—the essence of good classroom teaching, with elements quite familiar to us.

The first element is clarity of goal. Each team can set its sight on clearly stated objectives, whether self-initiated, as in the case of the successful instructional division; initiated by the state, as in our academic senate example; extended by administration, as illustrated by the enrollment management team; or mutually designed by faculty and management for successful contract implementation, as modeled by our contract review and mediation teams. In the words of Will Rogers, "If you don't know where you're going, any road will take you there." All good teachers know where they want to go with a class, every class meeting, well enough to adjust as needed and maximize the involve-ment of students in achieving the goal. Likewise, all good teams know the goal and maximize involvement in reaching it.

The second element is maintenance of the integrity of the team process, which requires that certain unspoken values be cultivated: respect for good work and good thinking; respect for diverse people and ideas; an etiquette of personal kindness and consideration both in and out of the team setting; resis-tance to "we-they" language and alliances for their own sake; a commitment to consult before deciding; and pleasure in the work and shared pride and credit in the results. This climate is no different from the environment created by a good teacher in the classroom. While DeAnza is a large college and can occa-sionally get stuck with either a short-circuited decision process or one so cum-bersome that nothing comes out of it, people generally understand that stu-dents come first, and creative teamwork across the organizational chart is the best way to improve what we do for them.

The third element is the responsibility of the leader of each team to tilt the bal-ance between process and product toward closure and accomplishment. While setting the agenda, creating a positive climate, and providing the necessary resources are fundamental to team accomplishment, it is also the leader's respon-sibility to move on; if a team is enjoying itself as much as it should be, the natural tendency of the group is to avoid the discomfort of the next challenge. Graceful prodding is the leader's job, just as it is the teacher's job in the classroom.

Finally, the academic team will be only as successful as the college as a whole is successful, under the leadership of the president, chancellor, and board of trustees, to meet the future as a united team in service to the community. Aca-demic teams must see themselves in this ever larger context and adjust, even follow, accordingly. Knowing when to lead and when to follow is a subtlety that all good teachers have mastered.

We thus find that we are, as organizations, blessed with an inherent supply of skilled team members and team builders for the academic team, as DeAnza College can certainly attest. The formal structures of the team will vary, man-agement reorganizations will occur, teams will cease to exist, and new ones will evolve, but the power of the team for the improvement of quality will endure and prevail. At DeAnza, we plan to perfect our running game well into the cyberspace of the 21st century.

References

Assembly Bill 1725. Chapter 973, Section 61 (a), California Administrative Code, Title 5, Subchapter 2, 53200, 1988.

Bacchetti, R.F. "A Proper Ecology for Board-CEO Relationships." *Leadership Abstracts,* 1988, *1*, (18).

Community College League of California. *Report of the Enrollment Growth Manage-ment Task Group*, Sacramento, Calif., 1992.

CHAPTER 6

BUILDING BRIDGES

A Team Approach to Transforming Student Services in the Community College

MARGUERITE MCGANN CULP

Introduction

A s Matson (1994) recently observed, major student development functions have remained consistent for three decades, although organizational patterns and the activities included in each function may differ as individual institutions respond to student demographics. Also remaining consistent for three decades are the debates over how to organize and lead student services in the community college (Miller & Prince, 1976; Phoenix, Flynn & Floyd, 1986; and Garland & Grace, 1993) and whether or not student development programming is effective (Medsker, 1960; Elsnor & Ames, 1983; Cohen & Brawer, 1989; and Creamer, 1994). For community colleges entering the 21st century, these debates take on a new meaning as institutions deal with increasingly complex educational missions in an era of dramatically reduced resources.

Is there a role for student development practitioners in the community colleges of the future? What impact will the current emphasis on teaching and learning have on traditional student development programs? Can student development practitioners compete in any meaningful way for a share of the reduced resources currently available to community colleges? Does collaboration with the academic side of the house dilute student development to the point that neither its programs nor its practitioners have any integrity? How do practitioners demonstrate that their programs are effective? This chapter describes how one community college used a team approach to redefine and reorganize its student development functions, outlines the principles and assumptions that guided the team-building process, provides an overview of data-gathering procedures, analyzes the programs and processes that the team created, and offers some insights into the leader's role in the team-building process.

Constructing a Philosophical Framework

In response to faculty concerns that student development "types" were either invisible or out of touch with reality, that programs were neither data based nor evaluated regularly, and that the resources allocated to student development could be used more effectively by instruction, Seminole Community College (SCC), a medium-sized Florida institution, decided in 1981 to reengineer the student development office. Located in Central Florida, Seminole was a comprehensive community college offering college credit, noncredit vocational, and adult and continuing education opportunities to the residents of its service district. The student development office provided traditional support services—admissions, counseling, financial aid, testing, and registration—to all areas of the institution, including an alternative high school on campus.

Before initiating the reengineering project, the dean of student development worked with practitioners and collegewide administrators to develop assumptions and principles to guide the process. These players based assumptions on the institution's culture and mission; principles evolved from organizational theory and research.

Assumptions
To reduce the anxiety that any change process creates, the college agreed that no one would lose his/her position during the reengineering process, although staff members understood that job responsibilities and assignments could change. The president established a positive framework for change by announcing that the student development office was an important part of the college team and would not be asked to sacrifice its identity during the change process. Supporting the positive framework with money, the college allocated staff and program development funds to the student development office to help staff members study new theories and acquire new skills. Because the creative tension produced by opposing views was a critical component of the change process, the college assumed that dissonance would occur and mistakes were inevitable—and that both presented student development practitioners with unique learning and problem-solving opportunities. Finally, the college adopted

the assumption that served as the foundation for the entire reengineering process: Seminole Community College was a teaching-learning institution where everyone was responsible for doing the right thing and doing it well.

Principles

After an extensive review of organizational and student development research, the college adopted five change principles:

Principle 1. A universally right way to lead, manage, plan, or evaluate people and programs does not exist. Systems that work well at one institution fail miserably at another because of dramatic differences in organizational culture, mission, and resources.

Principle 2. Education is the business of helping people learn. Like any business, the keys to success are customer satisfaction, a superior product, and competitive prices. Because education is a unique business, however, institutions must identify their product and their potential customers, define what they mean by customer satisfaction, and identify the outcome measures they will use to demonstrate their product's superiority.

Principle 3. A community college's resources are finite, while the many good things it can do are infinite. Change agents must clearly define each program and service, relate each to the teaching-learning mission of the institution, ensure each is based in theory and research and compatible with the campus culture, and demonstrate acceptable cost-benefit ratios.

Principle 4. Planning and evaluation are the keys to resource acquisition and management, but planning must be flexible enough to allow practitioners to take advantage of unexpected opportunities and respond to unforeseen crises. As the institution at the bottom of the higher education "food chain," the community college must respond quickly to changing student and community demographics. A rigid plan would cripple any community college's capacity to deal with unexpected threats and opportunities.

Principle 5. Technology is a tool; it does not drive the teaching-learning process, it supports the process. The fact that the technology exists to perform a specific function does not mean that it is in the best interests of the college to acquire that technology.

Creating a Climate for Change

Initial team-building activities led by external consultants revealed the presence of multiple cultures and confusing communication structures within the student development office. Staff members defined their roles inconsistently, relied upon an authority figure (usually the dean) to resolve disputes, and often competed with one another for recognition and rewards. Skill levels varied from practitioner to practitioner, even when two staff members had the same job description, and much of the staff resisted change.

To increase their ability to understand themselves and others, staff members volunteered to participate in a series of workshops built around the Myers-Briggs Type Indicator (MBTI). Almost immediately, the MBTI improved internal communication by providing everyone from the dean to the part-time clerk with a shared framework from which to view behaviors, a common vocabulary that allowed them to talk with one another about problems, and a neutral arena for management-staff interactions. The MBTI also provided the dean with working hypotheses about the type of leadership to which each staff member would respond, the strengths each would bring to a team, and the weaknesses with which each must deal. Table 6.1 illustrates a few of the strategies that proved effective in dealing with basic type differences and increasing the chances that all staff members would contribute positively to the student development team.

Knowledge of type produced some immediate changes in the student development office at the team level. To provide introverts with an equal opportunity to contribute during meetings, teams distributed agendas and all related material one week in advance, allowing introverts time to reflect on the issues

Table 6.1
Responding to Type Differences

MBTI Preference	Leadership Responsibilities
Extroverts	Focus their efforts. Help them think before speaking. Prevent them from dominating meetings or group activities.
Introverts	Provide reflection time. Do not require immediate answers. Create an atmosphere in which they feel comfortable sharing partially formed thoughts.
Sensing	Provide step-by-step directions, facts, and details. Help them look at the "big picture" and anticipate the long-range consequences of every decision. Develop their self-confidence by asking them to be responsible for practical, detail-oriented tasks.
Intuitives	Give them a global picture of a task, then help them understand how facts and details fit into the "big picture." Develop their self-confidence by asking them to tackle projects that require imagination and inspiration, but keep them anchored in the real world by establishing deadlines and requiring a product.

and prepare their positions. Type was a key factor in creating work groups, and members understood the unique gifts they brought to the problem-solving process because of their types. Teams used type as one of the criteria in determining assignments and building support systems. Most importantly, teams used their knowledge of type to improve programs offered to students, connect with faculty colleagues, and communicate more effectively with administrators.

To test out their hypotheses about the status of student development in the college, staff members gathered baseline data from administrators, faculty, staff, and students. Data were gathered in a variety of ways—formal needs-analysis and evaluation instruments, focus groups, informal department meetings, individual interviews—and evaluated with the help of the college's institutional research office. Seven questions yielded the most valuable data. They were: What skills and attitudes do students need to succeed at the college? How does the student development office increase the chances that students will succeed? What does the student development office do to decrease the chances that students will succeed? How can the student development office become one percent better? What are the threats and opportunities facing the student devel-

Table 6.1 (continued)

MBTI Preference	Leadership Responsibilities
Thinking	Recognize their accomplishments. Encourage them to compete with themselves, not with other staff members. Teach them to factor emotions into the work equation, to value harmony, and to function effectively in groups.
Feeling	Praise who they are rather than what they do. Provide them with opportunities to work in groups and create friendships among coworkers. Teach them to deal with disharmony and to feel comfortable identifying and dealing with people and program problems.
Judging	Provide well-defined objectives, limits, and timelines. Help them slow down their tendency to make quick decisions. Teach them to develop criteria that they can use to determine the effectiveness of a decision.
Perceiving	Provide as much autonomy and job variety as possible, but set limits and demand closure.

opment office in the next three years? What are the most significant threats and opportunities facing faculty and students in the next three years? and How can the student development office help students and faculty members deal effectively with their concerns and respond positively to opportunities?

The picture of the student development office that emerged was one of a division on the verge of being out of touch with the needs of students, the demands of faculty, and the goals of the college. For example, counselors wanted to spend at least 50 percent of their time providing personal counseling to individual students, while faculty and students felt counselors needed to spend more time dealing with students in groups and in the classroom. The registrar saw few advantages to computerizing the registration process, but faculty and students believed computerized registration would improve the college's competitiveness among Central Florida institutions. No one in the student development office placed high priority on either academic advising or career counseling, while faculty and students, however, agreed that academic advising and career counseling were essential services.

Providing the Tools for Change

As staff members analyzed baseline data, three facts became obvious: the division had to establish priorities, because needs were infinite and time was finite; many staff members did not have the skills to implement new programs; and without decision-making/conflict-resolution procedures, both the change process and the teams planning new programs and services would fail.

Establishing Priorities
Staff members in each of the major student development areas worked with the dean to develop a list of strategies to improve existing services and ideas for new programs and services. These lists were circulated to all faculty and administrators and to a random sample of new and currently enrolled students. Using a Modified Delphi approach, respondents selected the five critical programs or services in each area. Staff members tabulated the responses, selected the programs in each area that received the most votes, provided data about the costs and benefits associated with implementing each program, and asked respondents to again pick their top five. The voting process continued until respondents reached consensus. Practitioners used the Modified Delphi results as the starting point for improving existing services and designing new programs.

Acquiring New Skills
The dean of student services obtained grant funding to update staff skills. Each group within the student development office identified the skills its members needed to acquire in order to implement new programs or strengthen existing ones. The counselors, for example, used their money to update their career

counseling skills, to become familiar with new assessment instruments, to receive training in learning theory and teaching styles, and to learn how to deal with difficult students. To reinforce the team concept, consultants came to campus to enable staff members to complete training sessions together. In addition to formal in-service sessions, staff members with skills in critical-need areas agreed to either mentor other staff members or allow themselves to be videotaped for use in in-service training sessions. Staff members also created professional development plans that included attendance at state and national conferences, completion of credit and noncredit courses, and a commitment to reading journal articles.

Decision-Making/Conflict-Resolution Techniques

Dealing with conflict in a positive, productive manner proved a significant challenge to staff members until counselors teaching life/career planning courses suggested a seven-step decision-making model. Although team members used the model only when dealing with major decisions and team-threatening conflicts, the process increased the chances that staff members would view a problem objectively and reduced the tendency of staff members to become emotionally involved with an issue. The seven steps are:

1. *Define the problem/Identify the conflict.* Staff members learned to identify the real problem and who owned it, to ask the right questions to determine if a problem really existed, and to establish the real dimensions of the conflict.

2. *Gather and analyze the data.* Rather than rely on one data-gathering technique (usually hearsay), staff members learned to use a variety of data-gathering techniques and to rely heavily on subgroup analysis. This step challenged everyone analyzing the data to look at facts—even when the facts did not fit their assumptions—and to recognize that a solution that helped one student group might harm another.

3. *Identify alternatives and consequences.* The fun part of the process, this step encouraged staff members to recognize that most problems have multiple solutions, each with different positive and negative consequences, and to identify all possible options. Practitioners learned to weigh negative consequences very carefully and to imagine paying the consequences associated with each alternative.

4. *Choose an alternative.* All alternatives were not equal, and staff members eventually had to select the alternative that moved the team toward its goal at a price the team—and the college—was willing to pay. Once an alternative was selected, team members brainstormed strategies to minimize the negative consequences associated with their choice.

5. *Design a plan to implement the choice.* The team's responsibilities did not end when they selected an alternative. Teams had to design an implementation plan, paying special attention to the project's timeline, evaluation criteria, and feedback loop. The college was particularly concerned

that each team identify the different types of data they planned to collect to determine the effectiveness of their program.

6. *Implement and evaluate the plan.* The time and effort involved in identifying and resolving a problem or planning a new program often predisposed teams to view their solution or new program through rose-colored glasses. To increase objectivity, this step encouraged team members to look at both process and product data to determine whether or not a program was effective or a problem resolved. Team members were cautioned against forcing something to work, encouraged to collect evaluation data as the plan progressed, not just at the end of the trial period, and challenged to learn from and "celebrate" failures as well as successes.

7. *Institutionalize, modify, or abandon the program.* At some point, teams had to either institutionalize or abandon new programs. Teams learned to base this decision on hard data and consensus rather than emotional responses and a vote of the majority. They also learned that the stronger the evaluation/feedback loop in the original plan, the easier it became to decide whether to institutionalize, modify, or abandon a program.

Learning to Work as a Team: The First Steps

Armed with their knowledge of type theory and equipped with new skills and conflict-resolution techniques, staff members began to work in teams, the first of which were functional teams designed to create a mission statement and identify annual goals and outcome measures for each area within the student development office. When completed, each team's plan was reviewed by four cross-functional teams composed of members from each of the major departments within the student development office. Approaching each plan from an outsider's perspective, the cross-functional teams analyzed the plan's strengths and weaknesses, its impact on other areas of the college, and its potential to help students succeed.

During mandatory two-day planning sessions facilitated by the dean, all student development staff members discussed each plan, paying special attention to the modifications suggested by the cross-functional review team, and reached consensus on goals and outcome measures for each area. Because budget figures for the coming year were not available, staff members voted to prioritize objectives, so that no doubts would linger about what should be done first if budget cuts materialized.

At the conclusion of the two-day planning sessions, staff members offered five critical observations about the college, the change process, and the future of teams at the institution: (1) the lack of information about college priorities made it difficult to establish meaningful department goals and objectives; (2) until day-to-day operational activities were running well, the student development office should not inaugurate new programs and services; (3) saboteurs within the student development office were undermining the team-building process; (4) the college's weak communication system aided the saboteurs; and (5) both product and process data were critical to the team building and the change processes. After an extensive discussion, staff members developed strategies to respond appropriately to each challenge.

Collegewide Goals

The dean agreed to use two strategies, one long term and one short term, to deal with the issue of collegewide goals. The long-term strategy involved encouraging the president's council to develop collegewide planning procedures to produce institutional goals and outcome measures. Short-term strategies focused on meeting with the president, the vice presidents, the faculty senate president, the chair of the board of trustees, and individual academic departments both to clarify their goals for the institution and to measure their receptiveness to the proposed student development goals; publishing a planning and evaluation calendar for the student development office; and including faculty, staff, and community members in student development's planning process.

Operational Activities

Believing that faculty members would not trust student development until day-to-day services were performed effectively and efficiently, practitioners voted to spend one year improving existing programs while developing the skills to introduce new programs and services. As new programs were introduced, however, staff members identified nonessential activities to phase so they could continue to perform essential day-to-day activities efficiently while phasing in new programs.

Saboteurs

Staff members identified four types of people on each of their teams: the risk takers, those who supported the risk takers, the neutrals, and the saboteurs. The risk takers and those who supported them needed recognition and rewards—and occasionally protection—to function effectively, the neutrals needed information to make an informed choice about the team and the proposed change, but the saboteurs responded negatively to everything and needed to be "neutralized." To neutralize the saboteurs, staff members agreed to make every decision in the open, to share how and why each decision was reached, to tie every act and every decision to data, to engage in preemptive strikes by developing and using a campuswide communication network, and to confront inappropriate and unproductive behaviors immediately.

Communication

The student development office established a campuswide network that included four components: an electronic bulletin board that changed weekly with information about programs and challenges, new initiatives, and the dean's weekly schedule; a monthly newsletter to all faculty and staff describing the department's challenges and accomplishments, outlining future threats and opportunities, and providing basic campus, state and national information of value to faculty; suggestion boxes throughout the campus; and a "welcome wagon" program through which student development staff members introduced new faculty to the programs and services provided by their offices. At the most elementary level, the network kept faculty informed about who was doing what in the student development office. On a deeper level, however, the network educated faculty members, demonstrated the relationship between the teaching-learning process and student development, and provided practitioners with a vehicle they could use to shape the campus culture.

Information

The student development office created an information highway to provide team members with process and product data. Process data included midyear faculty, student, and staff evaluations of programs and services; "roses and thorns," a written analysis of department strengths and weaknesses completed each semester by student development practitioners; and preliminary program-effectiveness figures. Teams used process data to fine tune programs and services, or to make midcourse corrections. Product data included formal end-of-year evaluations of all programs and personnel, final program effectiveness figures, and needs-analysis information provided by faculty and students. Teams used product data to make decisions about the fate of current programs and to guide future programming efforts. To encourage teams to use data in an intentional way, the student development office published an annual calendar that identified the information each team would receive monthly, as well as major team assignments, due dates, and outcome measures.

Building Confidence in the Team

During the confidence-building phase of each team's development, it became apparent that some team members responded to team-building techniques that focused on creating harmony and a feeling of goodwill while others gained confidence only when the team accomplished something. For those who gained confidence in the team when its members were in harmony, the dean sponsored social events, offered gifts and cards on special occasions, wrote poems to celebrate landmark occasions, and provided lots of face-to-face feedback. The dean helped accomplishment-oriented team members attain confidence in their teams by encouraging them to define incremental outcome measures so that they saw many small day-to-day triumphs rather than one big end-of-the project success, nominating their programs for state and national awards, and celebrating achievements with plaques, poems, and an occasional party.

During their first two years, teams improved existing programs to the point that 85 percent of the faculty, students, and administrators evaluating student development services rated them three (satisfactory) or above on a five-point scale. As confidence increased, teams devised people and paper strategies to begin to shape rather than merely respond to the campus culture.

The first attempts to influence campus culture through people involved establishing paid summer internships for faculty in the student development office, electing or appointing a student services practitioner to every committee on campus, assigning a specific student services liaison to each academic department, and conducting an annual three-day faculty-student development open house in which participants talked about what went right and what went wrong in the preceding year. As each strategy increased the visibility and influence of the student development office on campus, confidence in the team and in the change process increased.

Paper strategies that had a positive impact on campus culture included publishing a detailed mission-and-goals statement for every area within the student development office, providing all faculty members with an opportunity to complete an annual report card on student development programs and services, and publishing an annual report. The annual report proved particularly effective, since it outlined major accomplishments in relation to previously defined outcome measures, clearly documented the relationship between student development programs and the teaching-learning process, and tied program costs to program outcomes.

During this time, teams used the Modified Delphi Technique to update job descriptions, create evaluation criteria and procedures for each position, and develop procedure manuals for each area. Since student development was the first campus office to tackle these projects, team members received considerable positive feedback from administrators and faculty. Encouraged by the positive feedback and the mounting number of successes in each area, student development practitioners recommended that the college change the name of the student development office to the student services office to send two messages to the college community: a new day had dawned, a new service-oriented office was born, and everyone was responsible for student development, not just student affairs practitioners. The college accepted the recommendation.

Increasing the Team's Influence through Partnerships

During their third year of operation, most practitioners reached the conclusion that the future of their team and the student services office was tied to partnerships—partnerships with other teams within student services, partnerships with faculty and students, and partnerships with the community. Teams consequently focused their energies on building, maintaining, and evaluating partnerships, a focus that led to the creation of cross-functional teams that designed and implemented solutions to specific problems then disbanded when data demonstrated that the problems were solved. Table 6.2 outlines a few of the internal (on-campus) partnerships developed as a result of team decisions, while Table 6.3 outlines external (off-campus) partnerships.

Partnerships paid off in many ways for the student services office as teams received state and national awards for the articulation office; the co-advisement program; the placement, planning, and evaluation models; the at-risk student tracking system; the learning-style workshops; and applications of the Myers-Briggs Type Indicator to the teaching-learning process. The student services office established a "victory wall" where plaques were hung with pride, but staff members were equally proud of the campus "awards" never displayed on the walls: focus-group results documenting that faculty, staff, and community members viewed the student services office as one of the strengths of the college; the number of student affairs practitioners elected as officers and at-large members of the faculty senate; and a satisfaction with services ratings that approached 95 percent among students, faculty, and administrators.

Empowering Team Members: The Final Steps

During their first five years, teams did an admirable job of reengineering the student services office. Every area enjoyed a high level of customer satisfaction as a result of mission-and-goal statements, operational and strategic planning procedures, and feedback loops that included process and product data. Each year, the student services office published a calendar, a progress report to the faculty, and program evaluation results. Each year, faculty, students, and administrators completed needs analysis and evaluation forms and had the opportunity to participate in open forums to discuss the strengths and weaknesses of the student services office. And each year, the student services office, with input from all areas of the college community, spent two days planning its future. But three elements were missing: although budgeting was tied to planning, team members did not control their budgets; program evaluations relied too heavily on customer satisfaction measures; and teams demonstrated that they used resources effectively and their programs were popular, but they did not demonstrate how (or if) their programs made a difference to the college's bottom line, the education of students.

Controlling the Team's Budget

During the first few team-building years, the college required the dean to control all of the budgets within the student services office. As each team demonstrated its ability to collect and analyze data, to design programs that supported the college's operational and strategic goals, and to make difficult decisions, the dean relinquished the purse strings. Only when teams began to allocate

Table 6.2
Internal Partnerships Created by Team Members

Partners	Program
Deans of instruction, applied technology, and student services	Articulation office, a cooperative approach to helping students transfer with no loss of credit to upper-division institutions.
Department chairs, faculty, institutional research office, assessment and testing center, counseling department	College credit placement model, a computerized system designed to place new college credit students in appropriate English, mathematics, and reading courses.
	Student tracking system, a computerized system to identify and track at-risk students from their first day at the college.
	Disabled Student Services, an office to deal with the needs of physically and mentally challenged students.
Data center, counseling department, registrar	GRAD check, a computerized degree audit and graduation check system.
Data center, admissions and records, counseling department	DCS, a computerized admissions and registration system.
Faculty, counseling department	Co-advisement, a cooperative advising approach that provided students with advising assistance from two- and four-year faculty members and counselors.
Faculty, counseling department	Counselor workshops for faculty, a series of twenty-four workshops designed to support the teaching-learning process.
Faculty, student activities	Campus Governance Association, an association of faculty, students, and staff working together to solve campus problems.
	Celebrating Diversity, a series of workshops, seminars, entertainment, and cultural activities designed to create a campus environment that values differences.

Table 6.2 (continued)

Partners	Program
	Co-curricular activities, a year-long series of speakers, films, entertainers, and activities designed to supplement classroom activities.
Counseling department, social science department	College credit courses, such as life/career planning and college success, taught by counselors but sponsored by the social science department, which also received the revenue generated by the course.
Assessment center, career center, counseling center	The career choice service, a series of career choice tests administered by the assessment center, interpreted by counselors, and followed up on by career center staff.
Assessment center, faculty senate	Make-up testing center, a place where faculty could refer students who missed an in-class exam.
Faculty, counselors	Learning style workshops, a series of workshops taught as part of a credit class or after the class for extra credit, to help students develop a study skills method to match their learning style.
	Teaching style workshops, a series of workshops to help faculty members discover their teaching styles and to explore the impact of their style on their classroom effectiveness.
Career center, cooperative education office, faculty	Placement center, a computerized center to assist current and former students in locating full- and part-time jobs.

resources and monitor the expenditure of funds did they have the power that matched their responsibilities; until then, each team planned, recommended, and evaluated, but did not have to make the hard decisions needed to move a program forward. Managing budgets was a challenging task for most teams,

Table 6.3
External Partnerships Created by Team Members

Partners	Program
Career center, area businesses	Outplacement services for employees whose positions were changed or eliminated.
Dean of student services, leadership	Training workshops for business and civic leaders.
Orlando counseling center, minority business community	Community mentor program to provide minority students with mentors and role models.
Career center, Central Florida business community	Job shadowing opportunities for students in life/career planning courses.
Articulation office, Florida community college system, state university system	Student bill of rights to define the rights of all community college students transferring to a Florida public university as well as the responsibilities of the receiving institution.
Articulation office, state universities, private colleges	Articulation agreements to protect the rights of and provide scholarships to SCC transfer students.
Counseling department, area high schools	High school counselor manual to provide detailed information about programs, services, and degrees. Annual high school counselor workshop to provide basic information about the college and in-service opportunities to Central Florida counselors.
Articulation office, Seminole public schools, University of Central Florida	Joint committees to solve shared curriculum problems and establish a seamless curriculum in all subjects from kindergarten through college.
Articulation office, University of Central Florida	Cross-town transfer agreements to allow students to earn credits at the university while completing their degrees at the community college.

Table 6.3 (continued)

Partners	Program
Counseling department, Seminole County public schools	Tech prep counseling institute, a seminar series for counselors, teachers, and parents to help them understand and use tech prep effectively.
Assessment and testing center, counseling center, Seminole County	Workshops to help middle and high school students develop self-esteem, career maturity, and the ability to study effectively, take tests, and make decisions.
Women's center, area businesses and foundations	Scholarships for at-risk females planning to enter nontraditional careers.

and more than one tried to avoid the task by returning fiscal control to the dean, but by 1994 each team controlled its own budget and was beginning to deal directly with three harsh realities: resources were finite, the costs of some programs were simply too high when weighed against the outcomes, and the productivity of some practitioners did not match their salary level.

Expanding Program Evaluation Procedures
Although important, teams soon realized that customer satisfaction was only the tip of the effectiveness iceberg. One by one, teams began to work with the dean of student services to design research studies to determine whether programs helped students succeed, the ultimate effectiveness criteria for a community college student services office. Studies completed by the adult high school counseling center, the articulation office, the assessment and testing center, the career/placement center, the college credit counseling office, the college retention project, and the college success team either demonstrated the effectiveness of or answered critical questions related to their program.

In a two-year study of the effectiveness of a peer-counseling course, the adult high school counseling center demonstrated that students who completed the class earned more credits toward their diploma and were more likely to graduate than students who did not complete the class. The same study used the Myers-Briggs Type Indicator to demonstrate that the peer counseling class enrolled more introverts (53 percent) than would be expected based on type theory, led to additional studies that documented the unique nature of adult high school students when compared to the general population, and resulted in the creation of new support services.

In cooperation with one state and one private university, the articulation office initiated an ongoing study of the effectiveness of the college's advising system. The study measured three elements: the quality of the advising information, student evaluations of the accuracy and timeliness of the information they received, and the number of credits lost by students when transferring to state and private institutions. The office measured the accuracy of advising information by asking all counselors each semester to earn 90 percent or above on a one-hundred-question test designed to measure mastery of advising information; the office tracked scores by counselor and by term to enable the college to monitor trends and take appropriate action to make sure that each counselor maintained a high skill level. The staff measured student perceptions of the accuracy of advising information by a paper-and-pencil instrument distributed annually to a random sample of currently enrolled students and all graduating students. The office analyzed results by ethnic subgroup to identify trends and modified the advising process each year until the satisfaction level in all areas reached 90 percent. To measure loss of credits, a private and a public university agreed to track Seminole Community College transfer students and provide a list of the credits these students lost when they transferred. Problem areas were identified and corrections made until fewer than 2 percent of the transfer students lost credits when transferring within the same major.

To increase the chances that students would succeed in entry-level math, English, and reading classes, the assessment and testing center worked with the mathematics, English, and reading departments to refine the state-mandated placement model for college-credit students. In mathematics, for example, center staff designed a series of research studies to determine the role that a student's high school math background and number of years since his/her last formal math course played in success in math. As a result of the study, the college required students not only to earn state-mandated cut-off scores but also to demonstrate that they had completed appropriate prerequisite courses within the last three years. To improve the testing climate for noncredit vocational-technical students, the assessment and testing team asked students to evaluate every aspect of the testing process from the way they were greeted to the temperature of the room. The team tracked responses and modified the testing process until 95 percent of the examinees reported satisfaction with all aspects of noncredit vocational testing.

Faced with conflicting claims about the effectiveness of various career counseling interventions for undecided students, the career/placement center team designed a longitudinal study to investigate the effectiveness of three counseling interventions: a three-credit course, a career counseling group, and no intervention. Using career maturity as the effectiveness indicator, the team used pretest and posttest measures to demonstrate that a three-credit class was the most effective intervention. A byproduct of the study, however, was the finding that any counseling intervention was better than no counseling intervention; undecided students in the control group who received no counseling became more undecided and less focused as the semester progressed.

Before offering a series of ten study skills seminars to at-risk vocational students, the counseling center team administered a pretest. Posttest results indicated significant gains in all study skill areas, while anecdotal data from faculty members credited the seminars with salvaging 25 percent of the LPN class. The counseling team used similar pretest and posttest measures to demonstrate the effectiveness of a variety of large and small group activities such as advising, orientation, test anxiety seminars, and math anxiety workshops. Test results were used continually to improve the programs until counselors reached a point where most services were rated three or above on a five-point scale by 90 percent of participants.

To convince the college curriculum committee that a two-credit college success course would increase retention, the college success team designed a longitudinal study to compare the retention and graduation rates of students who completed experimental college success courses with the retention and graduation rates of noncompleters. Because the study documented that completers were more likely to be enrolled in or graduated from the college at the end of two years, the curriculum committee approved the course for permanent inclusion in the curriculum.

The desire to know if the federal dollars allocated to retaining at-risk students produced results led the college retention project team to conduct a five-year longitudinal study of their program's effectiveness. The study examined six outcome measures for all students: successful completion of English I and intermediate algebra, the first college-level English and math courses; final or most-recent grade point averages; percentage of students on probation, suspension, or dismissal; percentage of students currently enrolled; and percentage of students who graduated. Although the study answered some questions, it raised many more. For example, even when all of the questions were answered in relation to college retention project students, it was impossible to determine the program's effectiveness for two reasons: the college did not routinely track graduation and completion rates for college credit students, and team members could not establish a link between services received and a student's success. Recognizing the problems the project faced, team members implemented procedures to capture baseline data on all new students, implement pretest and posttest measures for major interventions, record the services college retention project students received, and connect the services to student success in the classroom.

Demonstrating that Student Services Makes a Difference
To share the data generated by research studies and customer satisfaction measures and to demonstrate that student services helped Seminole Community College students succeed, practitioners developed a biannual publication titled

"Do We Make A Difference?" Distributed to administrators, department chair-persons, and faculty senate members, "Do We Make A Difference?" not only summarized research results but also demonstrated how each team used the results to continually improve programs and services.

Putting the Change Process in Perspective

At the end of its transformation, the student services office consisted of one administrator and two types of teams: functional teams, which were permanent and responsible for day-to-day operations such as advising, testing, registration, and counseling, and cross-functional teams, whose members came together to respond to specific challenges and disbanded when the challenges no longer existed. Team leadership varied depending on the challenges facing each team and the expertise of group members; all teams were committed to supporting the teaching-learning process, creating on- and off-campus partnerships, using student success as an outcome measure, and demonstrating daily that programs and practitioners were effective. What role did the dean of student services play in the change process? What mistakes did teams make as they worked their way through the transformation process? Was the pain worth it?

Leading...and Following
The dean's role in building teams and managing change was always challeng-ing, often frustrating, but eventually rewarding. The dean served as the holder of the compass, a coach, a mirror, and a cheerleader. As the pathfinder, the dean maintained a strong sense of where the student services office needed to go and kept teams focused on their destination. In her role as coach, the dean taught problem-solving and conflict-resolution techniques; assisted teams to access information, resources, and training; and provided enough discrepant information to disturb each team's equilibrium but not enough to discourage team members. Acting as a "mirror," the dean helped teams to scan their envi-ronment, monitor their progress toward a goal, anticipate consequences, and "see" the world from other perspectives. As a cheerleader, the dean encouraged teams to define realistic goals, learn from setbacks, value one another, and cel-ebrate victories.

Learning from Mistakes
Although every effort was made to minimize errors, staff members knew from the beginning that mistakes were an unavoidable byproduct of change and an important part of the learning process. Some mistakes were unique to Seminole Community College, others could have occurred at any institution, but all pre-sented challenges and opportunities to the staff.

In the beginning, most teams made mistakes in interacting with people: team members underestimated the impact that a negative person could have on

111

morale and effectiveness, hesitated to give honest feedback to their colleagues, buried problems instead of dealing with them honestly and openly, and lobbied to join a team where everyone shared their views. Teams consistently fell victim to errors of time, either attempting too much or too little, and occasionally succumbed to the box trap, believing that the price of solving a problem was too high—without either verifying the price or exploring other options. Maintaining a balance between the old and the new was a challenge for most teams; unable to agree on priorities, more than one team struggled to do everything and please everyone. For some staff members, particularly those trained as counselors, role ambiguity became a problem as staff members played one role on the team, another in the student services office, and a third on the campus. At one time or another, almost every staff member made the mistake of viewing the change process from a comparative framework ("compared to the blue team, we are not doing too well") rather than applying their own definition of effectiveness to their team's efforts. As teams became more sophisticated, however, these mistakes either decreased considerably or disappeared.

The dean made three major mistakes: underestimating the amount of time that teams needed to reach a decision, assuming that all groups would reach consensus given enough data and time, and shielding team members from harsh student and faculty evaluations, particularly during the initial stages of the change process. These mistakes led to the formulation of the three rules of change:

Rule 1: Teams will always take longer than an individual to make a decision, but the time "lost" will be recaptured during the implementation phase. Always overestimate the time a team needs to reach the implementation phase of the problem-solving process.

Rule 2: Teams sometimes cannot—or will not—reach consensus. When this happens, the dean must act on the data and establish direction. Teams are subject to political pressures, both within their department and in the community, and occasionally need someone else to "take the heat."

Rule 3: Teams benefit from contact with unhappy customers, whether those customers are faculty members or students, and the dean needs to arrange for these contacts.

Reaping the Rewards
Was the time and effort spent building teams and transforming student services worth it? The office, facing life-threatening challenges in 1981, won the 1992 Pyramid Award from the National Association of Student Personnel Administrators, the American College Personnel Association, and the American Association of Community Colleges as well as the 1985 and 1994 Outstanding Institutional Advising Program Awards from the American College Testing Program and the National Academic Advising Association. During the 1991–1992 self-

study process, a collegewide faculty committee concluded that student services was "doing a commendable job with allocated resources" (Seminole Community College, 1993, p. 160) and that its practitioners demonstrated "an attitude of achieving and maintaining excellence through continuous evaluation and change" (p. 143). At the conclusion of its 1993 visit, the Southern Association Reaffirmation Team praised the student services office for the "genuine team spirit among the staff" (Commission on Colleges of the Southern Association of Colleges and Schools, p. 82), complimented the college for "developing a student services model worthy of national replication" (p. 82), and commended the student services office "for its exemplary delivery of services and the comprehensive manner in which planning, policies, and evaluation are conducted" (p. 79). The time it took to build teams, create partnerships, and transform student development at Seminole Community College paid dividends for student affairs practitioners and their faculty colleagues by increasing their ability to help students succeed, the main mission of all two-year institutions, and by producing a powerful faculty-student affairs partnership whose primary goal was—and is—to improve the learning climate for students.

References

Cohen, A., and Brawer, F. *The American Community College*. San Francisco: Jossey-Bass, 1989.

Commission on Colleges of the Southern Association of Colleges and Schools. Report of the Reaffirmation Committee. Unpublished Report, 1993.

Creamer, D. "Synthesis of Literature Related to Historical and Related Functions of Student Services." In G.A. Baker III (Ed.), *A Handbook on the Community College in America*. Westport, Conn: Greenwood Press, 1994.

Elsnor, P., and Ames, W. "Redirecting Student Services." In G.B. Vaughan and Associates (Eds.), *Issues for Community College Leaders in a New Era*. San Francisco: Jossey-Bass, 1983.

Garland, P.H., and Grace, T.W. *New Perspectives for Student Affairs Professionals: Evolving Realities, Responsibilities, and Roles*. Washington, D.C.: George Washington University, 1993.

Matson, J. "The Role of Student Services in Response to Reduced Support." In G.A. Baker III (Ed.), *A Handbook on the Community College in America*. Westport, Conn: Greenwood Press, 1994.

Medsker, L. *The Junior College: Progress and Prospect*. New York: McGraw-Hill, 1960.

Miller, T., and Prince, J. *The Future of Student Affairs*. San Francisco: Jossey-Bass, 1976.

Phoenix, R., Flynn, D., and Floyd, D. "Opportunities through Interdependence." In D.G. Creamer and C.R. Dassance (Eds.), *Opportunities for Student Development in Two Year Colleges*. Washington, D.C.: National Association of Student Personnel Administrators, 1986.

Seminole Community College (1993). Institutional Self Study. Unpublished Report, 1993.

CHAPTER 7

THE TEAM APPROACH TO MANAGING RESOURCES

An Open Systems Approach

LESTER W. REED, JR.

Resource Management before Teams

Before the mid-1980s, community colleges usually delegated management of resources to the chief business officer, who played a solo part in the orchestration of the college's use and distribution of resources with minimum supporting efforts from the remainder of the institution's leadership team. In the era when the business officer reigned supreme in the resource allocation and management arena, the competition for what stakeholders perceived to be a "fair share of the budget" most often was termed as a budget battle. The term "battle" applied to resource management clearly signifies the general lack of mutual cooperation and group input, responsibility, and authority in the area of resource acquisition and allocation. Administrators thought of institutional resources as the allocation of the college's budget and rarely the more encompassing concept of those elements needed to effectively accomplish the educational mission of the college. Physical resources, procurement of goods and services, management of auxiliary services, human resource issues, and most recently, the management of information were rarely thought of as part of the team effort to effectively allocate all resources to meet the core mission of the institution in the most effective and efficient manner possible.

This unilateral management style concerning institutional resources came about during the formative years of the community college during which resources were normally plentiful with only short periods of constrained availability. Community colleges were growing; they were receiving funds from the state and federal sources as well as an ever-increasing flow of tuition. When short setbacks in resource growth occurred because of cyclical business downturns, managers quickly learned that incremental across-the-board cuts for a "few years" solved the problem until the stream of ever-increasing funds was reestablished.

A Changing Resource Landscape

In the mid-1980s, community college leaders began to recognize that what was initially thought to be a periodic short downturn in resource allocation was truly a structural change in how community colleges and other governmental institutions would receive support from state and federal resources. A report in November 1993 by the Pew Charitable Trusts identified a mix of political and social forces that would reshape higher education by creating different and higher expectations of verifiable performance as well as by providing reduced available assets "creating a need to find alternative sources of revenue and resulting in fewer discretionary funds for institutions" (Zemsky, 1993, p. 2A). The report identifies a sense of frustration in higher education institutions that the "expanding bureaucracy and control systems of governance threatens to consume them, on the one hand absorbing all available time and, on the other, dividing them into factions" (p. 5A).

In short, the flow of funding to the community college would never again reach the levels of the 1960s and 1970s, and the resulting stress forced these institutions to approach the use of their limited resources in a new way so they could continue to provide their constituents with quality educational opportunities. The lack of resources meant everyone had a stake in arriving at the most effective allocation to meet the primary mission objectives of the college. No longer could the chief business officer be the czar and other members of the leadership team be supplicants struggling for their perceived fair share.

At the same time that the permanent shortfall in funding occurred, the concept of systematic quality improvement came into its own in the United States. Although the total quality movement has had numerous approaches, including highly structured statistical methodology aimed at system improvement, an additional core concept identified the need to create teams of associates who could take charge of the evaluation and improvement of a system and ensure that the system best met the customer's needs. Kouzes and Posner (1987) reflect this changing philosophy and state that "Leaders build teams with spirit and cohesion, teams that feel like a family. They actively involve others in planning and give them discretion to make their own decisions" (p. 131). Francis and Woodcock (1990) express a similar theme while emphasizing the need to provide support and training for teams to ensure their effectiveness. Peters (1987) states, "One of the most dramatic requirements associated with increasing responsiveness is to shift the organization's entire way of being from a vertical (hierarchical) to a horizontal (fast, cross-functional, cooperative) orientation" (p. 366).

With this call for leaders to develop more participatory management styles, emphasizing team concepts and cross communications, and using the quality movement as a springboard, community college chief executive officers began to initially view the functions of the institution as a total leadership team responsibility whose decisions affecting the future vitality of the college had to be reached through consensus, with ownership of the decision and responsibility and authority to carry out the decision belonging to all members of the leadership team. This philosophy quickly percolated down through the organization and created a cultural change that allowed decentralization and delegation of functions and their operation to leadership team subordinates. Recognizing the broad base of customers who are served by the internal operations of the institution as well as its educational system, teams were quickly formed within and across functional areas to better tune the college's operation in terms of quality, customer satisfaction, and overall effectiveness and efficiency.

Examples of Resource Teams in Action

A microcosm of the changes taking place throughout the community college in its resource management is reflected at Midlands Technical College, Columbia, South Carolina. Midlands was a medium-sized institution of approximately 8,000 credit students and an additional 18,000 noncredit students served from three separate teaching locations. Before the mid-1980s, the allocation of resources was tightly held by the chief business officer who, with the president, predetermined most priorities that would receive funds. In addition, a large codified set of rules governed all resource activities, from the hiring and compensation of faculty and staff through the procurement of goods and services. Information management was consolidated under a director with little or no input from information users concerning their needs or the quality of services. The president and the chief business officer controlled physical plant decisions, from housekeeping and maintenance to construction of new facilities, with a concurrence of the governing board. Top officers generally informed senior leadership of these decisions but rarely allowed or expected those managers to participate in making resource decisions.

The system at Midlands before the mid-1980s worked. It worked because sufficient resources were available to meet most of the needs of the institution. Enrollment was growing, which both increased state funding and produced an ever-larger pool of tuition dollars. The state's financial condition allowed gov-

117

ernment to meet the funding requirements of the college at the high 90 percent rate. A managed contingency fund held in reserve by the chief business officer could easily meet any fluctuation in the income stream. Few problems arose because the system was only marginally stressed from lack of resources. Considerable dissatisfaction surfaced, however, in the perceived autocratic way in which administrators managed resources and provided services. Even when services were quite good, many individuals resented the fact that they had no input into the system. Of course, this resentment was not the exclusive realm of resource management but extended to faculty concerns about curriculum and student service professionals' concerns about their legitimate impact on student success. A history of collegiality in the academic and student services ranks, however, made shifting to team management an easier road than that associated with management of resources.

Midlands had appointed a new president in 1986. The senior business officer, who had the title of senior vice president, and the president mutually agreed that a more participatory style concerning resource management was essential if they were to accommodate reduced allocations of state funding with minimal disruption of the educational mission. The competency of the chief business officer or whether he could effectively manage resources was not in question; the issue was how the leadership team could agree to what was needed and take their rightful share of the responsibility in meeting the institution's priorities.

Organization and Communications

Midlands had a relatively standard organizational structure. The president as chief executive officer reported to a commission, which acted as a governance board. The commission's role primarily was the establishment of policy and the approval of budgets, curricula, and long-range planning, including construction activities. The commission did not involve itself in the operations of the institution, which was under the control of the president and his executive senior staff. The president directly managed the functions of marketing and institutional effectiveness and supervised three vice presidents who managed the areas of education, student services, and support operations. An organization chart of the college is shown as Figure 7.1.

The organizational structure, while relatively traditional in its formal form, had embedded in it some specific communications flows, which at Midlands Technical College were rigidly followed. Normally, bureaucratic organizations expect that formal communications flow upward through the organization and laterally across senior levels, particularly when decisions are involved. Most organizations, however, developed informal communications lines that allow information to move laterally without passing through higher organizational levels. At Midlands, the formal communications system, which is depicted as

Figure 7.1
Midlands Technical College Organizational Structure

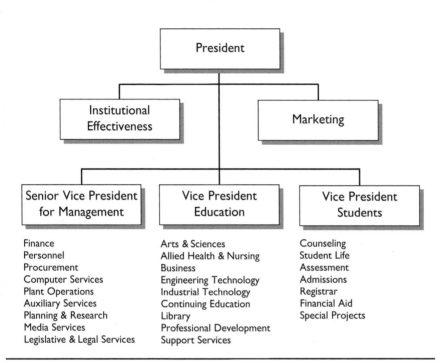

Figure 7.2, was also the informal communications pattern. Even routine matters moved vertically up "a chain of command" to the vice president level and then laterally across the organizational chart, if the vice president wished to involve units not under his or her authority, or from the vice president to the president down to a colleague at the vice president level. In short, communications were extremely structured and time-consuming; actions were often taken without coordination because the communications routes were so difficult to follow.

To break down the informal/formal communications structure and to accelerate both communications and decisions, the executive staff of the college began to encourage increased delegation of authority commensurate with responsibility and the establishment of lateral communications paths between units, both within major divisions and between the functional areas of the college. As part of this effort, the college adopted a modified quality management plan in 1988 (Reed, 1988a). The major component of this plan was the focus on improving systems to meet customer needs through the use of teams. As a collateral effort, routine communications between units were strengthened,

Figure 7.2
Midlands Technical College Formal Communication Flow

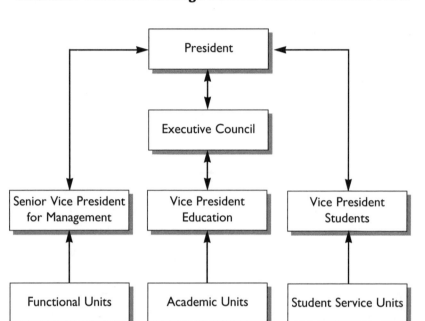

and authority for many of the college's decisions concerning routine operations were delegated to submanagers throughout the institution.

Because the resource unit had under its cognizance the majority of the functions that affected all members of the college community, the use of teams was most appropriate, particularly cross-functional teams involving players outside of the resource unit.

Resource Teams Created

The Parking Dilemma

The first major attempt to use the quality team approach to improve an ongoing system involved parking. As in most commuter colleges, parking was an ever-present issue at Midlands. As enrollments increased, parking was at a premium—particularly parking close to the building a customer was interested in reaching. Although efforts were under way to expand the number of parking spaces, the issue of parking management persisted. Recommendations by the operations staff appeared to be "traditional and unresponsive" to the majority of faculty, staff, and students.

Faced with an issue that would not go away, the vice president for management formed a cross-functional team consisting of faculty, staff, and students to resolve the problem and to continue to work toward a better system. Phase one of the team's effort involved analyzing the existing parking structures and identifying issues of concern and perceived inefficiencies. Based on this analysis, members presented, proposed, and debated numerous alternatives. Finally, the team selected an innovative option that was a major departure from the current practice of requiring decals for assigned parking locations.

The team proposed to implement an open parking plan, which limited reserved parking and allowed all customers to park on a first-come, first-served basis. Under the plan, only faculty and staff would be issued decals, and the student parking permit would be eliminated. As part of the analysis, the team examined the issue of revenues received from parking violation fines versus the effort expended in enforcing parking rules. The cost of issuing decals and maintaining the computerized file system was also examined. The data clearly indicated that the current permit system was not cost effective (Reed, 1988b). When coupled with the perceived fairness of the open parking situation, the recommendation won wide support among the various constituent groups.

With considerable reluctance, the operations unit implemented the option that the parking team developed. The team remained intact and was charged with following up the results of the open parking plan and fine tuning the implementation as needed. During the first two years, the team recommended several modifications particularly associated with the designation of reserved parking areas for visitors, loading areas near buildings, and the enforcement of handicapped parking privileges. By the end of the third year, the parking plan had become institutionalized, and the parking team dissolved itself and relegated future evaluation to the periodic surveys conducted by the institution concerning its customer services.

Registration Becomes a Resource Issue

The student registration process would not normally be considered an issue of concern for resource managers. Traditionally, registration is the province of student development services professionals. However, at Midlands Technical College, the consolidation of all information management within the resource unit placed a great deal of responsibility for the mechanics of registration within the resource management realm. As enrollments increased, the in-place system of holding registration as a collegewide event became totally impractical and threatened to overburden the administrative systems designed to implement student registration and scheduling. A general perception arose within the faculty and the student services staff that the real problem rested with the computer-driven information system, which had been implemented as a layer on top of the old manual approach. As a result, the senior business officer took over the responsibility of restructuring and managing the registration process from student services.

Recognizing that the process of registration involved more than processing students, the chief business officer elected to assemble a cross-functional team, which represented all of the major elements of the college affected by the registration process. The team consisted of faculty representatives; academic managers; representatives from the student services office of records, assessment and advisement, and counseling; operations personnel charged with preparing facilities; a computer specialist; and student representatives. This team was given the responsibility and authority to investigate the issues, design a solution, and implement that solution. Part of the charge also included an ongoing responsibility to continue to refine and improve the system as well as to manage the system with a team approach (Hudgins, 1989), which was the college's first attempt to move responsibility for a major function from an individual office to a collegewide cross-functional management team. Table 7.1 indicates functional units that obtained authority to implement team decisions without prior review and approval by senior staff.

The hierarchical bureaucratic organization most colleges employ is based on the assumption that a specific task is the responsibility of a specific office and, in turn, the manager who heads that office. In many ways, this bureaucratic organization offers a high degree of comfort to senior leadership, who can quickly pin responsibility on specific workers for what occurs in any particular aspect of college operations. When the college purposely eliminates that line-

Table 7.1
Registration Team

Senior vice president–chair
Academic dean*
Director, academic scheduling*
Faculty representative
Registrar*
Director, computer service*
Campus operations managers*
Assessment coordinator*
Counseling staff representative
Director accounting/cashiering*
Advertising and publications manager*
Student representative

* Indicates authority to implement team decisions.

authority model in favor of a team of individuals who have varying primary responsibilities and who report through numerous management channels, however, the senior leadership team is not as comfortable with knowing "who is in charge." Therefore, the senior leadership team approached the establishment of the registration team and assigning responsibility for the management of the registration process to that team with a great deal of apprehension. Since the college had committed itself to the principals of improved quality management and participatory management, however, the senior leadership team accepted the registration team concept as a function manager and gave the registration team all the necessary support to ensure its responsibility was matched with the authority needed to make changes and manage the critical process.

Over the next four years, the team continued to analyze and modify the registration processes. During this period, the team made changes in the dates class schedules were available, and instituted and expanded an open registration period, which encouraged students to register before the last day for registration. From the analysis of the registration process, the team made other changes, such as in the fee collection process, availability of automated information, dispersal of advisement and schedule input sites, reports, and real-time updates of class closings. The team devised a system to provide advisers with lists of former students or individuals who had been accepted but not registered so that follow-up with these individuals could be efficiently and effectively conducted. Within four years, the registration process changed from a dreaded nightmare to an efficient and effectively run customer-oriented process (customers include the college faculty and staff, as well as the students). Team members implemented decisions, modified processes, and ensured that resources were committed to make the substantial improvements needed. The senior leadership never had to intervene into the management of the registration process, and the experiment of using a team to improve as well as manage a major process was a total success.

The Budget Process

Technically, we can't view the activities associated with restructuring the college's budget process as a team approach. Because the budget affected all sections of the college and the formulation of the priorities for resource allocation stemmed from the college's strategic and operational planning activities, no single team could achieve the desired level of participation in the budget process. The college did form a team, however, to examine the budget methodology and to revise procedures used in the "budget call" to ensure appropriate input into the resource allocation process. In addition, this team was charged to review and revise as required the forms and administrative procedures associated with formulating the budget.

The team recommended the elimination of most budget data forms, and streamlining of the review process, including a major reduction in justification statements for various budget line items. The team urged that cost-center managers have greater autonomy in the distribution of allocated budget funds throughout the college. The budget team also reviewed the monthly reporting process associated with budget expenditures and recommended the institution of a "real time" budget report, which would be available to cost-center managers via the college's computer system. The college implemented the recommendation, which has greatly improved the internal management of budgets by cost-center managers and the supervisory staffs of various college units.

An outgrowth of the team's recommendation was that the budget process became more open, and the college granted greater authority to those managers/leaders responsible for various college activities to redirect and authorize expenditures within their budget. Although the chief business officer continued to serve as an adviser and a resource concerning the college's budget, the role of the resource management unit became one of accounting and providing information instead of control.

With the implementation of the revised budget process and the increased participation in developing and controlling budgets, the college undertook a major restructuring. This restructuring centered on prioritizing more than eighty-five key college functions, followed by a collegewide reallocation of funds to those functions enjoying the highest priorities. Although this effort resulted in a reduction of funding and staff in certain areas and a major reduction and realignment of senior leadership positions throughout the college, the effort enjoyed wide support because it reallocated funds for the hiring of additional faculty and for educational supplies associated with academic programs. Had these major changes been imposed from the top, significant resistance to the changes and an adverse impact on morale and performance would have surfaced. Since these actions were, however, a spinoff from the initial actions in implementing budgetary team recommendations, the actions strengthened the college's institutional effectiveness.

More Adjunct Faculty Means More Work

We've seen that Midlands Technical College was undergoing the phenomenon of an increasing enrollment. Sufficient permanent faculty to teach the increased number of sections were not available, and the reliance on adjunct faculty escalated dramatically. The college attempted to meet the challenge of the increased workload required to obtain the services of adjuncts and to effectively compensate them. The institution set aside the academic implications of an increase in adjunct faculty, which would have to be addressed through a major diversion of resources to permanent faculty salaries.

Initially, the resource unit attempted to resolve the problems of individual contracts for each course taught by an adjunct faculty member and the hourly compensation rates for these adjuncts through an internal review of procedures. Although recognizing the problems, the resource staff was hobbled by what seemed to be specific requirements of the statewide personnel and finance system. In short, the staff could recommend no way to improve the process.

Senior leadership considered this recommendation unacceptable; those in the academic unit where the burden of paperwork creation and processing had the major impact particularly insisted on improvement. As a result, the senior leaders formed a cross-functional team comprising deans, department chairs, department administrative specialists, finance and personnel staff, and computer staff and charged the group with reducing the administrative requirements of managing adjunct faculty.

After a detailed investigation of the current system and an analysis of specific state legal requirements and policies and procedures, the team designed a much less labor-intense process. Some of the actions resulting from team recommendations included a change from an hourly pay rate to a by-course pay process; establishing course compensation levels by discipline instead of an individual rate for each adjunct faculty member; issuing annual adjunct contracts with a verification process of actual courses assigned each term in place of individual contracts issued for each course taught; eliminating monthly time sheets and compensating adjuncts based on a percentage of the course completed during the pay period with verification required only before the final payment; developing a "by exception" verification process based on computerized records, replacing individual certification for each adjunct; and developing a budget tracking mechanism that allowed department chairs and deans to manage the allocated adjunct salaries within their units without consulting office records (Rhames, 1990). Table 7.2 reflects the major changes in the adjunct pay process.

The adjunct team still continues and monitors the process, making refinements. During the last five years, the college has, however, accommodated a 30 percent increase in the number of adjuncts and a 40 percent increase in the number of sections taught by adjuncts without an increase in personnel associated with processing the hiring and compensation paperwork. The adjunct team not only created these efficiencies, but increased customer satisfaction because of the reduced workload and fixed payment schedules for adjuncts, thus greatly increasing the perception of the resource management system as user friendly to those who rely on its services.

New Buildings

Just as at any community college, construction of new buildings at Midlands Technical College was somewhat of a rarity during periods of constrained resources. Enrollment growth during the latter 1970s and first part of 1980, however, made either the construction of additional academic facilities or curtailed enrollments imperative. The college successfully pressed its case to the state's legislature and county governments and received funding for a major academic facility. The competition over what activities would be housed in this new 80,000-square-foot building was intense. The building's functions were identified in initial planning stages and the funding proposal, but once the college received funding, all prior planning seemed to be jettisoned as senior staff and subordinates jockeyed for their perceived fair share of the new building.

Table 7.2
**Adjunct Faculty Management
Before and After**

	Before	**After**
Contracts	Required each term for each course	Annual contract covering all courses
Salary Schedule	Hourly rate established for each adjunct based on discipline and seniority	Course rate by discipline
Pay Documents	Monthly time sheets for each adjunct and each course	Term authorization listing covering all adjuncts and courses
Verification	By dean monthly for each adjunct and course	By inception prior to last pay
Payments	Monthly in areas based on hours/rate	For equal payments during semester
Budget Management	Posted after each pay period	Encumbered when authorized

The president and senior vice president wanted to ensure that the facility reflected the college's highest priority needs and would be viewed by the college community as a major positive improvement. Therefore, they elected to create a construction planning team. This team consisted of collegewide representation and was charged with determining which activities would be housed in the new facility. The operations staff of the college acted as "an adviser" to the team but was constrained from participating in this prioritization effort.

After approximately six months, the team was unable to reach a consensus. Not only did it fail to prioritize functions, its approach to allocating space was both unrealistic and unmanageable. Simply stated, this cross-functional team did not have the technical expertise to plan for the construction of a complex facility nor could it overcome its parochial interest in obtaining its perceived share of the facility.

Hence, the team was disbanded and a functional proposal that the resource staff created was presented to the senior management team for consideration. Senior management approved the plan, which became the basis for actual construction design and development. Although the construction plan had the endorsement of senior management, the majority of the college faculty and staff never fully accepted it. Although the operations staff and the architects made every effort to consult functional managers to be housed in the facility, the process never seemed to work effectively. Functional managers perceived needs well beyond the scope of funds available and were reluctant to change their requirements based on recommendations of technical staff at the college or of the architects. The facility was finally designed and constructed primarily as a resource unit project, not as a team effort. The application of team concepts to this major one-time function did not succeed.

The college, however, did learn several lessons from this experience and formed a cross-functional planning team for developing approaches to future new construction. This cross-functional team was used to identify broad priorities for future construction and to recommend modifications of existing space. Because the specific timeline when funds would be available for the construction projects could not be identified, however, team enthusiasm for the project was extremely limited. As a result, the senior leadership determined that broad-based cross-functional teams were not an effective approach to ensuring the quality of major construction activities.

Lessons Learned in Team Management of Resources

The use of teams to manage the resource process has proven to be highly successful. All members of the college community feel they have a legitimate way to express themselves concerning these critical issues and a stake in ensuring that the college effectively implements the decisions they reach.

Based on the experience at Midlands Technical College, the following conclusions concerning resource management teams are offered:

- The president's leadership style and philosophy are key ingredients in effective change strategies.
- The use of teams to manage systems for total quality is an effective approach in the resource area.
- The use of cross-functional teams both within the resource unit and across the college is the most effective way to apply total quality concepts to resource issues.
- The effectiveness of functional teams in the resource management area is limited because of the broad impact of most resource issues and should be restricted to internal processes.
- Cross-functional teams can be invested with overall management responsibilities and can effectively ensure implementation, control, and improvement of ongoing systems.
- To achieve effectiveness, teams must be given authority to implement recommendations if the required high level of energy is to be invested by team members in the quality improvement process.

- Willingness by resource managers to use cross-functional teams stimulates collegewide cultural change by increasing trust, cooperation, and a mutual commitment to support the primary educational mission of the institution.
- The use of teams in resource management eases the competition at the senior leadership level and allows the senior management team to increase the use of its talents for defining the future efforts of the college instead of the execution of day-to-day management tasks.
- Teams work when systems are in place that may be analyzed and adjusted to increase customer satisfaction, effectiveness, and efficiency.
- Quality teams may not be effective in arriving at broad-based consensus concerning priorities for major one-time events such as construction of facilities.

In summary, resource management is an area in which the concepts of total quality management through the use of team techniques is essential. Resources belong to everyone associated with the educational enterprise. Through effective leadership, the appropriate use of teams, and the systems by which the resource base of the institution is allocated and managed can be constantly improved and the degree of customer satisfaction and institutional effectiveness consistently increased. Institutional leaders must be willing to fully support the concept of resource management through the use of cross-functional teams and provide these teams their total support.

References

Francis, D., and Woodcock, M. "Teamwork: Pulling Together." In *Unblocking Organizational Values*. Glenview, Ill.: Scott, Foresman & Company, 1990.

Hudgins, J. *Internal Memo: Registration Committee Charge*. Columbia, S.C.: Midlands Technical College, 1989.

Kouzes, J.M., and Posner, B.Z. *The Leadership Challenge*. San Francisco: Jossey-Bass, 1987.

Peters, T.J. "Pursue Team Product/Service Development." In *Thriving on Chaos*. New York: Random House, 1987.

Reed, L.W. "Executive Council Decision Brief." In *Integrating Institutional Effectiveness and Quality Management*. Columbia, S.C.: Midlands Technical College, 1988a.

Reed, L.W. "Report to Executive Council," In *Results of Parking Taskforce*. Columbia, S.C.: Midlands Technical College, 1988b.

Rhames, R. "Report to Executive Council." In *Recommendations of Adjunct Faculty Review*. Columbia, S.C.: Midlands Technical College, 1990.

Zemsky, R. "An Uncertain Terrain." *Policy Perspectives,* November 1993, 5(2), Section A.

CHAPTER 8

TEAM BUILDING, QUALITY INITIATIVES, AND STRATEGIC PLANNING

A Consolidated Approach

CONSTANCE M. HAIRE
BARRY W. RUSSELL

S outhwestern Community College is a relatively small community college serving a three-county, sparsely populated region located within the western North Carolina mountains. To maximize the effectiveness of its resources and to better meet community needs and the increased calls for accountability, the college embraced a philosophy of continuous quality improvement in the early 1990s. This philosophy calls for an ongoing commitment to continually improve all of the programs and services offered by the college. In our continuous improvement journey, we have learned that a continuous improvement process cannot be fully implemented without giving equal attention to processes for ongoing planning and institutional effectiveness. These three processes share many common elements with our approach to continuous improvement and, if carefully integrated, can drive an institution through planned change.

Initially, Southwestern Community College viewed these three processes as separate strands. We quickly found, however, that not only are they closely related and share some common elements, but also that they are difficult and inefficient for a small college to manage as separate entities. Since this realization, we have attempted to integrate the three processes so that they function as one process serving continuous quality improvement, planning, and institutional effectiveness.

From the beginning, we have been committed to using team approaches wherever possible. Several reasons contribute to this decision. To truly achieve the campus climate necessary for this integrated process to lead effective change, we knew that widespread commitment and support from across the college community were essential. We also realized that this approach could work only if participants understood and supported the college's mission. We purposely chose to use teams because we felt that the team approach offered the best opportunity to gain the widespread input and support we needed to make our integrated approach work.

This narrative will offer a brief review of institutional effectiveness, planning, and continuous quality improvement and will then describe Southwestern Community College's attempt to develop an integrated model that effectively weaves the three strands into one process, concluding with a look ahead at future needs and implications.

Institutional Effectiveness

Community colleges face numerous challenges in addressing the mandates for responsiveness to community needs, accountability for resource utilization, and effectiveness in meeting the mission of the institution. With these calls for increased accountability has come the demand, "Prove to us that you are effective in using resources to accomplish your mission." Stakeholders have designed institutional effectiveness models to help answer that question. Data gathered through institutional effectiveness processes provide external groups, such as accrediting agencies and governing organizations, with insight about how well our institutions are performing. Just as important, however, is that these measures let the institution know how well their programs and services are meeting the needs of students and the community. It is through feedback that colleges learn where to focus improvement efforts.

The educational community has urged colleges to focus on outcomes, provide quantifiable data, use objective standards, and develop explicit statements of purpose (Burrill, 1994) as they implement strategies and plans to accomplish desired results. Colleges have implemented institutional effectiveness programs to determine how well they are meeting their goals and objectives as derived from the mission, which is the primary purpose of the institution. Additional questions about effectiveness of an institution revolve around the issue of quality: How well is an institution accomplishing its mission? Are the outcomes we achieve valuable to the students and community? Can we do better?

The National Alliance for Community and Technical Colleges provides a practical working definition for institutional effectiveness: "...the process of articulating the mission of the college, setting goals, defining how the college and the community will know when the goals are being met, and using the data to form assessments in an ongoing cycle of goal setting and planning" (Burrill, 1994, p. 285). Components of effectiveness include three P's: publics, performance, and perception (AACC, 1994). The publics are the external constituencies of the college; performance is related to meeting internally stated needs and expectations; and perception may be interpreted as the understanding of mission and purpose. At the heart of review for accreditation are questions about why and how an institution exists; the nature of its mission, goals, and objectives. These questions address the processes of planning, assessment, and outcomes, which together form a framework for institutional effectiveness. Healthy processes are effective, efficient, predictable, and adaptable. Employing quality processes and tools to organize work flow and encourage teamwork leads to data-based decisions and eventually a commitment to quality. These concepts are basic to successful quality programs that lead to an effective institution.

The Community College Roundtable Report cites and defines thirteen core indicators of institutional effectiveness. A core indicator is a measure that describes a critical, widely recognized outcome of mission. This outcome is clearly responsive to key constituent groups and is regularly produced (AACC, 1994). The thirteen core indicators provide a framework to measure student progress, career preparation, transfer preparation, developmental education, general education, customized education, and community development. Many colleges in the National Alliance for Community and Technical Colleges have adapted and incorporated these core indicators in their effectiveness and planning structure in ways that are meaningful to the institution.

A significant test of institutional effectiveness is the college's ability to convert information to meaningful actions that promote organizational change. The focus on using information forms the crux at which institutional effectiveness systems converge with other management functions and change the character of the institution. How we select the activities, allocate resources to support them, locate these activities in the processes and structures of the organization, and view the processes in the long term are important elements in achieving desired outcomes. The appropriate directing of funds and human resources is the result of joining thought and action to produce outcomes. Institutional effectiveness requires a definite link between planning and budgeting so that appropriate activities become part of the college structure and procedures.

The institutional effectiveness process of planning, assessment, and outcomes requires continual review and refinement, understanding the process of change, and organizational learning. Institutional effectiveness can provide the standards and benchmarks against which to judge progress. Continuous improvement must focus on collection of data and information that stakeholders can use to move the education process toward quality.

131

Planning

If institutional effectiveness answers the question "How well are we accomplishing our mission?" then planning addresses another concern: "Are we doing the right things?" This question is not as simple as it may first appear to be. While public institutions are normally given general mission and purpose parameters, and private institutions frequently have clearly defined philosophies often steeped deeply in tradition, institutions still face a seemingly endless array of options as they design appropriate mixes of programs and services. The aim of planning systems should be to bring optimum alignment and utilization of resources to the accomplishment of purpose. This alignment requires ongoing monitoring of internal and external environments. At Southwestern Community College, feedback provided through institutional effectiveness processes forms the basis for internal assessment. This assessment guides us in which processes are working effectively and which ones may need to be revamped, eliminated, or strengthened. Looking inward, however, while essential, is not enough. It is equally necessary for our college to continually monitor the external environment, identifying and following trends and events that may affect our college's ability to accomplish its purpose. These external events may provide opportunities for the institution, or if left unchecked, could pose threats to the institution's ability to serve its purpose.

In a presentation at the 29th Annual Forum, Association for Institutional Research, Lawrence Sherr (1989) contended that higher education has lost sight of who its customers are and suggested using a model based on the teachings of W. Edwards Deming, the key influential figure in the development of quality management. Deming maintained that the most critical concept is "constancy of purpose," with a core philosophy and a set of unifying goals (Seymour, 1992). Constancy of purpose is needed in higher education. Many institutions are unsure of their purposes or who their customers are. Institutions need mission statements, or statements of purpose, which are living documents with which everyone in the institution is familiar. Sherr (1989) believes that higher education should "figure out who our customers are and...make a commitment to excellence. Not just talk, but actions. A commitment to action throughout the entire organization" (p. 48).

Effective planning requires that an institution state its mission clearly and define goals from which the college can derive measurable objectives. The college must establish priorities that guide the development of programs, schedules, policies, procedures, and allocation of the college budget. A college must create outcomes for all its constituencies that allow the college to compare results to purpose. The comparison of outcomes to mission can provide a picture of the institution's effectiveness.

Community colleges addressing the critical issues facing them must be involved in strategic planning to develop the processes that align their resources with the needs of their constituencies. At Southwestern, strategic planning is a comprehensive approach to systematically screening the external and internal environments and assessing the institutional strengths and weaknesses in relation to opportunities and threats in that environment. Strategic planning differs from traditional planning because it considers the external environment as well as the internal needs of the institution. We have found that strategic planning is a process concerned with changing attitudes, behaviors, and work habits, as well as with setting organizational priorities (Richardson, 1988).

According to Wallin and Ryan (1994), the primary purpose of strategic planning is to determine the strategies and activities that will enable the college to grow and remain viable. Because of the external focus, strategic planning helps ensure that colleges make the right decisions for the future. Strategic planning has allowed our college a systematic approach to decision making, helping to eliminate haphazard or arbitrary decisions. Strategic planning allows the college to become more proactive and identify and act on opportunities and developments more quickly, thus assisting in anticipating community needs ahead of the demand curve. Strategic planning has allowed the college to be more efficient and effective in gathering and analyzing data upon which decisions are made. Information collected for strategic planning has helped us to better focus the efforts of the management team and the planning team and helped us to agree on goals and direction for the college. This focus enables our college to become more proficient at developing tools and processes to achieve those goals.

With a well-defined planning and effectiveness process, we are moving toward better assessment. Measuring the accomplishments of a college and activating its priorities are complex acts. Because of the delay in response on performance in the learning process, sometimes by years, an assessment component of institutional effectiveness should let educators know quickly and efficiently what facilitates learning and what does not. This process is not easy, but it is vital to finding ways to improve education continuously in community colleges. Our experience has shown that when key players agree on areas of strategic importance, they also agree on the indicators that measure performance in strategic areas.

Continuous Quality Improvement

If institutional effectiveness processes give us ongoing feedback about how we are doing, and if planning activities help ensure that we are doing the right things, then the final piece of the triad is continuous improvement processes to enable ongoing improvement in the quality of our programs and services. While these components in the process may seem to be common-sensical and almost all organizations can be said to be continuously engaged in improvement processes, the emphasis at our college has been on a formal, systematic improvement strategy. What makes this strategy different from nonsystematic approaches is that it attempts to make the improvement process operate more efficiently and effectively.

The philosophy of continuous quality improvement is manifested in several aspects of organizational life. Continuous improvement is key; it is foremost in meeting or exceeding customer needs; it is everyone's job; it requires measurement of improvement; it involves leadership, teamwork, and seeing the organization as a system, with systematic ways of problem solving. A side effect of continuous quality improvement efforts is the reduction of fear and an increase in intrinsic rewards offered through team efforts. One essential characteristic of quality is appropriateness to purpose. When the process helps our people and products to accomplish their purposes, we have achieved quality outcomes. The quality of production processes assures quality of outcomes. Quality results from frequent, informed interaction between our employees and the processes in which they work. At Southwestern, quality measures responsiveness and appropriateness to our customers' needs (Rhodes, 1992).

The story of "quality" began with American industry. Key concepts and philosophy were exported to Japan after World War II and were reintroduced in this country in the 1970s. According to Seymour (1992), David Garvin described four major quality eras, eventually ending with strategic quality management. Initially, observers viewed quality as a natural result of the application of skills by workers and artisans. With the advent of industrialization, the responsibility for quality shifted to the inspector at the end of the production line who detected defects. The era of "statistical quality control" began in 1931 with the work of W. A. Shewhart, a statistician at Bell Telephone Laboratories (Seymour, 1992). He introduced probability and statistics as a way to understand variability in processes. Knowing that variation was inherent in processes led to building quality in, rather than inspecting at the end, and during the 1940s and 1950s statistical quality control was practiced.

According to Needham (1991), the components of total quality management (TQM) are a blend of the ideas of three major theorists: W. Edwards Deming, Joseph M. Juran, and Philip B. Crosby. The blend includes the basic concepts of TQM, which include continuous quality improvement, focus on the customer, systematic improvement of operations, open work environments, long-term thinking, development of human resources, and management responsibility for total quality leadership.

Deming, Juran, and Crosby influenced the movement of quality from the factory floor to management. Deming advocated Shewhart's statistical methods and introduced a systematic approach to problem solving along with customer research, goal setting, and organizational issues. Deming's work was applied primarily in Japan until 1980 when a documentary featuring him was shown on network television. The public's question "If Japan Can...Why Can't We?" has been described as the turning point for TQM in this country, and American quality erosion began to be reversed. The broadcast galvanized several of America's corporate giants, including Ford Motor Company, American

Express, IBM, Xerox, and Motorola. Moreover, in 1987 the U.S. Congress created the Malcolm Baldrige National Quality Award, awarded annually after extensive on-site evaluations (Chaffee & Sherr, 1992). Although many corporations were looking for a quick fix, a new era of quality began to evolve. For the first time, businesspeople saw quality as a leadership function that could be managed in the daily life of an organization. Quality changed from its internal focus on internal standards to and emphasis on external customer considerations and further expanded to a management philosophy adaptable to all types of organizations.

Community colleges have evolved since the 1900s from extensions of the high school to the various forms of comprehensive community colleges that we see today. Accompanying management styles have changed, and the most recent is a philosophy focused on continuous improvement of all aspects of the college. Its origins stem from Deming's management philosophy, which centers around four major dimensions: profound knowledge, human psychology, the function of systems, and the theory of variation (Chaufournier, 1992). Knowledge comes from a better understanding of how people learn, how to develop people, and how to develop a learning organization. The human psychology dimension focuses on the basic theory that people are intrinsically motivated and want to do a good job. At Southwestern, we believe that all parts of a system are interconnected, and our college should aim to optimize the whole system, not just its parts. Variation is a natural characteristic of systems, and by reducing variation and continuously improving services, we are beginning to meet the needs and exceed the expectations of our customers.

According to Chaufournier (1992), TQM in higher education appeared to be nothing more than a mix of operations research, education, engineering, psychology, and organizational behavior and development. Total quality management has the potential to integrate these disciplines in higher education. Despite concerns about using a business management model in education, adapting management concepts and business practices is not new to education. Several examples include: multiple levels of management (supervision); formal chain of command; generation of forms, reports, and data; multiple checks and approval (inspection); use of evaluations; competitive bidding for low cost; elaborate planning systems that often do not work well (Sherr & Lozier, 1991).

Rhodes (1992) defines TQM as a value-based, information-driven management process through which the minds and talents of people at all levels are applied fully and creatively to the organization's continuous improvement. Several colleges and universities are recognizing what TQM has to offer higher education.

The factors that have prompted Southwestern Community Colleges to adopt quality management philosophies relate to competition, cost, accountability, and a customer (student and employer) service orientation. One of the first community colleges to adopt and implement a continuous improvement philosophy was Delaware County Community College (DCCC) in Pennsylvania. In 1985, led by president Richard DeCosmo, DCCC began a transformation toward a quality philosophy in both administration and classroom practice. The college identified three goals to guide the implementation:

- To transform our philosophy of administrative management to total quality (TQ);
- To develop training curricula and programming in TQ for business in our service area; and
- To incorporate the concepts and philosophy of TQ into our curriculum and into classroom management (Entner, 1993, p. 29).

Through the ensuing years, DCCC established goals, developed strategies for accomplishing the goals, and formulated ways of measuring the effectiveness of TQ. Top management leadership and support, strategic planning, customer focus, employee training and recognition, empowerment and teamwork, measurement, access, and continuous quality assurance are the hallmarks against which DCCC measures itself.

Continuous Quality Improvement at Southwestern Community College

Southwestern Community College (SCC) embarked on the journey to become a learning organization and made a deliberate decision to continuously improve teaching, learning, and service. With involvement of all college divisions and departments, the college examined its corporate philosophy and values and developed a mutually agreed upon statement of beliefs for ourselves and our students. The college philosophy statement is shown in Figure 8.1.

The mission of the college, shown in Figure 8.2, defines our purpose and direction for serving the constituents of the college service area and larger region.

In 1992, the college leadership adopted the philosophy of continuous quality improvement and began a learning process involving all college employees. Reading, studying, and visiting businesses and organizations practicing continuous quality improvement were the hallmarks of early efforts to inculcate leaders and administrators with the philosophy. Changing the culture of the organization began when all employees read and studied Stephen Covey's *Seven Habits of Highly Effective People*. The book's philosophy sent a signal that all levels of leadership at the college would embark on an empowering, participative, and collegial approach, with a renewed focus on individual responsibility. Another signal that culture change was imminent was the conversion of the organizational structure from a multi-level hierarchy to a flatter design, with just one layer of management that works with the president to guide the college.

Early efforts included the formation of the first team at the college: a quality council to oversee and guide the college quality initiatives on campus. The quality council represents administration, faculty, and staff. Membership

Figure 8.1
Philosophy

The faculty and staff of Southwestern Community College endorse the following beliefs and values in an effort to create a learning environment that will foster the development of human potential and service to our community. These principles serve as a measure for our decisions and actions:

Commitment to Students:
- To be responsive to our primary customers—the students.
- To treat students the way we want to be treated.
- To make decisions that reflect our concern for and commitment to students.
- To take students from where they are educationally and assist them to achieve their potential as productive and contributing individuals.

Commitment to Excellence:
- To expect and recognize excellence from everyone.
- To value the rich learning environment created by diversity in our college community.
- To continually improve our programs and services.
- To encourage creativity, innovation and responsible risk taking.
- To maintain a highly qualified work force through recruitment and professional development.

Commitment to the Community:
- To respond to community needs and enhance the economic vitality and quality of life in our service area.
- To work collaboratively with the community to achieve mutual goals.
- To ensure that programs and services are accessible to all.
- To be responsive to the changing needs of the labor market and society.
- To be responsible stewards of human, financial and physical resources.

Commitment to a Quality Work Environment:
- To maintain an atmosphere that is honest, fair, and respectful of the inherent dignity and worth of all employees.
- To provide a safe, secure, and supportive work place.
- To encourage cooperation and interdependence through teamwork.
- To provide employees with the resources and authority necessary to accomplish the College mission.

Figure 8.2

SOUTHWESTERN COMMUNITY COLLEGE

Mission of the College

PURPOSE

Southwestern Community College is a comprehensive, public, two-year college serving the people of western North Carolina with programs and services that are academically, financially and geographically accessible. Southwestern's quality educational programs prepare students to enter the job market, transfer to senior colleges and universities, and achieve their professional and personal goals. We seek to set the stage for students to experience success as we educate them to meet the needs of a constantly changing society. Southwestern Community College contributes to the social, cultural and economic development of the area.

VISION

Southwestern Community College recognizes that to meet the constantly changing needs of our region, we must be a community of learners committed to an ongoing pursuit of excellence. This quest for quality includes the following components:

1. Achieve Excellence in Student Learning and Support.

2. Achieve Excellence in Service to the Community.

---

changes annually, with the president as chairman and the deans as permanent members. Participation by these leaders ensures coordination between the college administration and the quality efforts led by the council. The deans are also included to facilitate the eventual dissolution of the quality council as continuous quality improvement efforts are integrated into the overall operation of the college.

Figure 8.2 (continued)

3. Create an Excellent Work Environment.

4. Achieve Excellence in the Utilization of Resources

To guide us in our pursuit of excellence, we envision the following:

Student Learning and Support

- Graduates will be highly competent within their fields of study and also be proficient in lifelong general skills required to succeed in the information age.
- Programs and services will be offered in a wide variety of formats, times, and locations to enhance accessibility for students with diverse social, educational, and economic needs.

Community Services

- As the community's college, Southwestern Community College will play a leadership role in enhancing community and economic development within the region.

Work Environment for Employees

- The College will be known for its exemplary work environment characterized by a total quality culture in which all employees are involved in continuous learning and development.

Utilization of Resources

- The College will be a model for achieving high productivity through continuous improvement processes, the aggressive application of technology, and regional collaboration.

Members of divisions and departments across campus participated in a brainstorming and prioritizing process to suggest systems and processes in need of improvement. The college faculty and staff generated more than 200 ideas for improvement; several were handled through executive decisions, and others were prioritized and determined to best be handled by a team. The first improvement team, not unlike those in other continuous improvement efforts in business and education, was chosen to evaluate the purchasing process. The college chose to move immediately into teams, assessing processes, and providing "just in time" training for teams, rather than training the entire college in anticipation of employees being on a team at some future time. Thus began our learning experience with teams and their role in our efforts to continuously improve the quality of services at SCC. With the full recognition that students are our primary customers at the college, the next improvement team dealt with the admissions process. The third improvement team investigated the process of textbook acquisition and sale and was followed by teams researching part-time employment, contracting, and orientation of new college students. Each of these team topics reflected the first five prioritized processes and systems recommended by collegewide input.

The college is committed to the idea of teams and teamwork. Effective implementation of continuous quality improvement depends upon widespread involvement and commitment of college personnel. Teams and teamwork enabled the campus community to be involved, participate, and cooperate with others in solving problems and creating solutions. The collective knowledge, skills, and tools of teams are much greater than those of individual members. Because people will help support that which they help create, teams provide a way for employees to create solutions and derive ownership for their successful implementation.

A key aspect of the learning organization is training. At Southwestern, trained team facilitators taught teams a problem-solving process, the mechanics of teamwork, and the personal and group skills of working together. The process used at SCC is total quality transformation (TQT) made available through PQ Systems in Dayton, Ohio. Total quality transformation is a seven-step process that includes analysis of the current situation, data collection and analysis, recommended improvements, trial of improvement theory, analysis of trial, and standardization of successful improvements. As teams begin working, they receive training in the TQT process. Additionally, all college employees receive a minimum of sixteen hours of training in the quality philosophy and basic tools. More than half of the college employees have participated on an improvement team or have served on the quality council. Because SCC is a small college, four active teams operating concurrently is the maximum the college can manageably support and continue daily operations. As one team completes its work, another team begins.

Improvement teams typically consist of six to eight members and meet an average of two hours per week. Early teams took twelve to eighteen months to determine customer needs, analyze the process, collect data, and recommend improvements. Quality teams require a major time commitment, and one criticism has been the length of time a team spends on an improvement project. Although teams have the authority, after preliminary investigation, to limit the scope of the project, no teams have yet elected to narrow their projects. Because team members sometimes grow tired of working so long on a project and begin to lose their effectiveness, the quality council makes every effort to limit the scope of the improvement problem to shorten the team-work time and accelerate improvements. People have been organized into cross-functional teams, with some department or division teams arising when experienced team members want to use the problem-solving process learned in a cross-functional team.

The student access team, charged with designing the way students access college programs and services, uses a quality planning process because of the potential impact and broad scope of this team's work. The product is a student access system by which a student enters and moves through the college with minimal barriers. Because this project is so broad in scope, the team is larger than others, and key college administrators are members of this team. The quality council imposed a deadline on the student access team because of the college's experience in allowing improvement teams to progress at their own pace.

Teams at SCC are responsible for achieving their goals and receive appropriate support from the administration. Teams select their own leader and recorder, and the quality council assigns a trained facilitator. The college administration is committed to implementing the teams' recommendations. The team makes recommendations with current budgetary and personnel constraints in mind, thus encouraging teams to carefully examine all other possible improvements that do not require additional funds. This limitation discourages teams from quickly concluding that additional personnel or funds will solve the problem and requires them to examine the system within which the process functions, to be creative, and to devise alternative potential solutions.

Upon determination of recommendations, each team reports to the quality council and later to the entire faculty and staff. The dean in whose area the improvement project functions formally responds to the recommendations and supports a trial period of implementation. Teams monitor the implementation and trial of recommended improvements and report their improvement findings to the quality council. Stakeholders standardize successful improvements and make further recommendations for continued assessment where improvement is needed.

Development of the Integrated Model

Concurrent with the improvement process, the college planning team began revising the planning process to integrate planning, quality, and institutional effectiveness. It refined the planning process to ensure inclusion of the major components of an integrated system. Figure 8.3 is a model to demonstrate how Southwestern Community College has integrated the concepts addressed in this chapter. The integrated system begins with review of the mission, then proceeds to a community involvement process of determining the vision for the

Figure 8.3
**An Integrated System for Strategic Planning, Institutional
Effectiveness, and Continuous Improvement**

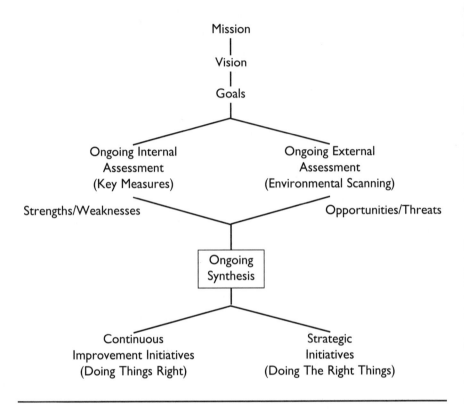

college, and then to a participative process for developing goals. The senior management team determines ongoing internal assessment measures and conducts external assessment, commonly referred to as environmental scanning. The internal and external assessments result in a synthesis that identifies processes to be reengineered. The synthesis also pinpoints strategic initiatives, which consist of new activities and frequently new programs or products that meet customer and community needs. Figure 8.4 provides a circular model demonstrating how the college's quest for quality can be disseminated and flows into various quadrants and spokes depicting how quality can eventually spread to all aspects of the college.

At the center of SCC's model is the college's quest for quality, representing the mission of the college. The planning process identified four major vision areas into which all college activities fit. According to the quality philosophy in the four vision areas, primary customers in the "excellent student learning and

Figure 8.4
Quest for Quality Wheel

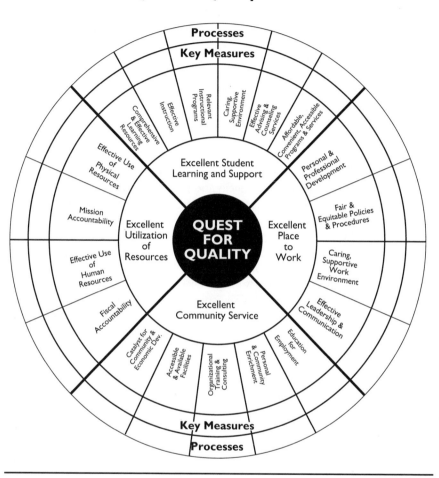

support" area were students; primary customers in the "excellent place to work" area were college employees; primary customers in the excellent community service" area were the community at large; and primary customers in the "excellent utilization of resources" area were state and local elected officials. This grouping of internal and external customers is not exclusive to education or to SCC. Gehris (1994) points out that you "review the mission of your firm to make sure it properly serves each of four groups: your customers, your employees, the community at large, and the ownership" (p. 6).

The planning team identified the perceived customer needs, and these became goals of the four vision statements. Because the goals were developed internally, the college needed to ensure that they were appropriate and accurately reflected the customer needs and expectations. Approximately 150 students, all 120 college employees, community groups representing 150 citizens, and most of the local and state-elected officials validated the identified customer needs. The planning team derived key measures or indicators of success from these customer needs. We ask, "To what extent are we meeting our customers' needs?" These measures or indicators form the basis for assessment of how effective SCC is at that particular moment and provides feedback for planning strategic initiatives for the future. The group specifies each goal's key measures and identifies processes that drive those measures. The team plans to monitor key measures regularly, and the results will provide an indication about how a process is working to meet customer needs. This monitoring function is one way to generate data that help to determine the effectiveness of the college.

A strength of this process is the facilitation of their employees' identification of the major process, or processes, most closely related to their jobs. Supervisors will coach employees to determine the degree of alignment of the job with the goals of the college, and adjustments will be made based on customer needs. Also, college staff will identify strengths, weaknesses, opportunities, and threats for each of the goals. They will identify and prioritize strategic initiatives for the future from this analysis and evaluate them in relation to the balance of the four vision statements. The college allocates resources to meet customer needs and to facilitate strategic initiatives that have potential positive impact for the college or to counter those that may have a negative result for the college. Budgetary decisions align closely with the strategic planning process, and the planning team monitors these decisions to ensure balance of the "wheel" regarding utilization of college resources and attention to strategic initiatives. The team carefully maximizes budgetary resources and ensures that initiatives do not diminish the quality of education at SCC.

Because the integrated model is a "work in progress" at SCC, and continuous improvement is the journey of the college, additional refinement will accompany the process. Clarification of the budgeting process will enable all employees to understand the allocation of resources and to support initiatives for the college. When all employees view the "wheel" as a whole, they can understand how their role and their job support the mission and are critical to the success of the college in meeting the educational and training needs of the community.

Future Trends and Implications

Continuous quality improvement is affecting higher education in significant ways. At the Third Annual Symposium on Quality in Action in Academe in 1992, more than 500 school, college, and business leaders from around the world agreed on several conclusions. These were: educational institutions must adapt TQM practices, TQM offers no quick fixes, TQM requires the transformation of an organization's culture to be effective, and the individualism and anti-authoritarianism of Americans must be accommodated (or at least recognized) in the implementation of quality processes (Godbey, 1993).

The external pressure from the public, state legislatures, education systems, and accreditation bodies will require that colleges and universities cooperate and share resources at unprecedented levels. Shrewd administrators will use a cooperative strategy to maintain or enhance their institutions. Developments such as distance learning, common informational infrastructures, and incorporation of "agile" production processes of the emerging "virtual corporations" will help create partnerships for K–12, higher education, and business (Godbey, 1993). Institutional autonomy will not disappear but will be preserved through transformation. Although cooperative strategies create more entanglements and obligations, they also create options not otherwise available. Emerging agile paradigms and changes in corporate cultures will affect the ways colleges organize themselves to teach and learn. An agile strategy assumes widespread adoption of TQM principles to produce a highly committed, highly skilled workforce and the development of a national informational infrastructure for the movement of voice, video, data, and documents (i.e., the information highway). Agile organizations will possess certain essential characteristics of core competence, technological information networks, flexible partnerships, and collaborations. In the future, colleges will depend on each other's strengths to compensate for each other's weaknesses, so they can serve students better.

The future will bring radical departures from traditional curricula, focusing more heavily on teamwork, problem solving, and involving faculty from various disciplines to deliver courses. Faculty will become facilitators of the learning process rather than deliverers of information. Students will be more involved and more responsible than ever for their own learning. Learning outcomes are not the result of the college's efforts alone but of such additional functions as student motivation, effort, and time on task.

Colleges must become learning organizations that can achieve meaningful change, transform themselves, and increase efforts to view themselves as a system. The next generation of leaders will be called upon to fulfill new roles: designers of environments that promote and enable learning, stewards of shared vision for the organization, and teachers who foster learning for everyone (Isaacson & Bamburg, 1992).

Needham (1991) states that TQM can provide a focus for institutional effectiveness that operationalizes both quality and accountability throughout the college. TQM can provide a structure for involving faculty and staff in problem solving and decision making in ways that are meaningful to them and the college, as well as provide a model for transforming a stagnant college organization to a new level of fitness. The values TQM espouses are the values of community colleges: commitment to quality, respect for people, focus on process, and the expectation of continuous learning.

Community colleges as well as universities and public schools will continue to face challenges to meet the educational needs of the people in society. The public will hold institutions of learning more accountable, requiring them to respond to community needs and reach new heights in delivering effective education. Formal education will continually change, and students of all ages will increasingly determine their own educational paths. The growth in the use of technology will require community colleges at least to keep pace, and in most rural communities they will lead the way. Cost-effective ways of meeting these responsibilities will mean changing processes to be more flexible, easily accessed, and responsive to student and community demands. Change occurs slowly; it takes time to integrate the principles and methods of total quality. According to Donna Shalala (1993), secretary of the Department of Health and Human Services, quality initiatives offer the best hope; however, education must collaborate with business in finding common goals and sharing initiatives and mutual eagerness to create, integrate, and disseminate new knowledge.

Southwestern Community College will continue its quality journey, work on refining its integrated process, and seek ways to change the organization to better serve internal and external customers. The college expects to expand its collaboration with neighboring community colleges, strengthen its relationships with area high schools through interactive instructional television, and build community leadership in its partnerships with business and industry. Technology advances will constitute a large part of the college's future delivery system for classes and courses, adaptable to the needs of the diverse adult learning population it serves. "If the quality movement carries the day, if across the institution there exists a collective responsibility for learning, a habit of listening to the people we serve, a preference for data, an ethic of continuous improvement, a determination to develop fully the talent of every learner, and an acknowledgment that we are professionally accountable to one another and to those we serve for results" (Marchese, 1994), we will be a truly effective college and will become a learning organization...a community of learners.

References

American Association of Community Colleges. *Community Colleges: Core Indicators of Effectiveness* (AACC Special Report No. 4). Washington, D.C.: AACC, 1994.

Burrill, D.W. "Institutional Effectiveness as a Leadership and Management Process." In G.A. Baker III (Ed.), *A Handbook on the Community College in America, Its History, Mission and Management.* Westport, Conn.: Greenwood Press, 1994.

Chaffee, E.E., and Sherr, L.A. *Quality: Transforming Postsecondary Education.* ASHE-ERIC Higher Education Report No. 3. Washington, D.C.: The George Washington University, School of Education and Human Development, 1992.

Chaufournier, R.L. "TQM in Higher Education." *Communiqué,* 1992, *15* (4), 1–5.

Entner, D. "DCCC Takes the TQM Plunge...and Tells How." *Educational Record,* 1993, *74* (2), 29–36.

Gehris, D.V.R. "Business Success in the 90's." *The Rotarian,* December 1994, 6.

Godbey, G. "Beyond TQM: Competition and Cooperation Create the Agile Institution." *Educational Record,* 1993, *74* (2), 37–42.

Isaacson, N., and Bamburg, J. "Can Schools Become Learning Organizations?" *Educational Leadership,* 1992, *50* (3), 42–44.

Marchese, T. "Assessment, Quality and Undergraduate Improvement." *Assessment Update,* 1994, *6* (3), 1–2, 12–14.

Needham, R.L. "Total Quality Management: An Overview." *Leadership Abstracts,* 1991, *4* (10).

Richardson, C.R. "Improving Effectiveness Through Strategic Planning." *Community College Review,* 1988, *15* (4), 28–34.

Rhodes, L.A. "On the Road to Quality." *Educational Leadership,* March 1992, 77–80.

Seymour, D.T. *On Q: Causing Quality in Higher Education.* New York: American Council on Education, 1992.

Shalala, D.E. "TQM Applications in Education." *Executive Excellence,* May 1993, 6–7.

Sherr, L.A. *Higher Education and the Future: Initiatives for Research.* Baltimore: General Session Presentations, 29th Annual Forum, Association for Institutional Research, 1989.

Sherr, L.A., and Lozier, G.G. "Total Quality Management in Higher Education." *New Directions in Institutional Research,* 1991, *71,* 3–11.

Wallin, D.L., and Ryan, J.R. *Essentialism: Common Sense Quality Improvement.* Washington, D.C.: American Association of Community Colleges, 1994.

CHAPTER 9

THE STAFF AND PROFESSIONAL DEVELOPMENT TEAM

Beyond Access

HELEN M. BURNSTAD
AMY LEE FUGATE

Introduction

All institutions of higher education are being forced to wrestle with public demands for greater accountability; increased competition for tax dollars; rapid developments in technology; increasingly diverse student populations in terms of age, gender, ethnicity, and preparedness; an aging faculty; and other related issues. For community colleges, adaptation has been a way of life. As Cohen and Brawer (1989) explain, "...their goals were to serve the people with whatever the people wanted. Standing outside the tradition, they offered access" (p. 23). This willingness to adapt seems unlikely to change in the near future.

This inherent willingness to change, offer new programs, and provide new services, however, has created a demand within the institutions for internal programs of staff development. Staff development programs differ from faculty development and management development programs in that they are designed to reach all personnel who staff the college, including full- and part-time employees who constitute the college's support staff, faculty, and administrators. The need for staff and faculty development is evident in that, while the external world changes, causing the need for adaptation, the competencies and skills of college employees and their arrangement in the organizational structure often remain relatively constant. As early as 1977, following the development of the National Council for Staff, Program, and Organizational Development (NCSPOD), community college theorists advocated the inclusion of a comprehensive staff development program in all institutions. Hammons, Smith Wallace, and Watts (1978) suggest that staff development is justified because of the acceleration of technology; an inability to cope with the needs of "high-risk" students now enrolling in community colleges; the redefinition of student clientele beyond the traditional eighteen- to twenty-one-year-olds; the increasing impact of the burden of proof in court decisions, collective bargaining, and state and federal regulations on institutional governance; the need for managers to become skilled in planning, implementing, and evaluating change; a growing recognition on the part of most staff that they have training needs as well as their expressed willingness and desire to participate in viable staff development programs; all depend on the ability of the community college and its staff to adapt to the changing environment. During the past seventeen years, changes have enlarged the need for staff development in community colleges. In *Building Communities: A Vision for a New Century*, the Commission on the Future of the Community College called for active staff development initiatives including faculty renewal efforts (1988). Most recently, the Board of NCSPOD reaffirmed its commitment to comprehensive staff development programs (Hoss, 1994). Unfortunately, history indicates that although these programs have been advocated for all colleges, financial belt tightening has often prevented development, reduced the scope of the staff development program, or in some cases eliminated it.

The continuation and further development of staff development programs, however, seems in keeping with the trends toward participative management. Bolman and Deal (1991) argue that in a human resource frame, the key to effectiveness is "to find an organizational form that enables people to get the job done while feeling good about what they are doing" (p. 15). Twombly and Amey (1994) suggest that, based on information in the Educational Resources Information Clearinghouse (ERIC), many community colleges are implementing participative forms of governance. Acebo (1994) argues that community colleges are seeing a paradigm shift to team leadership. Katzenbach and Smith (1993) claim, "Teams represent one of the best ways to support the broad-based changes necessary for the high-performing organization" (p. 25). Yet as this shift to teams occurs, it is important for those involved to remember that putting a group of people together and labeling them a "team" does not alone create effective team management. Twombly and Amey (1994) explain it as follows: "Building communities and effective teams requires the ability to articulate visions, goals, and ideals; to create functioning teams aligned with the pursuit of common goals; to assume team membership, which may not always mean team leadership; and to educate constituents about consensus building, teamwork, information sharing, and shared decision making. Learning environments for members need to be provided where people can learn how to work together and depend on each other as a team" (p. 272). Established staff development programs already provide the learning environment, and new staff development programs quickly create such an environment. Staff development seems a logical home for creation of teams and training in teamwork. An additional benefit is that, by its definition, staff development serves the entire college staff, not just a particular group. This composite make-up provides the opportunity for development of cross-functional teams. Baker and Upshaw provide the definition of cross-functional teams in Chapter 1:

> A *cross-functional* team occurs across several units. Members of a cross-functional team may represent many organizational units and a variety of leadership levels. A cross-functional team concentrates on tasks that require coordination and cooperation among different units in the institution. Cross-functional teams expand relationships between people and divisions within the institution, and thereby increase the global perspective of activity within the institution. (p. 4)

To delineate the specifics of how cross-functional teams can work within staff and professional development, this chapter analyzes several teams operating within our staff development program at Johnson County Community College. This analysis is not intended to be all-inclusive, but rather an attempt to provide a framework for development of cross-functional teams in other institutions.

Purpose

S.C. Acebo (1994) wrote:

> Most colleges are experimenting with ways to involve staff at every level in building a vision of service to students and to the community, and developing innovative, cost-effective ways of providing that service. Cross-functional teams are becoming the basic organizational form. (p. 587)

Katzenbach and Smith (1993) suggest that "Executives who really believe that behaviorally based characteristics like quality, innovation, cost effectiveness, and customer service will help build sustainable competitive advantage will give top priority to the development of team performance" (p. 25) In the case of a community college, the commitment should begin with the board of trustees and be carried out through the administrators. Such a commitment may appear in mission statements, in institutional master plans, in contracts negotiated with various employee groups, or in personnel policies.

151

The primary cross-functional team in staff development is a comprehensive body whose goal is to determine the professional development needs of the staff. The purpose grows out of the institutional commitment to staff development for all employees. Such teams can have a variety of names, including "staff development council," a "professional and organizational development committee," a "staff and professional development committee," a "faculty and staff development advisory committee," or a "staff development advisory team."

The sabbatical committee is an additional cross-functional team established through the staff development mission; its purpose is to make recommendations to the board of trustees as to which employees should be granted a sabbatical leave.

The wellness task force is a cross-functional team developed on an administrative initiative to provide wellness programs for all college employees. Because it deals with personal development, it is also housed under the staff development umbrella.

In a recent review and revision of the college mission statement, one of the goals was to increase diversity at the college. A cross-functional team composed of board members, administrators, faculty, staff, students, and community members developed the revised mission and goals statements. One of their recommendations was to create the diversity task force whose purpose is to develop means for implementing diversity goals throughout the college.

Mission

The person or persons responsible for the creation of the team usually determine its mission. This person could be the college president or his/her designee. In the case of our staff development council, the director of staff development set the mission, which stems directly from the mission of the staff development center as stated in the staff development directory. The mission includes serving the training needs as well as the personal and professional development needs of all employees at the college. The staff development council serves an integral function of carrying out the mission of the college as it relates to human resources. The team reexamines the mission annually during the orientation of the council so that each member can not only understand the mission but contribute input to further development or changes. The staff development program also undergoes a program review every five years. During this program review, all employees respond to a comprehensive questionnaire about the effectiveness of staff and professional development. Feedback from this review can then be used to adapt and revise the mission, the program, and the operation of the staff development council as well.

The development of the sabbatical committee's mission is an outgrowth of examination and interpretation of the staff development mission.

Administrative leadership, in conjunction with those with expertise in the specific areas, created the wellness task force and the diversity task force missions. For instance, the program director in health and physical education helped to determine the mission of the wellness task force. Each of these teams conducts an annual self-review and reassessment. The institutional program evaluation of the entire staff development program also provides feedback.

Systems Thinking

In Chapter 1, Baker and Upshaw suggest that cross-functional teams differ from functional teams in that they are usually a less permanent team and that they may require a rethinking of the organizational structure and relationships between departments. For cross-functional teams within staff and professional development, the "team" concept is permanent, but the team membership turns over periodically. Members usually serve two-year terms on a rotating basis, which allows for consistency in team knowledge, as well as the opportunity for new input. Because these teams consist of members from all areas of the institution, the rotation of membership is a necessary and beneficial part of the system. For our college, the rethinking of the organizational structure took place when staff development was incorporated into the holistic structure. The cross-functional teams identified fit into the system through the staff development program. Because staff development programs are by their nature cross-functional, a focus on relationships between departments is not needed as much as in other cross-functional teams in the institution. For example, our student affairs committee is a cross-functional team that has to continually focus on the impact of their policies between departments at the college. For instance, how does a change in the withdrawal date affect faculty, the registrar, the counseling department, selective admissions programs, financial aid, and the student body?

The development of systems thinking is a natural outcome of the cross-functional teams within staff development, since the teams are charged with care and concern for each employee. For example, the discussion of the institution's need to be in compliance with various federal laws, such as hazardous materials handling or the Americans with Disabilities Act (ADA), is far reaching when taking into account the various standpoints of the full-time faculty member, the student life secretary, the technician in the science lab, or the member of the audio-visual staff. The shift to a systems approach can be difficult for some team members. A representative of a particular area needs to present the perspective of that area but also to be willing to consider a systemwide perspective. Part of becoming a real team is taking the risk to overcome constraints imposed by individual, functional, and hierarchical boundaries (Katzenbach & Smith, 1993).

Membership

The membership of cross-functional teams should reflect all relevant employee groups. Our staff development council, for instance, is made up of representatives from each branch, all divisions, an employee group, and various administrative levels. The membership is selected by the administrators of the groups to be reflective of the institutional culture and commitment. As we've noted, members serve staggered two-year terms, which may be renewed. This cross-functional team, with twenty-five members, is larger than is usually recommended but is highly representative, as specified in the criterion. The team meets monthly and provides a vital communication link between employees and the staff development function. The wellness task force and diversity task force draw on a similar pool for their membership.

Representatives of all employee groups who are eligible for sabbaticals comprise the sabbatical committee. The span of representation is approximately one per thirty. The group includes counselors, library, continuing education, administrative branch, a representative from midmanagement, and faculty from each division. Given their task of determining who should receive sabbaticals, the members of this team meet in larger time blocks for a more limited period of the year than other groups.

Process

Collaboration within a team is essential, and both leaders and participants to should realize that cooperation doesn't just happen because one is part of a team. Some people feel uncomfortable speaking up within a group; others are concerned over having to depend on others within the team; some dislike controversy; some may never have participated in a team; and still others may enter the group with past experiences that make them feel teams are a waste of time. While these factors can inhibit any team, these concerns may be even more evident when the team represents cross-functional units. An additional concern is the potential for competition among areas and perceived status differentials of team members. To assist in eliminating the sense of competition, tasks should require people to exchange ideas and resources. By working together and seeing that they need the information from each other to be successful, the team realizes that cooperation rather than competition will allow successful task completion (Kouzes & Posner, 1993).

Given the potential harm to the goal of collaboration, a team orientation stage is critical. During this stage, each group member must internally answer the core questions: "Why am I here?" "Do I belong in this league?" and finally "Do I want to be here?" Rees (1991) points out that "One must believe that the group's task is valuable and useful for the organization or for society in order to completely 'buy into' the team's mission" (p. 258). In addition, members of the group must believe the group rather than an individual can or should be doing the task, that their skills will be used, they will be heard, their presence matters, and that they have the power to influence the direction and outcome of the group's task (Rees, 1991). During this phase, the leader should create a climate that convinces the team members that collaboration is the real goal. If the leader ensures that collaboration begins immediately, members will not view the leader's collaborative message as mere rhetoric. Thus, team members will be motivated "by believing that the leader stands for and does what they believe in; in this way, motivating becomes leadership by example" (Twombly & Amey, 1994, p. 273). As team members believe in the credibility of the leader, they will also begin believing in themselves. Kouzes and Posner (1993) describe this idea: "Working with credible leaders bolsters people's self-efficacy and fosters greater self-confidence. Leaders take actions and create conditions that strengthen their constituents' self-esteem and internal sense of effectiveness. From this process comes the repeated sentiment 'my leader believes in me and so I can also believe in myself'" (p. 164).

Once the members of the team have bought into the mission, the group should examine its norms or working rules. In the case of the staff development council, all position power is removed, and everyone has an equal and valued voice. The most critical assumption of the team is that input and expertise from all staff are valued (Anthony, 1989). The success of the council also depends on all members' providing support and feedback. In establishing group norms, the team decides and verbalizes how an effective team should work. They then agree on such norms as: only one member speaking at a time, listening and responding are necessary and valued, asking questions to clarify understanding, seeking additional information if a point is unclear, and supporting decisions by all members. This step is also valuable in building awareness of individual differences and will enhance contributions to the group effort.

At the meetings, the teams deal with the missions of their teams. The staff development council, for instance, deals with staff development programs, issues, or problems in the functioning of the staff development center. An agenda is prepared a week in advance of the meeting and distributed to all members. A team member keeps detailed minutes and distributes them within a week of the meeting. The minutes and agenda allow each member to come to the meeting prepared to offer observations, solutions, insights, and constituent feedback. Each meeting always allows for the addition of other items solicited from team members.

The wellness task force and diversity task force follow similar processes. As newer teams with a still-developing mission, however, these teams need an orientation session that empowers team members to implement some of their creative ideas. In a new team, fear may arise that institutional bureaucracy will limit creativity, and thus teams must establish a supportive environment. The team often benefits if the leader ensures the specifics of the commitment made to the teams, particularly the financial commitment. Unless team members are able to see and experience the benefits of their work, they won't care (Kouzes & Posner, 1993).

The sabbatical committee operates according to a somewhat different process. This cross-functional team meets for approximately a month. The orientation process is critical for this group because the process of sabbatical selection is competitive. There are always more applicants than there are sabbaticals. Since various attitudes exist on campus about both the purpose for sabbaticals and the "right" to them, the orientation and training of this group takes longer. The group initially has to get to know one another. Although the team establishes group norms, some norms are imposed externally. The team must recognize and accept specific contract statements regarding sabbaticals, for example. The sabbatical process consists of three orientation sessions open to all applicants: the submission of a written proposal from the applicants, which follows the carefully spelled out requirements of the application form; the committee's review, rating, and group ranking; and the team's interview of each of the candidates, followed by the team rating and ranking the applicants again. The final tabulation is a result of the averaged committee members' scores (lowest and highest dropped), which are rank ordered. The committee meets a final time to review the results and affirm their recommendations, which then go to the president who submits them to the board of trustees for final approval. Because the process is so highly competitive, the internal workings and discussions within the group are more effective when the team accepts the norm of confidentiality. Nonagreement on confidentiality negatively affects the quality of the process. The competitive nature of sabbaticals also makes this team subject to criticism resulting from the disappointment of applicants not selected. If the decision-making process has been effective, the team members are usually more than willing to defend their team decision.

Communication

According to Katzenbach and Smith, "Excellent communication skills, some understanding of small-group dynamics (particularly facilitation skills used in conducting meetings), skills in motivating others, and conflict management skills are the major abilities needed in a good team leader" (1993, p. 173). Team members, too, need good communication skills and an understanding of group dynamics. Some members may bring these skills to the group, but far more often, members require some help in these areas. Most complaints about teams focus on the fact that the team approach is too time-consuming, too uncertain, or too risky. In cross-functional teams, the time issue can become even more apparent.

Initially, communication should focus on who the team members are. Our teams undertake initiatives to ensure that team members know one another. Cross-functional team members are more likely never to have met, much less worked together, on a project. Team members complete self introductions, which include information about their use of staff development opportunities, a concern they bring from their employee group, or a staff development success of which they are aware.

Communication on group norms provides an opportunity to impart information on how groups function. The explanation of task and maintenance functions within a group doesn't help the group function but often helps a team member find a role to play within the group. Task functions include the initiator, who defines problems and suggests strategies; the classifier, who clears up confusion; the summarizer, who pulls together related ideas; and the consensus seeker, who checks to see how much agreement the group has reached. Maintenance roles include the harmonizer, who decreases tension and reconciles disagreements; the encourager, who accepts others and their contributions; and the gatekeeper, who facilitates the participation of those not speaking up within the group (Benne & Sheats, 1948). Groups may need to identify potentially destructive group roles, including the blocker, who resists ideas and is negative; the recognition seeker, who boasts and acts superior; the dominator, who tries to manipulate the team; and the avoider, who resists passively (Benne & Sheats). Some teams have found it beneficial to assign some of the task roles initially until the team members assume them naturally.

A group may choose to discuss or obtain training in listening skills. In cross-functional teams, this communication strategy is essential; members must go beyond hearing what the other person said to being able to understand the other person at least from the other's perspective. Kouzes and Posner find that "as individuals are listened to, more information becomes available, and people discover greater common ground and reasons to engage in cooperative behavior" (1993, p. 168). Communication research supports the idea that listening is the most often overlooked skill, the absence of which hinders effective communication.

In some instances, the cross-functional team benefits from opportunities for uninterrupted communication. Special attention is given, for instance, to setting the annual agenda for staff development with the assistance of the staff development council. Many schools with this type of organization hold annual retreats using either an internal or external facilitator/trainer. The development of the institutional commitment and longevity in a staff development program seems to dictate the selection. Many colleges undertaking a new staff development program elect to hire an external facilitator who can not only direct the group through its planning, but who also knows about various issues surrounding staff development implementation and can train the group simultaneously. On the other hand, schools with more developed programs may choose to strategize planning using an in-house facilitator. Either approach will work nicely; the key issue is to determine the outcomes of such a retreat.

Communication in a team should not be taken for granted. The team leader and team members must be aware of communication breakdowns. If a member of the team perceives communication problems, the team may need to shift from a particular task item to a focus on the communication problem. The task item will be more effectively considered when positive communication is restored.

Outcomes and Rewards

Acebo concludes that "...the most important value of the team is that it can produce results: Through the diverse talents of its members, an end product will be created that is beyond the capability of the members acting individually" (1994, p. 583). Staff development cross-functional teams can particularly produce results because they have the opportunity to produce outcomes that affect the entire employee population.

The staff development council celebrates its outcomes by initiatives such as the all-staff picnic, in which many council members assist with the planning and production, and the "Extra Efforts" program, a recognition program for employees who have helped out the college. The wellness task force has developed a number of wellness initiatives open to all employees, including a life fitness center and the creation of a part-time wellness director position. The diversity task force, while in initial stages, is already working on programs that will provide opportunities for diversity awareness training. The sabbatical committee has worked to revise the sabbatical process, including moving the selection date up a semester so applicants can plan more effectively.

Team members are personally rewarded by seeing their suggestions initiated, which is possible because of the institutional commitment made when the cross-functional teams were established. Team members can reap the further reward of promoting positive feelings about each other based on the interaction of the team.

The cross-functional teams also produce enlightening and healthy ways for the institution to increase participation and commitment. Members take back to their respective groups a better understanding of the complexity of our institution and a willingness to appreciate the contributions of other employees to the institutional mission.

Conclusion

While cross-functional teams are vital, they are also difficult to develop into a cohesive unit. They come from various levels in the organization and are asked to shift their thinking to systemwide concerns. Staff development provides a natural home for cross-functional teams, given the mission of staff development programs to serve the needs of all college employees. The success and effectiveness of cross-functional teams depend on multiple factors: a clear purpose and mission for the team, membership by people with a working knowledge of the goals and missions of the institution, a membership willing to buy into the team concept as opposed to individual decision making, an orientation process that serves to clarify the team mission as well as communication skills, and the ability to see their recommendations coming to fruition.

Success is apparent when team members ask to be renewed at the end of their term and when a staff development council member, reflecting on his or her term, says, "I liked being with this group because we discuss things and get things done!" The continued expansion of the role of staff development as the participants in staff development, the employees, expand their programs not as a result of the action of an administrator but through their own cross-functional team participation is another mark of success. For those schools fighting to either establish a staff development program or expand a limited one, the use of cross-functional teams may provide the needed energy to develop the program.

References

Acebo, S.C. "A Paradigm Shift to Team Leadership in the Community College." In G. A. Baker III (Ed.), *A Handbook on the Community College in America*. Westport, Conn.: Greenwood Press, 1994.

Anthony, J.H. "Therapeutic Leadership." *Leadership Abstracts*, 1989, 2 (13).

Benne, K., and Sheats, P. "Functional Roles of Group Members." *Journal of Social Issues*, 1948, 2, pp. 42-47.

Bolman, L.G., and Deal, T.E. *Reframing Organizations: Artistry, Choice and Leadership*. San Francisco: Jossey-Bass, 1991.

Cohen, A.M., and Brawer, F.B. *The American Community College*. San Francisco: Jossey-Bass, 1989.

Commission on the Future of the Community College. *Building Communities: A Vision for a New Century*. Washington, D.C.: American Association of Community and Junior Colleges, 1988.

Hammons, J., Smith Wallace, T.H., and Watts, G. *Staff Development in the Community College: A Handbook*. Los Angeles: ERIC Clearinghouse for Junior Colleges, 1978.

Hoss, C. Interview with H. Burnstad, November 29, 1994.

Katzenbach, J., and Smith D. *The Wisdom of Teams*. New York: McKinsey and Company, Inc., 1993.

Kouzes, J. and Posner, B. *Credibility*. San Francisco: Jossey-Bass, 1993.

Rees, F. *How to Lead Workteams*. San Diego: Pfeiffer & Company, 1991.

Twombly, S., and Amey, M. "Leadership Skills for Participative Governance." In G.A. Baker III (Ed.), *A Handbook on the Community College in America*. Westport, Conn.: Greenwood Press, 1994.

CHAPTER 10

GENDER AND EQUITY ISSUES IN TEAM BUILDING

A New Management Paradigm

ROSEMARY GILLETT-KARAM

Women represent approximately 47 percent of the workforce today. They account for the majority of the new entrants to the workforce through the year 2000 and beyond. Minorities (as nonwhite populations) now account for a third of the new entrants into the workforce. More immigrants are joining the workforce. The population and the workforce are getting older. Quality of life now depends on examining this new workforce, its attitudes and problems. Stakeholders are calling for a new managerial paradigm—one that integrates both the new and existing workforce with quality in the workplace. To compete in world markets, business demands continuous quality in the workplace. Business leaders expect the new workforce to become part of the quality movement and its members to become effective team members (Lewis & Smith, 1994).

This author intends to suggest that team development and team building offer new grounds for addressing the gender and equity issues, which in other contexts may seem insurmountable. While in other contexts, discussions about diversity might center on issues such as underrepresentation, inequality, and limited access (Gillett-Karam, Roueche & Roueche, 1991), the appeal of using the quality model and team building to address gender and equity issues is compelling. We begin by exploring the concepts of quality and teams. Team building may be thought of as developmental, like leadership in this context; Bensimon and Neumann (1993) provide an exceptionally good model for teams in higher education. They think of leadership in terms of teams—the concept of interactive and collective leadership. A team-centered managerial approach enhances the capacity of organizations to master new knowledge and to use it effectively to improve innovation, problem solving, and productivity. To Bensimon and Neumann (1993), the key to understanding teams is using the cultural metaphor rather than the athletic one: a team as a cultural entity is "a body that simultaneously coheres and fractures in its meaning, relationships, and work dynamics" (p. 26). Patterns of success, as well as patterns of hardships and contradictions, are equally important in discerning the developing stories of teams.

Through the team development, this study argues, the disparities associated with diversity can be fine tuned. According to team-building strategists, effective teams turn obstacles into opportunities; they are motivated toward continuous improvement.

One model of motivation, equity theory, suggests that people strive for fairness and justice in social exchanges and cooperative relationships. Based on the cognitive dissonance theory developed by Festinger (1957), equity theory maintains that individuals tend to preserve consistency between their cognitive beliefs and their behavior. Perceived inconsistencies create cognitive dissonance, which motivates corrective action. Adams (1963) pioneered application of the equity principle to the workplace. Critical to Adams's equity theory is an awareness of key components of the individual-organizational exchange relationship. Input by an employee to the organization includes education, experience, skills, and effort. On the outcome side of the exchange, the organization provides pay, rewards, and recognition. On-the-job feelings of inequity revolve around a person's evaluation of self, other, and system.

Studies demonstrate that people have a low tolerance for negative inequity but that men seem to respond more strongly to negative inequity that do women. Moreover, equity perceptions seem to vary from culture to culture. Some basic considerations are possible, however, from equity theory and the explanation of how beliefs and attitudes affect job performance. Not only do organizations and their leaders need an understanding of cognitive processes, but they also need powerful motivation to correct inequities when intolerant people squelch ideas of fairness and justice, abrogate ideas of respect and esteem of individuals, and point out marked differences of race, gender, age, or handicap. No doubt the case of the disgruntled ex-worker returning to the workplace to exact revenge on a boss or coworkers is the extreme example of the psychological dimension of equity theory. When people believe they have been slighted, they feel the need to repair the perceived damage done to them. Problems arise when the slight appears of small consequence to the boss or coworker, and of significant consequence to the worker who feels harmed. People have a low tolerance for negative inequity (someone else enjoys greater outcomes for similar inputs); when they feel shortchanged, they feel they need to correct the situation. The delicate balance between inputs and outputs is critical here. Good leaders must learn how to reduce inequity; better still, by working in teams, resolution of inequity issues means working through perceived injustices as team members share responsibility for change. If inequity exists in the college, and women and ethnic minorities are underrepresented in staffing patterns, in leadership positions, and on cross-functional teams, the leader is responsible for making adjustments as necessary.

The example of the "glass ceiling" offers insight into the application of equity theory (Morrison et al., 1992). When women consistently have difficulty in achieving promotion and positions of authority and feel passed over because they are female, they are responding from dissonance and the need to correct job position inequity. Certainly organizations must promote training in equity issues but, so too, should the impression that perceptions of fairness and equity be regarded as real enough to have an effect on policy, procedures, and reward systems.

Equity theory can aid in understanding issues related to sexual harassment in the workplace. Men and women see the concept in almost diametrically different ways. The perceived inequities are, however, real as the principle of retaliation becomes a more litigious one. Too, the economic impact of racism and sexism is often apparent from an analysis of salary scales. Here perceptions of input and negative inequity are strong; the same work for different pay hardly seems fair (Hayes & Colin, 1994). Quality teams can work to understand these disparities and to "fine tune variations" that impede the productivity of the system.

Quality and Teams

W. Edwards Deming, the father of the quality movement, taught that quality products depend on quality processes. The core of his teaching deals with reducing variation in manufacturing systems. By using statistics to measure variation in manufacturing systems, Deming demonstrated that the more fine-tuned the system, the more the product improves. In a constantly improving system, the process of improvement is more important than the product.

Process, not product, is the focus of continuous quality improvement. The process for reducing error is one constantly monitored by the quality team. Teams and teamwork, therefore, are popular terms in management circles. Research shows that teamwork is having diverse and substantial impacts. In the view of management expert Peter Drucker (1988), tomorrow's organizations will revolve around teams. According to Aldefer (1987), teams are an officially sanctioned collection of individuals charged with completing a mission by an organization and who must depend on one another for successful completion

163

of that work (p. 211). Buchholz and Roth (1987) noted eight attributes of high-performance teams in a nationwide survey of team members. They include the following:

- participative leadership (creating an interdependency by empowering, freeing up, and serving others);
- shared responsibility (establishing an environment in which all team members feel as responsible as the manager for the performance of the work unit);
- aligned purpose (having a sense of common purpose about why the team exists and the function it serves);
- high communication (creating a climate of trust and open, honest communication);
- future focused (seeing change as an opportunity for growth);
- focused on task (keeping meetings focused on results);
- creative talents (applying individual talents and creativity); and
- rapid response (identifying and acting on opportunities).

This writer would add a ninth attribute, a representative team. If the team does not reflect the diversity in the institution, the college community will not accept its work as representative.

Consideration of "powerlessness" in typical work situations is an area of strong contention today. Women and members of minority groups often feel powerless in organizations because they fail to succeed to position or authority. People trying to build teams must question this idea that power is position. Power shifts from position, reward, or coercive bases to information, role-modeling, and networking bases. Participative leadership and shared responsibility replace authoritative or even paternalistic leadership, as stated earlier. The design of the team is a leadership responsibility.

Work Team Effectiveness

Other theories, too (Sundstrom, deMeuse & Futrell, 1990), make reference to work-team effectiveness models in which team effectiveness depends on team viability (team member satisfaction and continued willingness to contribute) and team performance (acceptability of output to customers within or outside the organization who receive team services, information, decisions, products). Measuring team viability and performance results from gauging team cohesiveness and team interdependence. Thamhain's (1990) model of team effectiveness includes three principal factors that are *people related* (characterized by personal work satisfaction; mutual trust and team spirit; good communications; low unresolved conflict and power struggle; low threat, fail-safe, good job security); *organization related* (characterized by stability and job security; involved, interested, supportive management; proper rewards and recognition; stable goals and priorities); and *task related* (characterized by clear objectives, directions, and project plans; proper technical direction and leadership; autonomy and professionally challenging work; experienced and qualified project team personnel; team involvement; and project visibility). These factors, in turn, result in effective team performance (innovative ideas, goals accomplished, adaptable to change, high personal/team commitment, rated highly by upper management).

Determinants of teamwork and team effectiveness are similar to those routine aspects of good leadership and good management in organizations. It is important to note that these factors are interdependent and complex; it is not enough to maximize a few and ignore the rest to accomplish team effectiveness.

The pursuit of team effectiveness and teamwork is an endless battle in the eyes of some and a struggle for continuous improvement for others. Katzenbach and Smith (1993) say it best: "Working through the obstacles make teams stronger" (p. 149). Work teams and cross-functional teams approach diversity issues through a vision of quality, not through a sense of social responsibility or legal mandate. High-performance participation requires valuing the uniqueness that each person brings to the organization. In many colleges, diversity training has become little more than a mandated session; it should be more. Team building is a leadership training process in which members bring personal visions together. Team building becomes the goal of discussions.

By examining the nature of groups and their transformation to teams, by focusing on trust, by evaluating their performance, and by scrutinizing communication, change, collaboration, and conflict (elements and skills necessary to team building), teams can discover ways to increase fairness, tolerance, and justice.

From Groups to Teams

What distinguishes a group from individuals is that its members share status and, by their interaction and challenges, gain a stronger sense of common identity and purpose; thus, the more they interact, the more they feel like a team. Although groups may vary in the amount time they spend on task behavior (accomplishing a task) and socioemotional behavior (managing tensions, building friendships, being mutually supportive), groups tend to collaboratively make decisions by moving through a process of gathering and sharing information, debating the suggestions, accommodating differences within the group, and readjusting to the group. The more alike the group members are in status, gender, or ethnicity, the faster the group can solve a structured problem (a problem for which a known solution exists). Yet, if the group violates the principle of equitable representatives, the larger community will often not support its decision (Hampton, Summer & Webber, 1987).

For the most part, group traditions and the studies of groups reflect major, or dominant, group traditions that in turn establish norms of homogeneity.

Culture becomes compliance to the dominant norms. The equity issue here is one of either acceding to acculturation or enculturation, or resisting the dominant group norms and "fighting" for cultural persistence. Most nonwhite groups in America have had to come to grips with this issue, as have women. Is there just "one best culture in America?" they ask. The characteristics of groups may reveal this paradox.

Groups tend to develop in sequential phases that Tuckman and Jensen (1977) call forming, storming, norming, and performing. At the *forming* stage, a group must get acquainted, define its roles, select a decision-making method, construct an agenda, and set goals. Uncertainty is a problem for the group at this initial forming stage. Here a single leader may bring the group together and act as its first facilitator. When a group is forming, members cautiously explore the boundaries of acceptable group behavior. Like hesitant swimmers, they stand by the pool, dabbling their toes in the water; they experience excitement, optimism, pride in being chosen, tentative attachment to the group, and exhibit suspicion and anxiety about the job ahead (Scholtes, 1988).

To account for equity and gender issues at the formation stage of the group, the issue of representation is important. Who to include in the group is as important an issue as is the process of exploring differing beliefs, behaviors, and values that individuals bring to group membership. Inclusion is a concept worthy of debate. Often minority representation is token membership, and because only a few women may be presidents or engineering faculty, or a few African-Americans who are faculty members, every group asks them to join, and they soon question their "real" input and contribution to the group. Personal and group conflict is sure to arise over such issues.

In the *storming* stage, the group will benefit if differences are expressed. The most important problem-solving process during storming is idea generation. Ideas, distinct from solutions, are the key to group creativity. The assumption is that structured group storming produces more and higher-quality ideas than people would by working alone. Storming may not result in conflict resolution, which may become a problem for the group. If the members of this group of hesitant swimmers decide to jump into the water without adequate instructions, they may drown. At this stage, participants exhibit sharp fluctuations in their attitudes about their group and their project (Scholtes, 1988).

Conflict is an expected norm in group development; equity issues are uncomfortable. Raising the question of discrimination based on race or ethnicity, gender, age, handicap, or sexual orientation is disconcerting to some, problematic to others. Many would prefer to ignore controversial topics. Usually, noncommunication and angry silence or hostility replaces open dialogue around these issues. Storming suggests that groups must face and resolve tough, uncomfortable personal issues.

Norming implies that a collection of people has become a group. Norms imply informal rules that regulate group behavior (Feldman & Arnold, 1983). Groups use norming to reduce differences among group members and to encourage the group's common identity of values and goals. One danger in norming is the tendency of groupthink to occur; here cooperation and "getting along" may become more important than creative thinking and the expression and communication of individual misgivings and doubts. At this stage, the participants who thought they were drowning, now see a chance to help each other stay afloat (Scholtes, 1988).

More than any stage of group development, norming is the one in which the group should exercise. If norms are standardized, they must reflect the needs, wants, and aspirations of the whole group and its identities. If these norms are based on dominant cultural values in which expectations of convergence and compliance occur, alienation results. Alienated group members are unproductive, and eventually the group eliminates them as "problem" people. In team development, a collaborative effort at rule making ensures that individual respect and integrity are honored.

Performing occurs when the group fully mobilizes its resources to achieve a goal; group members are interdependent and get down to business. Performing is the implementation stage of group work. Leaders delegate responsibilities and empower others. Foot-dragging, a tool of the uncommitted and powerless, can be a problem, as can poor follow-through, which sometimes results from a shortage of doers or by a lack of ownership. The ideal time to address these problems is before they occur. At the performing stage, group members know each other's strengths and weaknesses; here they may learn to swim in concert (Scholtes, 1988).

All the caveats refer to the "deviant's behavior." The group must determine reasons for foot-dragging and noncommitment. Why do only some group members "own" the goals of the group, and others not? Team performance depends on relating and finding consensus around people, tasks, and organizational orientations. Consensus can occur when teams share visions by working through conflict, a process that eliminates hidden agendas, rule by tyrannies or autocrats, and tense atmospheres. Teams should expect an informal, tension-free work atmosphere, pertinent discussions and participation, well-understood tasks and objectives, listening that gives every related idea a hearing, disagreement and frank criticism, and an ongoing model of evaluation that monitors inequity.

The use of the term *transforming* here means the group transforms itself into a team. In much the same way that Burns (1978) uses the concept of transformation, we use the word here. Just as good leaders transform followers into leaders, so, too, does group transformation allow the building of a cohesive, effective team of equals. Team development and team building spur the process of transformation. The concept of teamwork suggests that where once barriers, rivalries, and distrust existed among group members, the quality organization fosters teamwork and partnerships as a common struggle to benefit the good of the organization (Scholtes, 1988).

Groups work independently; teams are interdependent and mutually supportive. Leaders tell groups what to do; team members contribute to an orga-

167

nization's success by applying their own talents and knowledge to team objectives. Teams work in a climate of trust, openness, and honest communication. Teams recognize conflict is a normal aspect of human interaction and view conflicts as opportunities for new ideas and creativity. They work to resolve conflict quickly and creatively (Maddux, 1992; Mears & Voehl, 1994).

In their book *The Wisdom of Teams*, Katzenbach and Smith (1993) point out that teams align because they want to contribute to the well-being of an organization or idea; they feel challenged to perform with excellence. The authors believe teams achieve results based on their mutual accountability, their skills in problem solving, technology, and human relations, as well as their commitment to specific and commonly agreed upon goals that have a meaningful purpose. Scholtes (1988) and Katzenbach, as well as Smith, offer recipes for successful teams. Goals, planning, and roles provide one category for team development. Clarity in team goals means the team agrees on its mission and works together to resolve disagreement; the team has identified the resources it needs and follows a plan (which it may revise) that focuses on constant improvement of the team; and the team finds it operates most efficiently if it uses every member's talents and carefully defines members' duties and roles. Teams begin their development by practicing trust.

Trust

When Madison wrote *The Federalist Papers*, he referred to the natural coalitions of groups. Groups, he said, formed and coalesced out of agreement around special interests. Translating those shared interests into policy transformed and institutionalized the interests as law. Later, competing groups would challenge the special interests of previous groups and establish their laws; hence, we had the principle of pluralism—majority rule with minority rights. Minority rights were the natural order of varying coalitions; minority interests had the same privilege as majority interests. Madison, too, was interested in determining how variation was fine tuned. As a student of the enlightenment, he explained that trust between individuals and groups was an expectation of competing groups. He warned, however, that tyranny and trust are in competition.

Trust is the belief in the integrity, character, or ability of others, and it is essential if people are to achieve anything together. Unfortunately, trust is no longer expected. The book *Credibility* examines leadership from the constituent's perspective; it explains how leaders earn the trust and confidence of their constituents (Kouzes & Posner, 1993). According to Kouzes and Posner, these new leaders cannot champion their own agendas, their own advancement, and their own well-being if they want team members to follow them. They must clarify their values and beliefs. A credible leader truly understands and appreciates the aspirations of others. A new ethic is in order: Shifting the focus from self to other. This ethic is reminiscent of the works of Simone de

Beauvoir, Paulo Freire, and Carol Gilligan, all of whom are attuned to the ethic of the other. All three speak to the importance of listening to the voice of silenced peoples. Listening is the operative word here. It is not telling; it is not selling. Kouzes and Posner reclaim the notion that leaders of the 21st century must value diversity if they want to be future leaders.

Equal representation is a great motivator; most people want access to training and certification to become leaders. The concern is that the achievement nature of leadership will replace the ascriptive nature of leadership, where status replaces individual achievement. If people are willing to train to be leaders—if their achievements position them to compete for roles—then they must question and renegotiate poor hiring practices such as those referred to as selection of sameness or positions of perfection (Gillett-Karam, Roueche & Roueche, 1991).

What makes for good working relations among people with different demographic characteristics? Understanding the nature of trust and values is a good beginning. Zand (1972), an authority on trust, believes that trust is the key to establishing productive interpersonal relationships. The primary responsibility for creating a climate of trust falls on the manager/leader. Trust initially encourages openness and honesty. People talk *with* others rather than *at* them. A trusting person exhibits a willingness for others to influence him or her and to change if the facts show that change is appropriate. Mutual trust encourages self-control, rather than control from the top. Confidence abounds that others will perform as agreed, and mutual commitment to success emerges. Full disclosure of relevant information, feelings, and opinions is a necessity.

Trust is fragile. It grows at a slow pace. It can disintegrate in an instant. Bartolome (1989) suggests six ways to build trust: good information and communication; support and coaching; respect, delegation, and listening; fairness; predictability; and competence. Trust seems to grow from decent behavior and from valuing others.

Each person has a self-concept; we think of ourselves as physical, social, and spiritual beings. Carl Jung noted that individuals have unique cognitive styles; two dimensions of the human character influence our perceptions: sensation and intuition; and two dimensions affect our personal judgment: thinking and feeling. From Jung we know that individuals with different cognitive styles should seek different kinds of information when making decisions. From Milton Rokeach we know that people have and share enduring beliefs as preferable modes of conduct; these are their values. As we share those characteristics, culture emerges, expressing a collective frame for values, beliefs, and dispositions. What good leaders know is that value conflict is real and can occur interpersonally, intrapersonally, and between individual and organization. Consider how President Nixon's aides failed to apply the value of honesty during the Watergate era. Consider how the concept of equity was not an issue when laws allowed separate schools for whites and blacks. Rokeach suggests that even instrumental and terminal values clash in an individual; if we are serious about our ambitions, we may forgo equality or equal opportunity for all. Most critical here is reconciling individual values and organizational values; if employees are at odds with their organization's values, they find themselves at a decisive point: Do they quit? Do they change their values? Do they fight? Do they become alienated? Understanding conflicting values may hinge on combining trust with good communication.

Communication

Another category for team building includes the development of good communication skills. Good discussions depend on how well information moves between and among team members. Noncommunication is the chief reason for conflict. Effective team members are good communicators; they exhibit the characteristics of assertive communication: knowing when to talk, when to listen, and how to assert their needs and limits. They are fair, tolerant, and nonjudgmental; they know how to meet the whiners, moralizers, labelers, silents, and attackers (those who display passive or aggressive communication behaviors). They also know the power of constructive confrontation, that period of communication in which a person takes the heat of criticism.

Effective communication skills require that people listen actively, exploring, rather than debating, another speaker's ideas. Skilled communicators know how to use open questions, encouraging statements, and reflecting comments. Effective communicators avoid interrupting and talking when others are speaking. "Why" questions tend to discourage positive communication by implying criticism or judgment. Assertive communicators demonstrate various levels of shared information; these levels include the sensing, thinking, feeling, and action statements described below:

- Sensing statements—I don't hear any disagreement on X's point. Do we all agree?
- Thinking statements—The number of errors and the volume of work seem to correlate.
- Feeling statements—A question was raised that seemed to be directed at X, when really the questioner wanted more information.
- Action statements—Let's explore this debate by distributing an inventory to collect our thinking.

Scholtes (1988) points out several indicators of potential trouble surrounding poor communication behaviors, and although many of these are common (poor speaking skills including mumbling, rambling, and monotone speaking), others show how people abuse speech and listening. The use of tentative statements such as "Do you think?" and "Maybe" suggest that speakers may be cautious, afraid, or unable to say what they really feel. Opinions expressed as "the law" may intimidate others. People's words do not match their tone, manner-

170

isms, or expressions. Bullying statements, discounts, and plops are among other abuses. A bullying statement says, "What you don't understand is...." A discount statement says, "That's not important; what's worse is...." And finally, a plop receives no acknowledgment or response.

In a discussion of communication in the workplace, Tannen (1994) monitors conversation between men and women. While acknowledging that she cannot entirely generalize, Tannen paints a picture of gender differences; women, for example, are apologetic in their conversations and are more likely to make "plop" statements that later re-emerge as another's idea. Men often use banter in their conversations and are socialized to respond aggressively when they think they are being "put down." Tannen suggests that we attempt to discern meaning and understanding between sexes and reports that in conversations, men do not want nurturance and that women do not want solutions.

Beneficial team behavior means team members initiate discussions, seek information and opinions, suggest procedures for reaching a goal, clarify or elaborate on ideas, summarize, test for consensus, direct conversational traffic, make room for reserved talkers, keep the discussion from digressing, note the hidden agendas, compromise, ease tension, refer to references, praise and correct others equally, and encourage the group to agree on procedures. A dialogue process that involves the learning of positive and assertive communication skills will allow conflicting parties to explore differences, clarify areas of disagreement, and search for common ground without the expectation that binding agreements will emerge. Here the focus is on exchange of information and possible generation of proposals for consideration. Effective communication is the surest way to maintain the linkages between actors in a conflict or confrontation. Improved communication can strengthen productive relationships. Good leadership can aid team communication. Effective leaders are good communicators.

Change Strategies

Senge (1990) suggests that change in organizations and their leaders must come through "generative learning." Organizations should be places that nurture new and expansive patterns of thinking and that set free collective aspiration. People in organizations should continually expand their capacity to create the results they truly desire and continually learn how to learn together. Learning organizations actively seek opportunities instead of waiting for problems to occur. Continuous quality improvement encourages innovation and provides an atmosphere of tolerance and growth.

The structure of organizations, according to the quality theorists (Deming, Juran, Baldrige) should become less top heavy, and the leaders of organizations should be willing to transfer power and share authority. Organizations expect managers accustomed to planning, scheduling, and controlling to transform the managerial position. Change leaders as team participants know that workers no longer need to know a particular set of skills, but to understand *how to learn*.

Change creates pressure in any organization but especially in traditional hierarchical organizations where top management may have the hardest time coming to grips with the direct implications of change. In a study by Scott and Jaffe (1989), traditional leaders often underestimated the impact of change on employees, and although they engaged in strategic planning, they avoided communicating with their followers. Scott and Jaffe conclude that these leaders did not take the time to understand the changes that were occurring all around them and thus, when change was unavoidable, they felt betrayed especially by middle management and employees. While middle management felt the pressure to make organizational change, they were pulled in different directions (between top management and workers) and lacked the information to focus on multiple priorities. According to the authors, resistant or withdrawn employees besieged managers, who felt deserted, blamed, or misunderstood by their superiors. Employees in changing organizations often felt attacked and betrayed. Responding angrily or in confusion, many "retired" on the job; they experienced a loss of traditional relationships, familiar structure, and predictable career advancement. These traditional organizations label top management's "isolated"; middle management's "squeezed"; and employees' "resistant." Specifically trained to view change as an opportunity, change leaders help to guide and develop an organizational culture based on collaborative decision making and teamwork.

Change requires the following: preparation and planning, transition and communication, and implementation and rewards. Preparation for change involves an understanding of organizational and worker readiness around potential change; it also suggests that workers know about options, alternatives, and have thought through contingencies. During the change process, people may focus on the past and deny the change. Activity may occur, but not much gets done. Next, everyone goes through a period of preoccupation, wondering where they stand and how the change will affect them. This stage is where resistance occurs, and anger, blame, anxiety, and depression may mark this phase. When workers begin to work together, they begin to build their commitment to change. The Transition Grid (Scott & Jaffe, 1989) presented in Figure 10.1 marks the four stages of personal transition through change—denial, resistance, exploration, and commitment.

Change leaders delegate and communicate control to the team. To implement change, appropriate training and coaching must take place, feedback must be constant so that people know where they stand, and rewards for their efforts and contributions should be in place. Finally, teams must build bridges to other teams and organizations; they accomplish this process through collaboration. Collaboration occurs when the organizational or personal identity of leadership is subordinated to the team.

Figure 10.1
The Phases of Personal Transition Through Change

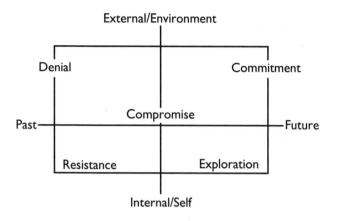

Collaboration

Fisher and Ury (1981) suggest that even well-intentioned decision makers do not really understand the interests they are trying to reconcile. The option for decision making that Gray (1989) advances is the assembling of a representative sample of stakeholders (those involved in goal outcomes) to work out an agreement among themselves; she sees teams as collaborators, parties who value differences and search for solutions that go beyond their own limited vision of what is possible.

Collaboration usually follows a prescribed three-phase sequence on what it takes to "get to the table and to explore, reach, and implement an agreement." *Phase 1* is the problem-setting phase, or the "how to get to the table" phase. This phase requires a common definition of the issue or problem and a commitment to collaborate. The team identifies and legitimizes stakeholders in this phase. Who convenes is critical, as is the identification of resources. Teams in *Phase 2* prescribe direction setting, set ground rules and an agenda, and form subgroups to access information. Teams discuss options and reach agreements in this phase. In *Phase 3*, the implementation stage, teams consult internal and external constituencies, ensure monitoring and compliance, and institutionalize the issue/problem (Gray, 1989).

Opportunity, a key word for change, is also a key word for collaboration; the opportunity for collaborating arises because stakeholders recognize the potential advantages of working together. Here, working together means that teams are formed representing gender and ethnicity ratios in the organization. These

173

opportunities can be classified into two general categories: resolving conflict and advancing shared visions (consensus building).

Conflict Resolution

Conflict is unavoidable because people with varying personalities and values must work together to solve problems. People have different needs, interests, and values; even their goals and activities may be incompatible. Conflicts may occur in many areas, including, but not limited to, resources, ideas, turf, race, ethnicity, and lifestyle values and norms. Unresolved conflict is destructive and can escalate into violence and permanent schisms. The challenge is to resolve conflict constructively. When people discuss common goals around issues in an open, positive atmosphere, and defer individual claims to territory or ideas in the interest of satisfying the identified recommended need, they reduce potential conflict.

Over the last several decades, a quiet revolution has been taking place in the methods used to deal with conflict (Canfield, 1992). The alternative dispute resolution movement uses win-win negotiation and mediation rather than win-lose negotiation and litigation. We use several terms to describe different conflict resolution techniques, including negotiation, which is direct back and forth communication between or among people involved in a disagreement with the intention of agreeing. Collaborative or win-win negotiation attempts to help all parties meet their needs by focusing on underlying interests and developing mutually beneficial alternatives. Mediation uses a neutral third party to assist disputing parties. Arbitration is similar to mediation, but an arbitrator determines the facts in a dispute and recommends a solution.

In their book *Getting Disputes Resolved*, Ury, Brett and Goldberg (1988) describe three approaches to resolving disputes: reconciling differences, determining who is right, and using power. Reconciliation of differences addresses each person's interests, needs, and values through negotiation or mediation. Independent standards determining legitimacy or fairness under the law may be applied to disputes that seek to decide who is right. When threats and physical and emotional violence occur, and status inequalities surface among actors in a dispute, the use of power (as in a more powerful military force) is inevitable.

Ideally, among groups who are working together to resolve common goals, negotiation, collaboration, and mediation (and sometimes arbitration) are preferred uses of conflict resolution. These unified groups rule out competition, which involves a win-lose situation, as an undesirable dispute resolution solution. Canfield (1992) suggests that complex organizations, such as colleges, should have some type of ombudsman whose only role is to facilitate conflict resolution. This role may be designated, however. A facilitator dealing with conflict has two major tasks: probing (examining beneath the surface to discover the real issues and the issues in conflict) and generating (suggesting alternative solutions that meet the needs of the parties).

Probing allows the facilitator to examine negative feelings, usually expressed by anger and/or hostility. When participants express negative feelings and the rest of the group accepts those feelings, they often lose their strength. The facilitator's responses are nondefensive even when anger is directed to him or her. Giving an angry person an opportunity to express anger in a private, nonthreatening environment usually can defuse the situation. Fisher and Ury (1981), in *Getting to Yes,* suggest separating the people from the problem. The goal for relational issues is to establish a respectful business relationship in which parties can work together. Probing allows a facilitator to move to the actual issues at hand after the anger dissipates. Probing beneath the surface allows an examination of the concerns and needs of the individuals. People in conflict need to tell their story. Identifying values that the disputants hold in common is worthwhile. A consensus of values is the foundation for the beginning of a solution. Finally, the disputants can clarify the real problem and separate it from their anger and their need to express their own needs, concerns, and values.

Generating solutions is the opposite of probing. It is exploratory and open ended. Problem solving begins with a wide-open look at all the potential options and focuses on the present or the future, not the past. Fisher and Ury (1981) suggest moving away from personal blame to generating objective criteria such as precedent, scientific judgment, and specified procedures. Agreement on criteria means the solution is more fair and objective. The parties should feel that they have won; having a loser means a continuance of problems. Win-win solutions include "expanding the pie," or finding a way to generate ideas about increasing resources: if it is a matter of money, look to foundation support. Another suggestion for generating solutions is "bridging common interests." Finding out how to meet both persons' interests may seem difficult, but a facilitator can accomplish this task. In politics, the concept of "log-rolling" may offer a generating idea. Each person gives up what is of little value to help each other get what is of greater value. Finally, the team should not rule out compromise as a solution to disputes.

Table 10.1 makes a comparison between adversarial and collaborative methods of dispute resolution.

Collaboration, which uses conflict resolution, allows shared visions (Gray, 1989). But to understand collaboration as shared visioning is to understand that collaboration is not cooperation. Cooperation entails partnerships and agreements to work together to meet goals but does so without substantially changing the services provided or the rules and regulations governing the separateness of cooperating institutions, individuals, or groups (Melaville & Bland, 1993). Cooperation usually does not result in coalition building.

Collaboration is also not coordination. Coordination refers to formal, institutionalized relationships among the existing networks of organization (Mulford, 1984). To presume that the parties in a collaborative effort are already part of an organized relationship underrepresents the developmental character of the collaborative process. Collaboration creates a forum within which teams

Table 10.1
Methods for Dispute Resolution

Adversarial	Collaborative
Rules position parties as adversaries	Parties positioned as joint problem solvers
Third parties intervene before issues are mature	Issues can be identified before positions crystallize
Characterized by positional bargaining	Characterized by interest-based bargaining
Facts used to buttress positions	Joint search used to determine facts
Characterized by polarization of parties/issues	Characterized by search for underlying interests
Face-to-face contact is restricted/contending parties	Face-to-face discussions encouraged/all parties
Seeks winning arguments	Seeks workable options
Yields all-or-nothing resolution of issues	Yields resolution by integrating interests
Narrows options quickly	Broadens field of options
Authority for decisions rests with judge	Authority for decisions rests with parties
Characterized by suspicion and high emotion	Characterized by respect/application of reason
Parties often dissatisfied with outcome	Outcome must be satisfactory to all parties
Often fosters bitterness and long-term mistrust	Promotes trust and positive relationships

(Gray, 1989)

can seek consensus about the problem, develop mutually agreeable solutions, and implement solutions through collective actions.

Collaboration occurs when partners share a vision, establish common goals, and agree to use their power to achieve common goals, including commitment of resources and the willingness to alter existing policies. Collaboration points to an opportunity for divergent groups, different levels of information, and varying degrees of motivation among individual members to come together because these people recognize the potential advantages of working together.

Collaboration implies synergy and team building. The products resulting from collaboration are greater than the sum of the separate work of individuals working independently. Collaborative solutions to issues emerge by dealing constructively with difference. Collaborators examine culture and behavior for similarities and laud differences. Collaboration operates on the premise that assumptions and values that one side has about the other side and about the nature of issues are worth testing. Testing assumptions and allowing constructive confrontation of differences in values or ways of thinking are potentially healthy benefits of collaboration. Collaboration asks individuals to reexamine their own separate identities or turf. Collaboration allows joint ownership of decisions and suggests collective responsibility for issues.

Team Building

To address gender and equity issues in the community college, this chapter suggests that through the process of developing a team for a quality institution, participants consider the unstated and often misunderstood differences among people and integrated them into the process of team evolution and team building. This chapter has suggested several strategies to enhance representation in team building and to use such concepts as work-group effectiveness, team building, trust building, effective communication, change strategies, and conflict resolution to help organizations achieve their missions. Team members and college leaders play important roles in this development. The evolution of the team from sociological group to work team is a crucial goal. So, too, are the concepts addressed in this chapter. Team members confront and work through misunderstandings over gender and equity issues by developing skills addressed in this chapter. Team building is an essential ingredient for cultural reintegration, and stakeholders may accomplish it, not as a social responsibility or as a federal mandate, but through the shared leadership of a team powerfully structured to solve major problems together.

References

Adams, J.S. "Toward an Understanding of Inequity," *Journal of Abnormal and Social Psychology*, November 1963.

Aldefer, C. "An Intergroup Perspective on Group Dynamics." In J. Lorsch (Ed.), *Handbook of Organizational Behavior*. Englewood Cliffs, N.J.: Prentice-Hall, 1987.

Bartolome, F. "Nobody Trusts the Boss Completely—Now What?" *Harvard Business Review*, 1989, *67*.

Bensimon, E., and Neuman, A. *Redesigning Collegiate Leadership*. Baltimore: The Johns Hopkins Press, 1993.

Buchholz, S., and Roth, T. *Creating the High Performance Team*. New York: Wiley, 1987.

Burns, J.M. *Leadership*. New York: Harper & Row, 1978.

Canfield, M. *Conflict Resolution*. Center for Policy Negotiation, George Mason University, 1992.

Drucker, P. "The Coming of the New Organization." *Harvard Business Review*, January-February 1988, *66* (1).

Feldman, D., and Arnold, H. *Managing Individual and Group Behavior in Organizations*. New York: McGraw-Hill, 1983.

Fisher, R., and Ury, W. *Getting to Yes*. Boston: Houghton Mifflin, 1981.

Festinger, L. *A Theory of Cognitive Dissonance*. Stanford, Calif.: Stanford University Press, 1957.

Gillett-Karam, R., Roueche, S., and Roueche, J. *Underrepresentation and the Question of Diversity*. Washington, D.C.: Community College Press, 1991.

Gray, B. *Collaborating: Finding Common Ground for Multiparty Problems*. San Francisco: Jossey-Bass, 1989.

Hampton, D., Summer, C., and Webber, R. *Organizational Behavior and the Practice of Management*. New York: Harper Collins, 1987.

Hayes, E., and Colin, S. *Confronting Racism and Sexism. New Directions for Adult and Continuing Education*. San Francisco: Jossey-Bass, 1994.

Katzenbach, J., and Smith, D. *The Wisdom of Teams: Creating High-Performance Organization*. Boston: Harvard Business School Press, 1993.

Kouzes, J., and Posner, B. *Credibility*. San Francisco: Jossey-Bass, 1993.

Lewis, R., and Smith, D. *Total Quality in Higher Education*. Delray Beach, Fla.: St. Lucie Press, 1994.

Maddux, R. *Team Building: An Exercise in Leadership*. Menlo Park, Calif.: Crisp Publications, Inc., 1992.

Mears, P., and Voehl, F. *Team Building: A Structured Approach*. Delray Beach, Fla.: St. Lucie Press, 1994.

Melaville, A., and Bland, I. *Together We Can*. Washington, D.C.: U.S. Department of Education, Office of Educational Research and Improvement, 1993.

Morrison, A.M., White, R.P., and Vab Velsor, E. *Breaking the Glass Ceiling: Can Women Reach the Top of America's Largest Corporations?* Reading, Mass.: Addison-Wesley, 1992.

Mulford, C.L. *Interorganizational Relations: Implications for Community Development*. New York: Human Sciences Press, 1984.

Scholtes, P. *The Team Handbook*. Madison, Wisc.: Joiner, 1988.

Scott, C., and Jaffe, D. *Managing Organizational Change: A Practical Guide for Managers*. Menlo Park, Calif.: Crisp Publications, Inc., 1989.

Senge, P. *The Fifth Discipline*. New York: Currency, 1990.

Sundstrom, E., deMeuse, K., and Futrell, D. "Work Teams," *American Psychologist*, February 1990.

Tannen, D. *Talking from 9 to 5*. New York: Morrow, 1994.

Thamhain, H. "Managing Technologically Innovative Team Efforts Toward New Product Success," *Journal of Product Innovation Management*, 1990, *7, 7*.

Tuckman, B.W., and Jensen, M.A. "Stages of Small Group Development Revisited." *Groups and Organizations Studies*, 1977, *2*, 419–427.

Ury, W., Brett, J., and Goldberg, S. *Getting Disputes Resolved*. San Francisco: Jossey-Bass, 1988.

Zand, D. "Trust and Managerial Problem Solving," *Administrative Science Quarterly*, 1972, *17*.

CHAPTER 11

TEAM BUILDING FOR COLLABORATIVE LEARNING

A Quality Initiative

GEORGE A. BAKER
ANN V. DOTY

The Milieu

Wherever we in education look today, the message is clear: all American institutions must become more effective and productive in manufacturing goods or providing services. For education, that means the production of universal literacy of a high order. To equip students with the tools to perform, to contribute individually and in teams, and to be employable is also the first social duty of America's educational system (Drucker, 1994).

Writing in the *Community College Journal*, Baker and Reed (1994) call for a continuous process of educating citizens. They averred that, starting in high school, students could first choose from multiple pathways, with distinct career and personal objectives. The challenge for American education is not to abandon the current structure but to reengineer the structure. Each pathway chosen would produce motivated and competent human beings who would join a workforce that employed quality and team-oriented principles.

Baker and Reed (1994) conclude that the race to reengineer American education is more of a marathon than a sprint and that the more than 1,200 American community colleges are strategically placed to attack the problem from the middle. We can expect K–12 to begin to produce more literate graduates in the near future. The pressure from external sources is coalescing, and these sources are mandating accountability both explicitly and implicitly. We can expect the university and college systems to continue to emphasize the development of new knowledge and to produce the theoretical engineers, doctors, lawyers, politicians, teachers, and the top and executive level managers. It is the community college that must produce the knowledge worker. Drucker (1994) adeptly describes the transformation of the social structure that is taking place. He characterizes the "knowledge worker" who will gain specific knowledge, learned first in formal education, and continuing to grow significantly through lifelong education in schools or in the workplace. Faculty members will lead teamwork within departments of the college and in community collaborations. They must be able to work within and between organizations as team players. Teams rather than the individuals will become the work unit.

The Organization

In the era of the knowledge worker, the organization becomes critical because only the organization can provide the basic continuity that these workers need. The managers, the planners, and the designers must all become a part of the larger team. Some knowledge workers may become consultants, meaning that they apply their knowledge only when required, while others will use their knowledge for the entire cycle of operations. All workers, however, full or part time, produce in an environment where the organization becomes the center for measuring quality. Simultaneously, the team performs the tasks needed to construct the products to market for return on investment. The managers and the producers come together to analyze the quality of the components and performance, as well as to gather data to reinvest in planning the next cycle of operations. College leaders and curriculum planners will need to understand the relationship of learning to working.

What educators must develop is Senge's (1990) learning organization in which participants practice leadership in a way that leads to participation and empowerment. We must develop situations in which communication is positive, timely, and accurate, in which people work together in teams and share information both vertically and horizontally, in which the college is organized situationally and flexibly, and in which stakeholders act on decisions. Executive suites should not be the origin of decisions; the workplace, where tasks are designed, should generate decisions so that people feel comfortable working together, feel that their work is important, and expect to succeed in what they do. In these college environments, the student is central to what the college does and how it is organized, and the major purpose of the college is to help students learn to learn and to treat the students as adults who are moving toward independence. Senge helps us summarize this section of the chapter on the milieu in which colleges expect faculty to work with students in their own effective, quality-driven, and collaborative classrooms and laboratories. Senge notes that the most striking aspect of the response when you ask people what it's like being a part of a great team is their description of the significance of their collective experience. He says people talk about being a part of something larger than they. They talk of being connected, of being in a position to generate something new and different. He concludes that being a part of a great team stands out as the period of their lives lived to the fullest.

The Quality Era

The late W. Edwards Deming, internationally known, well-recognized expert in all aspects of organizational life, successfully rebuilt Japanese industry after World War II. Returning to the United States, Deming saw his ideas fall on the deaf ears of most American industrialists who had just provided the means for a total defeat of what had been a collective German-Japanese attempt to conquer the world. Today it is well documented that during the 1960s and 1970s, most domestic U.S. companies lost their quality leadership to the same defeated and devastated industries that their weapons and munitions had destroyed. By 1980, foreign companies had gained a significant share of the North American market in such goods as stereo components, medical equipment, television sets, hand tools, radial tires, electric motors, athletic equipment, computer chips, industrial robots, machine tools, and optical equipment (Juran, 1992).

It is also safe to say that in American education and corporate training in the 1980s teachers and trainers prepared American students using foreign technology, sometimes with Deming's ideas imported from Japan. Today we find many applications of Deming's ideas and many subsequent writers who have interpreted them for other than manufacturing organizations. The fourteen principles, according to Deming (1986), apply directly to education institutions and specifically to the teaching of adults.

Table 11.1 relates Deming's fourteen points to the climate, the student, the instructor, and the instruction and provides a framework for this chapter, which is designed to assist the college, its leaders, and its faculty to apply the concepts of team building and quality to these aspects under their control.

The purpose of this chapter is to bring together two of Deming's general themes to improve the quality of teaching and student success in North American community colleges: quality in organizations and the leader's role in improving team commitment, both focused to improve learning. Crosley (1988), Deming (1986), and Juran (1992), for example, have written extensively about quality in organizations. Covey (1989), Drucker (1994), Gardner (1990), Hersey and Blanchard (1982), and Ouchi (1981), among others, have written about the leader's role in improving individual and team commitment.

Table 11.1
Deming's Concepts Applied to Quality
and Team-Oriented College Teaching

Point 1: Effective teachers employ systems thinking, personal mastery, mental models, shared vision, and team learning in the development of academic programs, courses of instruction, and the interaction with students in the learning-to-learn process (Senge, 1990).

Point 2: Through shared vision, effective teachers employ leadership principles to establish situational roles among themselves, the instruction, and the students. The key teaching role is one in which the teacher's main task is to support and enhance the learner's desire to learn to learn and to move the student toward independence (Baker, Roueche & Gillett-Karam, 1990).

Point 3: Effective teachers build quality into the course (mental models) by increasing the student's motivation and responsibility to achieve mastery over the span of the course through constant and accurate feedback on performance (Hersey & Blanchard, 1982).

Point 4: Effective teachers accept the challenge (personal mastery) of preparing the learners for a complex world in which they will solve complex tasks while working in teams (Drucker, 1994).

Point 5: Effective teachers set high goals for themselves (shared vision) and for the student. They expect that they and the student will achieve these goals together (personal mastery). They celebrate success in a classroom environment where progress is expected and learning is rewarded (Covey, 1989).

Point 6: Effective teachers believe that all learning is experiential and continuous (shared vision), and that adults undertake formal and informal learning tasks for self-renewal and advancement (personal mastery). Effective teachers consider themselves adult learners who are highly motivated to acquire new knowledge and to apply it in the exercise of their profession (Angelo & Cross, 1993; Cross, 1993).

Drucker (1994), Peters and Waterman (1982), Senge (1990), and others have written about systems and organizations and have developed paradigms, ideals, models, and patterns to help organizations improve. Government leaders, such as most governors, Presidents Reagan, Bush, and Clinton, other government officials, along with Malcolm Baldrige and Robert Reich (1992), have helped to develop links among economic development, leadership, and quality initiatives. In higher education and community college literature, Angelo and Cross

Table 11.1 (continued)

Point 7: Effective teachers consider all learning as developmental. Adults seek competency in knowledge and in the transfer of that knowledge to problem solving and decision making in life and at work (personal mastery) (Kolb, 1984).

Point 8: Effective teachers build an effective team within the course structure so that activities in the course can reinforce the learning to learn process. In the effective team, members help each other so that they use many mental models in the problem-solving process (Jaques, 1992; Kadel & Keehner, 1994; Slavin, 1988).

Point 9: Effective teachers shift the emphasis from knowledge acquisition to knowledge application so they can teach higher level problem-solving skills (mental models) (Paul, 1992).

Points 10 and 11: Effective teachers employ quality concepts in teaching learners to learn to learn. Quality concepts are modeled in the course structure and used by the teacher and the students in making decisions and solving problems (personal mastery, mental models) (Juran, 1992).

Point 12: Effective teachers resist all efforts to consider quantity over quality, both in measuring success and in reporting student outcomes. The goal must be to hold all students to the same high standards and to expect that each student can achieve those standards (Bloom, 1976; Jaques, 1992).

Point 13: Effective teachers deserve to be supported by the leaders who hired them. Teachers must constantly seek opportunities to learn to learn, and the college must provide leadership and a climate that expects and supports lifelong learning (Baker & Associates, 1992).

Point 14: Effective teachers see collaborative and systematic instruction as a means of sharing power with their learners. Adult learners immediately apply in their lives and on the job what they are learning in instructional sessions. Effective teachers understand that students individually and collectively have power. The secret is to harness this influence potential for effective individual and collective learning (Yukl, 1994).

(1993), Baker and Associates (1992), Cohen and Brawer (1994), the Community College Roundtable (1994), Gillett-Karam, Roueche, and Roueche (1991), Roueche, Baker, and Rose (1989), and Vaughan (1986), among many others, have written about quality, leadership, and teaching in more than twenty-five major publications from the 1980s until today. Some community college presidents most active in the quality movement—for example, Boggs (1983), Burrill (1994), Hudgins (1990), Lingle (1994), McCabe (1991), and many others—have written about leadership and the development of quality-oriented institutions. Presidents of the American Association of Community Colleges, such as Edmund J. Gleazer, Jr., Dale Parnell, and David Pierce, have made quality and excellence the association's major agenda from the 1970s until today.

This Chapter

This chapter focuses on two key aspects of the quality movement in North America. The first is the cooperative or team approach to learning, with the instructor working with students in a classroom context. The second is faculty's employment of continuous quality concepts as they teach adults in any educational setting. The quality aspects adapt Deming's fourteen points (see Table 11.1). The paradigm in Figure 11.1 depicts these concepts. The student is bound to the instructor through instruction. Around these three central concepts lies the organization, its climate defined "as the informal day-to-day behavior, with its underlying attitudes and values that make up that aspect of the organizational life" (Baker & Associates, 1992, p. 17), the physical environment, and the external surroundings of the community. In the introduction to this chapter we have addressed the larger issues affecting teaching and student learning in community colleges. A discussion of these points provides a framework for this chapter.

The Student and Teacher Environment

The key part of our model is the relationship between the student and the teacher. In 1988, the Commission on the Future of the Community College published *Building Communities: A Vision for a New Century,* which reemphasized the relationship of the student to the college and to the teacher. It is worthy of reprinting here:

> The community college should be the nation's premier teaching institution. Quality instruction should be the hallmark of the movement.... We agree with Mortimer Adler's conclusion that "all genuine learning is active, not passive. It involves the use of the mind, not just the memory. It is a process of discovery in which the student is the main agent, not the teacher." (p. 25)

Well-run groups and a well-designed curriculum must support students with a climate of both structure and consideration. Students must enjoy their learn-

Figure 11.1
The Paradigm

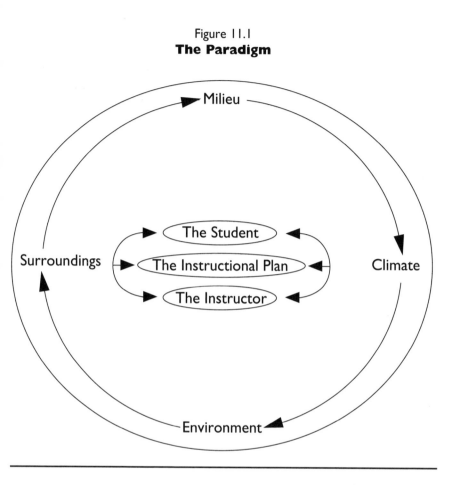

ing, be committed to their goals, and understand the basic tenets of good communication skills. Perry (1968) notes that the way we understand learning and knowledge accompanies social change. Where learners were once assumed to have a single frame of reference, learning is now assumed to be contextual and relative.

Faculties understand the importance of these interactions among group members as well as within the larger arena of resources, other professionals, and the workplace. Not only must faculty members disseminate knowledge, but they must gather information about their effectiveness in raising students' cognitive and affective skills. At the community college level, we assume that learning is directed toward adults; however, many students in their late teens are still maturing as they cope with identity crises (Erickson, 1968) and their fledgling relationships with academic authority. Knowles (1990) describes adult learning as andragogy, which promotes the productive scenario of adult-to-adult teaching/learning relationships. Accrual of team building and cooperation skills increases a sense of responsibility among all group members for cognitive gains.

Leading team and collaborative learning researchers have studied faculty interactions and the benefits of team building; these researchers include Bruffee (1993), Gamson (1994), Johnson, Johnson, and Smith (1991), and McKeachie (1978), who have based their definitions on theories of group dynamics and interaction, experiential learning, and leadership. Gamson (1994) offers the following:

> Collaborative learning is always cooperative, but takes students one step further: to a point where they must confront the issues of power and authority implicitly in any form of learning but usually ignored.... Collaborative learning always takes both the student and the professor into "enemy territory." (p. 9)

Student Team Building

Student team building toward subsequent learning is a positive method for achieving goals associated with the community college mission. Colleges are learning to measure how students reach their goals. Researchers have investigated the power of teaching and learning in small groups to promote student engagement with academic staff. Teaching and learning in groups also allows the full consideration of student expression through improved listening, persuasion, and presentation skills. Further, observations of group or team learning, reflection, and examination contribute to experiential learning (Kolb, 1984). Kolb offers three assumptions that support increased interaction of student and faculty:

- Students learn best when they are personally involved in the experience.
- Knowledge is significant for the student who chooses to learn through initiative, insight, and discovery.
- Learning occurs best when both the student and professor set and value goals.

The student is the focus of instruction and is thus at the center of learning organizations such as community colleges. It is not the organization, however, that directly changes the student in some positive way; it is the teacher. Certainly the design of the learning organization must fully support the activity that occurs between student and teacher. Team building for students challenges the model of powerful teacher versus powerless learner that is the status quo at many colleges. Schmoker and Wilson (1993) claim that the most important elements of Deming's principles for education are to build democratic atmospheres that support educational learning, to eliminate coercion, and to foster an ongoing relationship between the organization and improvement. Roueche and Baker (1987) report on a community college that reengineered itself to powerfully support and foster an environment where quality teaching could occur. Miami-Dade Community College, Florida, dedicated all support elements to the proposition that all students could succeed if they had sufficient motivation and if teachers maximized the quality of the learning environment.

Learner Characteristics

There is no doubt that the typical teacher of adults works from a set of assumptions about how students learn that fails to match the learning styles of the typical adult learner (Cross, 1981; Kiersey & Bates, 1978; and Schroeder, 1993). Adults enter college classes with varying ability and skills, and teachers intuitively know it. Research has shown that "...although an instructor may have a dominant teaching style, in those cases where his or her teaching meets generally with unsuccessful responses, the instructor can and does modify the approach almost immediately to accommodate students' needs and levels of readiness" (Baker, Roueche & Gillett-Karam, 1990, pp. 256–57). The body of research on teacher behavior is vast and ranges from personality to perceptions, to attitudes, to motivation and human response. In this section we will limit our discussion to instructor and student personality. The instructor's role is to motivate and influence the student to accept, to find satisfaction with, and to demonstrate by performance, a common path toward reaching his or her internalized goal (p. 92).

Kiersey and Bates (1978) write that nothing is more fundamental than the fact that people are different from each other; they want different things; and they have different motives, purposes, aims, values, needs, drives, impulses, and urges. Swiss psychologist Carl Jung theorized that perception and judgment form the basis of the personality. Myers and McCaulley (1985) write that these preferences affect not only *what* people attend to in any given situation, but also *how* they draw conclusions about what they perceive.

To understand the various learning styles, we study individual personality and seek to identify differences among students with different ways of behaving, deciding, and perceiving. Jung posited individual trait personality differences in 1921. Later Myers and Briggs developed the Myers-Briggs Type Indicator (MBTI) to establish individual preferences and to promote a more constructive use of the differences between people (Kroeger & Thuesen, 1988).

Just as people are born brown-eyed or blue-eyed, left- or right-handed, people are predisposed to be either Extroverted or Introverted (E or I), Sensing or iNtuitive (S or N), Thinking or Feeling (T or F), and Perceiving or Judging (P or J). Kiersey and Bates (1978) further the research by forming four typologies of temperaments. They included the Dionysian SP temperament (ISTP, ESTP, ISFP, ESFP), the Epimethean SJ temperament (ISFJ, ESFP, ISTJ, ESTJ), the Promethean NT Temperament (INTP, ENTP, INTJ, ENTJ), and the Apollonian NF temperament (INFJ, ENFJ, INFP, ENFP). (See also Chapter 6.)

Baker (1993) adapted items from the Myers-Briggs, Kiersey-Bates, and similar instruments, all of which employed forced-choice requirements, and developed an instrument that allowed the respondent to distribute ten points across a pair of items, based on their most recent experience at work. While this instrument correlates closely with Myers-Briggs (IE scale .83, SN scale .81, TF scale .83, JP scale .82), respondents enjoyed the ability to distribute points across two preferences without the requirement to choose one preference over another. Tests of validity have been remarkably similar to the Myers-Briggs instrument (Myers & McCaulley, 1985).

The Situational Temperament Sorter

Friedman (1995) conducted a study with Baker's Situational Temperament Sorter (STS) instrument to examine the correlation of the personality types of the instructors when compared with the personality types of their students. In this study, each community college faculty member who taught one or more classes during the winter quarter of 1993–94 participated in the study. A person other than the instructor administered the STS to each instructor's class, and analyzed all responses to determine relationships of personality types and satisfaction levels of the more than 700 students who participated in the study.

Friedman found that almost half of the community college students, as "concrete active" learners, preferred Extroverted and Sensing category and are identified by the ES pattern. These learners prefer action-oriented learning. More than 25 percent of the students fell within the IS pattern. They prefer concrete learning but seek a reflective learning environment. In the iNtuitive category, another 15 percent were EN students who prefer an abstract, action-oriented learning environment, and the remaining 10 percent were IN students who preferred an abstract but reflective learning environment. After surveying the instructors, Friedman (1995) found that almost half were concrete active or ES instructors, thus aligning well with the student learning styles. One fourth were abstract active (EN instructors), and a few were IS or IN, reflective or concrete/abstract. While these data suggest a good match between the student and faculty temperaments, the study demonstrates a need for more concrete active instructional strategies.

The sensing students prefer practical and immediate payoff for learning. These students often express a lack of confidence in their ability to learn and are most comfortable with concrete ideas. They do not immediately grasp complex ideas, and they express a low tolerance for ambiguity (Schroeder, 1993). The intuitives are significantly different. They are "big picture, global learners." They enjoy assignments where they can employ perceptive or imaginative new ways of thinking. These students love new concepts, ideas, and abstractions. Their learning pathway is from theory to practice. They enjoy more open-ended, less-structured instruction (Schroeder, 1993). When

Schroeder compared his findings with research synthesized at the Center for the Application of Personality Type at Gainesville, Florida, he discovered that the majority of students in higher education today are sensing types. Schroeder and his colleagues argue that instructors should be aware of student learning patterns and attempt to accommodate learning differences in their students.

When we compare Friedman's research to Schroeder's, we find that community college teachers are more like their students than university instructors are like theirs; however, community college instructors do not necessarily attempt to adapt to the different learning styles of their students.

The Active Student

It is easy to predict that the student who is strongly sensing will not do well with an intuitive instructor. Furthermore, the feeling of defeat in the IN teacher who attempts to teach the ES student is devastating. These personality differences could be a source of the burnout experienced by many teachers of adult learners.

An instructor who realizes that he or she strongly prefers intuition as a teaching style and realizes that the majority of the students prefer sensing can change to a student-active approach. Students can take a temperament-type instrument. The instructor can explain what these temperaments mean and ask students to write about how they like to learn. Employing temperament information, the instructor can form students into teams (built on unlike profiles). The instructor can assign outside projects and use case method in which students who are intuitive help students who are sensing and the reverse. Figure 11.2 shows how Sensing and iNtuitive functions can be grouped according to thinking and feeling preferences to solve problems in cooperative learning settings. From Figure 11.2, we can conclude that student groups should contain sensing and intuitive students and thinking and feeling students.

Schroeder (1993) develops several ways that intuitive teachers can help sensing students to learn, but concludes that after the third year of success, the Sensing student becomes more like the iNtuitive instructor. The instructor must first adjust to the needs of the learner by understanding how students learn and what strategies are more likely to work. Many paths to excellence are open, but the greatest task is to learn that the paths and many of our students' paths are different.

Course Design

Figure 11.1, the paradigm, conveys the idea that the student is bound to the teacher through the instructional plan. Stark, Lowther, and Smith (1986), in *Designing the Learning Plan,* present a substantive review of research and the-

Figure 11.2
Group Problem-Solving Functions

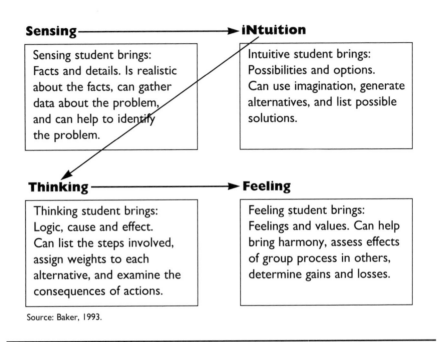

Sensing ─────────────▶ iNtuition

| Sensing student brings: Facts and details. Is realistic about the facts, can gather data about the problem, and can help to identify the problem. | Intuitive student brings: Possibilities and options. Can use imagination, generate alternatives, and list possible solutions. |

Thinking ─────────────▶ Feeling

| Thinking student brings: Logic, cause and effect. Can list the steps involved, assign weights to each alternative, and examine the consequences of actions. | Feeling student brings: Feelings and values. Can help bring harmony, assess effects of group process in others, determine gains and losses. |

Source: Baker, 1993.

ory related to college curricula. They studied different types of research in the higher education literature, such as faculty evaluation, teaching styles, and student outcome measures, and focused on the fine points of the learning plan, such as educational goals, discipline structure, learning objectives, course design, and program design. We cannot address all aspects of Stark et al.'s model within the confines of this chapter; however, we will attempt to develop aspects that relate to the chapter's major thesis. Included is Schwab's (1973) idea that there are four common elements in working with students: the learner, the teacher, the milieu, and the subject matter. Combining Schwab's idea with Stark's working definition results in the concept that the curriculum is an academic plan that includes:

1. The selection of knowledge, skills, and attitudes that are to be learned.
2. The selection of subject matter or content within which the learning experiences are embedded.
3. A design or structure intended to lead to specific outcomes for learners of various types.
4. The processes by which learning must be achieved.
5. The materials to be used in the learning process.

6. Evaluation of strategies to determine if skills, behaviors, attitudes, and knowledge change as a result of the process,

7. A feedback loop that facilitates and fosters adjustments in the plan to increase learning (Stark et al., 1986, p. 75).

Competencies, Knowledge, Skills, and Attitudes

Klemp (1982), among others, has helped the teacher of adults to view as competent those students who are able, sufficient, and capable. Yet measuring competencies is a complex and difficult task. One way is to develop a competency list for a course and program and then to have the students evaluate themselves against the list at the beginning of the course and at the end of the course.

The community college and higher education program at the University of Texas developed a list of twelve competency areas and more than sixty-four competency statements. Graduates of the program participated in a research project in which they developed a competency list and evaluated it against on-the-job activity. Three questions were possible for each competency. The first could be, "On a scale of one to five, express your perception of how competent you think you are on each competency." The second question could be, "On a scale of one to five, express where you would like to be on this competency at the end of this course." The gap between each answer provided the basis for analysis for the students in the class and could become the goals for students and instructors. These same questions were fair game for student answers during the course, and the instructor could analyze the data to determine the perceived progress for each student and for the entire cohort. This information is valuable to the instructor and the student.

At the end of the course, a third question regarding each competency was possible: "Where, on a scale of one to five, do you believe you are now that you have completed this course?" This process is akin to Angelo and Cross's (1993) Teaching Goals Inventory except that it measures student competency gains instead of teaching goals.

Long-Range Objectives

Adult learners would like to know how the content of their learning will help them achieve future success personally and in the workplace. Educators can design long-range objectives to be measured after the student is on the job or at the next level of higher education. From the discussion in the previous section, one can see how a survey instrument could determine the extent to which former students on the job are using those concepts that they learned in the academic program. An instructor might adapt a version of the competency instrument explained in the previous section to obtain specific levels of competencies actually used on the job. The instructor could compare these data to exit levels that the students described at the end of the course or program. These research data provide opportunities for the course design team to ascertain how to reengineer the program to meet student needs or how to make small changes that can enhance competency development. A sample of long-range objectives could appear as follows: Within two years after completing the course, 90 percent of the students will employ systematic decision processes, problem-solving techniques, and leadership theory in solving leadership dilemmas.

Course Terminal Objectives

Course terminal objectives are the outcomes that the course designer seeks to achieve at the conclusion of the course. They relate directly to the evaluation scheme developed for the course. Table 11.2 is an example of a set of terminal objectives visualized for leadership development. Each course developer could create a set of measurable objectives that signal to the students what products the instructor expects them to produce for the course. Alpha-numeric codes are listed at the end of each objective in Table 11.2. An instructor can use these codes in the course design and to inform students of the level of competency that he or she expects them to attain, as well as the level of supervision under which they will work. Klemp (1982) defines knowledge as a set of usable information around a specific content area and related to a specific set of competencies. He defines skills as the ability to demonstrate a set of related behaviors or to develop a set of related processes. Traits are dispositions or characteristic ways of responding to equivalent perceptions. (See the previous discussion on the use of temperament instruments to discover learner preferences.)

In the learning model presented in this chapter, we can reasonably assume that no course can successfully deal with all of the knowledge, skills, and traits necessary to move students from a degree of competence to fully competent. Teachers design instructional programs to deliver significant competency gain, but students completing any instructional program, whether two years, three years, or more, are unlikely to be ready to enter the workforce or higher learning fully equipped to employ knowledge and skills and to demonstrate the necessary traits to function as a fully effective team member. As we have stated earlier, the two basic outcomes of the instruction of adults are the learning-to-learn process and the commitment to quality performance within a team.

One way of signaling instructional intent to students and other team members is to predetermine the amount of supervision that will be expected once the adult learner is on the job. If students are working toward an entry-level job, we can assume they will receive a high level of supervision in most jobs. We certainly would expect that our entry-level workers, if working in a team arrangement, would have considerable supervision. On the other hand, professionals or managers who engage in continuing education might work with lit-

Table 11.2
Course Terminal Objectives

1. Upon completion of the course, all enrollees will be able to analyze a leadership case problem at the 90 percent mastery level or above. (D-4)

or

2. Upon completion of the course, all enrollees will be able to develop and analyze the key aspects of a leadership problem employing the model and examples that the instructor provides. (D-4)

3. Given appropriate instruction during the course and acceptable criteria, student teams will be able to successfully analyze and present findings of leadership instruments designed to evaluate leadership traits and performance. (D-4 and H-4)

4. Given appropriate instruction and an environment conducive to effective team management, each enrollee will develop the traits of cooperation to the extent that maximum development occurs for all enrollees (the instructor will provide criteria). (H-4)

5. Given appropriate instruction, each learner will be able to evaluate competency development during assigned sessions according to the criteria that the instructor provides. (D-4)

---

tle supervision or may be the supervisor. The course designer will find it helpful to conceptualize this dimension of work and account for it in the instructional plan.

Coding Levels of Objectives

Most curriculum designers follow researchers such as Bloom (1974), Krathwohl, Bloom, and Masias (1964), and Popham and Baker (1970) in developing taxonomies of educational objectives. Taxonomies are wonderful applications of the systems approach to problem solving and excellent intellectual exercises for an instructional theorist, but they provide little help to the teaching professional in instructional design. Just as the designer cannot account for all knowledge, skills, and traits necessary to develop a competent worker, neither can the instructional design account for all levels of behavioral objectives necessary for the student to accomplish a specific set of learning tasks.

Table 11.3 presents a systems-thinking method of developing objectives in a competency-based instructional design. In this model, knowledge-level objectives (Code A) represent entry-level concepts within a discipline or field of study. The objectives generally come from the content students will review in preparation for a particular unit of instruction. The instructor expects the student to recognize, recall, or identify information required to solve problems in class or in exam settings. Code B–level objectives will generally be employed in class discussions and can be based on exercises in preparation for assign-

Table 11.3

Baker's Taxonomy of Mental Skills A through D

Code/Name	Definition	Example
A. Knowledge	The individual can recognize, identify, or recall previously learned facts, dates, concepts, or principles.	Given a list of management terms, individuals can identify from memory each term.
B. Understanding	The individual can explain, summarize, detect similarities and differences, and analyze problems or situations beyond those previously learned and practiced by relating to those previously learned problems and situations.	Given basic understanding of performance criteria, individuals can examine two like criteria and determine which to employ.
C. Application of Knowledge	The individual can use previously learned knowledge to solve a familiar problem and apply a learned knowledge to a situation *already experienced.* Solutions are considered routine.	Having completed a lesson in decision making, individuals can solve a problem employing decision-making techniques of the type studied during each lesson.
D. Application of Understanding	The individual can solve new problems, create new entities, or successfully operate in unfamiliar situations.	Having completed a course in management theory, individuals can apply such theory properly on the job.

ments. Code C–level objectives require the student to solve problems, under supervision with feedback, and often in groups. Code D–level objectives require students to solve new problems or extrapolate problems that require mastery of A–, B–, and C–level objectives.

Affective Outcomes

We know that attitudes, values, and traits are important to the development of learners. Table 11.4 presents a paradigm for the development of affective skills. If the goal of instruction is to help the student learn to learn (apply D-level objectives on the job and in higher learning) and to become independent, course and program designers must also account for the affective development of learners. The codes E through H are based on Krathwohl, Bloom, and Masias (1964) affective taxonomy of educational objectives. They also employ Hersey and Blanchard's (1982) and Baker, Roueche, and Gillett-Karam's (1990) idea that teachers employ behaviors to match the students' readiness to learn. Early in a new instructional experience, teachers direct student learning. As students mature, they coach or support the learner, and when students display readiness for assuming more responsibility, teachers delegate more responsibility and allow students singly and in groups to implement problem solving at high levels of cognition. None of these tools is a panacea. No universal remedies are available for designing instruction to meet all of the needs of the adult learner. Faculty should seek to build quality into their courses so that they can increase their effectiveness with their students.

From Objectives to Evaluation

Perhaps a greater challenge for the quality course developer is measuring the attainment of course objectives. We have discussed the measurement of adult student competency attainment in a previous section of this chapter. Two evaluation processes follow. They provide criteria for the evaluation of the student's writing and evaluative criteria for teamwork. These forms are condensed for simplicity.

The Written Requirement Evaluation in Figure 11.3 contains six selected criteria, each with a ten-point Likert scale. This form, supplementing comments on written work, provides the adult learners with feedback on the quality of their writing. In using this technique, midterm grades have averaged, out of a possible score of 100, 86.2, and by the end of the course the final exam averages have been 93.7, a gain of 7.5 points. When the instructor requires three or four written assignments, the gain from the first assignment to the fourth is 11.3 points. Clearly, the more often students have an opportunity to write and receive timely and accurate feedback, the more competency they gain as measured against these specific objectives (Baker, 1993).

Table 11.4
Baker's Taxonomy of Affective Skills E through H

Code/Name	Definition	Example
E. Acceptance of Direction	Individuals respond to requirements placed upon them so they can achieve a favorable reaction. The behavior is adapted to gain a specific reward or to avoid punishment.	Individuals study assigned work out of fear of punishment for not completing it.
F. Acceptance of Values	Individuals believe the values or behaviors of an instructor or leader are similar to their own. This similarity reinforces the individual's attitudes toward the outside influence.	Individuals consistently perform well within their group because they want to live up to the standards of excellence and professionalism.
G. Commitment to Values	Individuals adopt the values and behaviors of an instructor or leader as their own. There is a real motivation to act out the behavior and values of the instructor or leader.	Individuals help team members study for promotion because they enjoy contributing to the success of the group. Individuals organize their values into a priority system, placing loyalty to the organizational team higher than personal ambition.
H. Characterized by Values	Individuals consistently demonstrate the values and behaviors desired by the instructor or leader to such an extent that they become an example for others to follow.	Individuals, over time, consistently exhibit the trait of cooperation so much so that they can be depended upon to be "team players."

Figure 11.3
Written Requirement Evaluation

Name: _____

Requirement: _____

Topic: _____

Criteria:	High									Low
1. Identifiable Outcomes Stated	10	9	8	7	6	5	4	3	2	1
2. Evidence of Creative Thinking	10	9	8	7	6	5	4	3	2	1
3. Accuracy of Information	10	9	8	7	6	5	4	3	2	1
4. Power of Description	10	9	8	7	6	5	4	3	2	1
5. Quality of Analysis	10	9	8	7	6	5	4	3	2	1
6. Quality of Insights	10	9	8	7	6	5	4	3	2	1

(Additional criteria may be developed as needed.)

Group Performance

A similar criteria sheet (not shown here) relates to the evaluation of group performance. Such a form again could contain several criteria, each with a scale from a high of 10 points to a low of 1 point. The course designer could modify this set of criteria based on the type of tasks assigned to the group. When groups work to complete tasks, the instructor should often allow the group to work under his or her supervision before assigning a task for completion outside class. Invariably, some students will commit greater effort to the group effort, while others will not contribute as much. Introverts will need to be drawn in, and extroverts will need to be patient and allow the group process to work. Assigning a team leader or allowing the team to select a leader frequently works well. In any case, the role of the team leader will vary as will the team's acceptance of the leader.

When the instructor is not present to evaluate the team's effort, the team can usually use a Peer Review Process. Table 11.5 is a truncated example of a peer review process. Note in the example provided that students will typically

Table 11.5
Peer Review Process

Directions: In the space provided below, please list the members of your team. DO NOT include yourself.

Team Members	Intellectual Ability	Personal Responsibility	Decisiveness	Energy	Leadership	Ability to Support Others	TOTAL/MEAN	RANK
B. Cashbell	8	9	9	10	10	10	56/9.3	1
D. Kildeer	9	8	9	10	9	9	54/9.0	2
S. Marson	7	9	8	10	9	8	51/8.5	3

Scoring Instructions:

Assign to each individual a score between one (1) [low] and ten (10) [high] based on the team members' contributions to group activities and presentations during the course. Total the scores assigned and divide by six (categories) to obtain a mean score for each team member. Finally, rank order each team member based on the mean score assigned. Fold your evaluation and return to the professor. These evaluations are private between the professor and you and will be used to develop a participation grade for the course.

give each other high marks. Students also will not generally downgrade peers who have not contributed. The course designer may need to weight the advantages of a forced distribution (see rank column) against the possibility that all students contributed equally to the success of the project. The course designer should consider carefully to what extent peer evaluations will count in the evaluation of each student.

Methods of Instruction

Appendix I presents eleven methods (A–K) by which instructors may work with students to help them learn to learn and to move toward independence. Brookfield (1986) offers six principles that he and others believe foster successful selection of instructional strategies.

Brookfield (1986) believes that, first, learning cannot be demanded; it must be voluntary. Instructors cannot assume that adults possess the motivation to learn what the instructor has to offer. Second, some methods of instruction increase motivation to learn. Others send a message that the desire to teach exceeds the teacher's desire to instill learning. Third, all adults must sense that they are worthy, valued, and deserving of respect. The instructor does not have to agree with every idea or attitude, but he or she should only challenge students within a climate of respect. Fourth, instructors must choose methods of instruction that convey to learners that the instructor is a collaborator in the learning process and is not the power broker. Fifth, the instructor should employ strategies that quickly involve the student in learning and provide quick and frequent feedback on performance. And sixth, effective instructors realize that learning is a loop—a continuous process of activity, reflection, analysis, and renewed activity.

Effective learning strategies inspire individuals to think reflectively about their own experiences and to envision what their new experience will be. Finally, effective learning strategies encourage adults to become more self-directed. When faculty envision a course of instruction as experiences that adults "go through" to gain competency, and advance in their commitment to excel in new experiences, or to improve performance in existing experiences, they will choose methods of instruction that embody these principles.

Appendix I also includes a grading scale on the extent to which each method enhances the self-directed goal. It is interesting to note that the most often used strategy, lecture method, has the weakest evaluation. These writers believe that the lecture, strategically placed and not exceeding twenty minutes, is an excellent way of illuminating the theory of text assignments. The effective instructor quickly moves to methods where students are active. If the desire is to help concrete (sensing students) to become more abstract in their thinking, the lecture can unfreeze the concrete and help the student be more reflective but generally cannot increase skills where the student must be an active partner in the process.

The Management Team

Management teams work with the instructor to set the topics each group will be responsible for preparing. The student teams must then brainstorm questions they have about the topic, plan its coverage, develop strategies for each group member's work, research a variety of sources, and put together a presentation to the whole class (Ventimiglia, 1994). The instructor engages the students in discussions, helps to facilitate their presentations, and notes points of interest from the presentations that might come up in subsequent essays, papers, or exams. By bringing the discussion of the whole class to closure on these points, the students agree on the information accepted and the course content that they are responsible for knowing.

The management team in charge of that week's instruction makes a presentation. Following its efforts, the other students in the class provide feedback to the team. The team will analyze those data, employing continuous quality improvement techniques. The following week, the team leader reports to the class on the likes, dislikes, and recommendations for improvement. The instructor grades the presentation on specific criteria and can then use these data to improve the next class and to revise the course at the end of instruction. Examples of the criteria may include how they have linked their presentation with previous studies; whether they have a clear rationale, theory, observations, and point of view; if they used time effectively and focused on their topic; and how they use technology. The management team learns how to better manage future assignments, and the management teams for subsequent weeks receive timely feedback for their upcoming efforts.

Putting It All Together

Appendix II is an example of a unit in a course that employs the principles of cooperative learning and quality initiatives. We will summarize this chapter by reviewing the components that have served to guide its development. The first unit serves as an introduction to the course. Students will have attended two previous sessions, however. In the first session, students will have completed the Situational Temperament Sorter (STS). They will know their four-letter profile as it has emerged from the previously mentioned E/I, S/N, T/F, and J/P. They will know their leadership style from the Kiersey-Bates (1978) research as SJ, SP, NF, or NT. From the results of this instrument, they will know how they best learn and how the instructor plans to teach. They will have formed groups where they must solve problems and make decisions with people who learn differently, process information differently, and see the world from a different perspective. They will struggle to solve problems in this context, often feeling frustrated, but all the while learning the power of the team to accomplish tasks through team learning that are quite impossible for the individual working alone.

In the first two weeks, the student will have completed a competency assessment instrument and will have assessed current competency levels and set goals for the end of the course. The instructor will have led a group discussion of the content of the course and the course terminal objectives and will have covered in detail the evaluation instruments, the grading procedures, the timelines, and the expectations for each adult learner. This discussion centers on the environment, the instructor's and the adult student's role, and the course of instruction for improving the student's knowledge, skills, and traits toward applying these competencies on the job. The course rationale, how the course is validated, the learning objectives, and learning activities are explained in detail with the expectation that students can see a pathway to their goals by forming a partnership with the instructor and other adult learner students, employing the course as a vehicle to move ahead with self-development.

The unit objectives in Appendix II also involve the sequential enhancement of knowledge (A and B levels), the sequential development of skills (C and D levels), and the development of affective traits (F through I) (shown in Tables 11.3 and 11.4).

In the sample, the instructor will combine a guided discussion method, which is a self-instructional method (completion of the STS), and the completion of the competency instrument, also a self-instructional method (see Appendix I). By the end of the course, the instructor will have employed all eleven methods of instruction and will have increased student and student team activities as the course progresses. The instructor will have facilitated textbooks, the package of course methods, case studies, simulations, films, role playing, tutoring, team building, and quality initiatives to achieve the course objectives. The instructor and students can employ computer technology for classroom research, and instructors will have encouraged the students to gather data on class activities as they evolve, create quality processes, produce matrices or process maps (of the learning cycle, for example), and combine concepts in illustrative ways for group presentations. Any of these tools generate, store, replicate, transform, and transmit electronic impulses in ways that humans can read and reproduce aspects of mental processes and reality. (Copies of the instructional plan discussed in this chapter are available from the writers.)

Summary

This chapter has attempted to convey a model of effective teaching and student learning that employs concepts of collaborative learning and quality principles. We have explored the environment (the organization designed to support teacher and student collaboration), the instructor (the leader of the collaboration, who provides influence when and where the students need it [Hersey & Blanchard, 1982]), and the adult student (who seeks competency development for achievement motivation, but gains better interpersonal skills and learns how to use influence to accomplish problem-solving and decision-making tasks). The instructional plan should include carefully designed specifications of knowledge, skills, and attitudes that students should learn; the selection of subject matter needed to improve the student's competencies; a structure of activities from simple to complex, from teacher centered to learner centered; and the processes and materials necessary to motivate and excite the learner. We have discussed evaluation strategies designed to provide both "just in time" and summative feedback to students and student teams and a feedback loop necessary to improve the succeeding units and the ultimate course improvements.

The writers of this chapter are aware that the concepts and models described herein do not constitute all of the variables necessary to produce effective collaborative learning in college and that instructional plans designed for mature adult learners will not always work for less mature learners. One cannot improve everything at once, however, nor does one necessarily need to discard strategies that have worked in the past. By employing team concepts and continuous quality improvement principles, we have presented a paradigm that can improve current practice in preparing adults for future roles. We are excited about the many teachers of adults who will adopt the ideas presented in this chapter and will constantly revise their courses to accommodate their learners. We also are excited about the possibility of veteran instructors who may make changes as appropriate or whose current approaches are reconfirmed. We also hope that leaders in the instructional area will read this chapter and apply these ideas in the development of new faculty and in influencing program leaders to plan programs from a team perspective and with the strong emphasis on appropriate quality tools.

Appendix I
Methods of Instruction

During the course, the following methods of instruction will be employed:

A. LECTURE METHOD
    Rating: C- *

Excellent means of conveying what students have already read. Should be short and sweet.

Definition: A lecture is a discourse of events, facts, concepts, principles, or explanations for instructional purposes presented by an instructor before a class or an audience.

B. DEMONSTRATION METHOD
    Rating: B-

One of the steps in the learning process is to have learners understand the actions necessary for them to perform the tasks themselves.

Definition: An accurate portrayal of the precise actions necessary to perform skills or processes. An instructor, by performing an operation, shows a student what is to be accomplished.

C. PERFORMANCE METHOD
Rating: A-

Here the student is able to apply learning and gain skills necessary to master the interface with technology.

Definition: The student practices, performs, and applies, under controlled conditions and close supervision, the skills or knowledges that have been previously explained and demonstrated. The student learns the desired behavior through "hands-on" experience.

D. GUIDED DISCUSSION METHOD
Rating: B

A form of team instruction often best performed by students in small groups who have been provided discussion guide sheets.

Definition: Interaction between students and/or an instructor in order to analyze, explore, and/or debate an issue, topic, or problem and achieve a stated objective.

E. CONFERENCE GROUP METHOD
Rating: A-

Excellent for adult learners who have gained in competence and commitment and who are at advanced stages of course or program completion.

Definition: The act of consulting together formally; an appointed meeting for discussing some topic or business; a pool of experiences and opinions among a group of people who are capable of analyzing the problem from information provided by the conference leader.

F. SELF-INSTRUCTIONAL METHOD
Rating: A

Self-instructional methods are exceptional for learning tasks requiring drill and practice. If the computer is employed, it is an exacting teacher that never forgets to provide timely feedback and cues to improved problem-solving strategies.

Definition: Self-instruction is a student-centered process of instruction. Instructional materials are prepared specifically to employ programming techniques.

Appendix I (continued)

Classical programmed instruction variables include small steps, carefully sequenced and cued to reduce errors; immediate feedback; and freedom on the part of the student to vary the normal rate of learning.

G. ROLE-PLAYING METHOD
Rating: A

Role plays can simulate team requirements demanded on the job. Not only is knowledge brought to bear, but skills can be enhanced. The most powerful aspect of the role-playing method is in the development of traits necessary to work in a team.

Definition: An improvisational acting out of parts in a job or instructional situation.

H. CASE SITUATION METHOD
Rating: A+

Case analysis is a powerful tool for the effective instructor. Cases taken from the workplace can teach adults to avoid the mistakes of others. A skillful instructor can exercise all levels of learning, both cognitive and affective, in the same context.

Definition: Students attempt to solve real or hypothetical problem situations by applying sound principles developed through analytical thinking based on the presentation of a written case or an appropriate film.

I. SIMULATION
Rating: A+

Simulations in their richest applications allow students individually or in teams to work with technology in problem-solving techniques. Often the simulation can become a part of a case situation.

Definition: Representation of some aspects of reality (either a process, event, or hardware) by symbols or devices that can be manipulated more readily than their actual counterparts. (See also Performance Method.)

J. FIELD TRIP METHOD
Rating: A

Field trips are excellent strategies for use by the effective instructor. Field trips where "hands-on" opportunities exist or where simulations are a part of the process are even more powerful learning devices.

Definition: A planned learning experience in which students observe actual operations that illustrate the classroom area of study.

K.   TUTORING
Rating: A

A tutor can enhance adult learning by creating a one-on-one opportunity to allow the adult learner to practice skills where he or she is weak. Other students who have successfully mastered the course or a learning center specialist who can help the student use self-paced or other material is also a form of tutoring.

Definition: A method of direct, one-to-one instructor-student relationships.

———

*Ratings are based on the writer's estimate of the effectiveness of these strategies when employing the collaborative/team-building model present in this chapter.

Appendix II
Sample Unit from an Existing Course
Unit I
Introduction to Strategic Issues in the Community College

Instructor: Dr. George A. Baker

Rationale: Graduate students enrolled in this course are expected to seek careers in organizations somewhere in the world. These organizations may be for profit or not for profit. They may produce products or offer services. They may be formal or informal, permanent or ad hoc. They may be in the United States or in other places in the world. This course seeks to help you develop the conceptual, interpersonal, and communication skills that are needed for effective management in organizations. The development of individual and team competencies is stressed throughout this course.

Some organizations are designed to enhance human resource development. North Carolina State University is a land-grant institution designed to develop human capital, create new learning, and serve other organizations in the public and private sector. A key learning task is to clearly understand why you are taking this course, what you expect to gain from it, how it will be conducted, and what is expected of you in this course.

Objectives:

1. Explain the link between the competencies, methods of instruction, and long- and short-range objectives of the course. (B)

2. Describe the case study method of instruction and why it is deemed appropriate for graduate students who seek to be managers in organizations. (B)

3. Outline and discuss the major responsibilities of the instructor, the guest instructor, the seminar member, and the management team as they relate to this graduate-level course. (B)

4. Define and explain each of the six learning principles upon which this course of instruction was developed. (B)

5. Explain the two-level learning model described in the syllabus and describe how this learning model will be central to your mastery of this course. (B)

Appendix II (continued)

Roles Enhanced: Visionary, task giver, motivator, disseminator, entrepreneur, negotiator.

Methods of Instruction:

- Lecture
- Guided discussion
- Case situation method

Resources: Syllabus 696U
The Case Study Method: Concepts and Synthesis
Baker, G. A. III (Ed.) (1994). *A Handbook on the Community College in America.* Westport, CT: Greenwood Press, preface, pp. xi–xxiii.

Concepts and Synthesis:

- Graduate education
- Instructional systems
- Case study method of instruction
- Competency-based education
- These concepts are taken from assigned readings:
    Historical Development of the Community College
    Mission and Functions of the Community College
    Curriculum and Instruction in the Community College
    Leading and Managing the Community College
    Resource Development in the Community College
    Human Resource Management in the Community College
    Student Development in the Community College
    External Forces in the Community College
    The Future of the Community College

References

Angelo, T., and Cross, P. *Classroom Assessment Techniques: A Handbook for College Teachers.* San Francisco: Jossey-Bass, 1993.

Baker, G.A., III. Unpublished research report of the National Initiative for Leadership and Institutional Effectiveness. North Carolina State University, Raleigh, N.C., 1993.

Baker, G.A., III, and Associates. *Cultural Leadership: Inside America's Community Colleges.* Washington, D.C.: The Community College Press, 1992.

Baker, G.A., and Reed, L. (1994). "Creating a World Class Workforce." *Community College Journal,* 1994, *64* (5), 31–35.

Baker, G.A., Roueche, J.E., and Gillett-Karam, R. *Teaching as Leading: Profiles of Excellence in the Open-Door College.* Washington, D.C.: The Community College Press, 1990.

Bloom, B.S. *Taxonomy of Educational Objectives.* New York: David McKay Co., 1974.

Bloom, B.S. *Human Characteristics and Student Learning.* New York: McGraw Hill, 1976.

Boggs, G.R. "Faculty Evaluation." *Community College Review,* 1983, *11* (2), 34–41.

Brookfield, S.D. *Understanding and Facilitating Adult Learning.* San Francisco: Jossey-Bass, 1986.

Bruffee, K.A. *Collaborative Learning: Higher Education, Interdependence, and the Authority of Knowledge.* Baltimore: The Johns Hopkins University Press, 1993.

Burrill, D. "Institutional Effectiveness as a Leadership and Management Process." In G.A. Baker (Ed.), *A Handbook on the Community College in America.* Westport, Conn.: Greenwood Press, 1994.

Cohen, A.M., and Brawer, F.B. *Managing Community Colleges.* San Francisco: Jossey-Bass, 1994.

Commission on the Future of the Community College. *Building Communities: A Vision for a New Century: A Report of the Commission on the Future of Community Colleges.* Washington, D.C.: The American Association of Community Colleges, 1988.

Community College Roundtable. *Community Colleges: Core Indicators of Effectiveness.* Washington, D.C.: American Association of Community Colleges, 1994.

Covey, S.R. *The 7 Habits of Highly Effective People.* New York: Simon and Schuster, 1989.

Crosley, P.B. *The Eternally Successful Organization: The Art of Corporate Wellness.* New York: McGraw Hill, 1988.

Cross, K.P. *Adults as Learners: Increasing Participation and Facilitating Learning.* San Francisco: Jossey-Bass, 1981.

Cross, K.P. *Involvement in Teaching.* Speech, North Carolina State University Forum Series, Raleigh, N.C., September 1993.

Deming, W.E. *Out of the Crisis.* Cambridge, Mass.: Massachusetts Institute of Technology, 1986.

Drucker, P.F. "The Age of Social Transformation." *The Atlantic Monthly.* November 1994, 53–80.

Erickson, E.H. *Identity: Youth and Crisis.* New York: Norton, 1968.

Friedman, D. "An Analysis of the Relationship Between Instructors' and Students' Personality Types to Evaluations of Course Satisfaction." Dissertation in progress. North Carolina State University, 1995.

Gamson, Z.F. "Setting the Stage: Collaborative Learning Comes of Age." In S. Kadel and J.A. Keehner (Eds.), *Collaborative Learning: A Sourcebook for Higher Education, Vol. II.* University Park, Penn.: National Center on Postsecondary Teaching, Learning, and Assessment, 1994.

Gardner, J.W. *Leaders and Followers.* New York: Free Press, 1990.

Gillett-Karam, R., Roueche, S.D., and Roueche, J.E. *Underrepresentation and the Question of Diversity: Women and Minorities in the Community College.* Washington, D.C.: The Community College Press, 1991.

Hersey, P., and Blanchard, K. *Management of Organizational Behavior.* Englewood Cliffs, N.J.: Prentice-Hall, 1982.

Hudgins, J. L. Institutional Effectiveness: Mastering the Process Before It Masters You. (ERIC Document Reproduction Service No. ED 322 981.) Columbia, S.C.: Midlands Technical College, 1990.

Jaques, D. *Learning in Groups.* Houston, Tex.: Gulf Publishing Company, 1992.

Johnson, D.W., Johnson, R.T., and Smith, K.A. Cooperative Learning: Increasing College Faculty Instructional Productivity. Washington, D.C.: ERIC Clearinghouse of Higher Education, 1991.

Juran, J.M. *Juran on Quality by Design.* New York: The Free Press, 1992.

Kadel, S., and Keehner, J.A. (Eds.). *Collaborative Learning: A Sourcebook for Higher Education.* University Park, Penn.: National Center on Postsecondary Teaching, Learning, and Assessment, 1994.

Kiersey, D., and Bates, M. *Please Understand Me.* Del Mar, Calif.: Prometheus, 1978.

Klemp, G.O. "Assessing Student Potential: An Immodest Proposal." In C. Taylor (Ed.), *New Directions for Experiential Learning: Diverse Student Preparation: Benefits and Issues.* San Francisco: Jossey-Bass, 1982.

Knowles, M.S. *Handbook of Adult Education in the United States.* Chicago: Adult Education Association of the U.S.A., 1990.

Kolb, D.A. *Experiential Learning.* Englewood Cliffs, N.J.: Prentice-Hall, 1984.

Krathwohl, D.R., Bloom, B.S., and Masias, B.B. *Taxonomy of Educational Objectives. The Classification of Educational Goals Handbook II: Affective Domain.* New York: David McKay, 1964.

Kroeger, O., and Thuesen, J.M. *Type Talk.* New York: Delacorte Press, 1988.

Lingle, R. "Economic Development: A Powerful Tool for Building Business, Industry, and Political Support for the Community College." Presentation to Strategic Issues in the Community College. EAC 696U, North Carolina State University, 1994.

McCabe, R. *The Miami-Dade Community College's Teaching/Learning Summary Report.* Summary Report (Year 4), 1989–90. Miami, Fla., 1991.

McKeachie, W.J. *Teaching Tips: A Guidebook for the Beginning College Teacher* (7th ed.). New York: Heath, 1978.

211

Myers, I.B., and McCaulley, M.H. *A Guide to the Development and Use of The Myers-Briggs Type Indicator.* Palo Alto, Calif.: Consulting Psychologists Press, 1985.

Ouchi, W. *Theory Z.* Reading, Mass.: Addison Wesley, 1981.

Paul, R. *Critical Thinking: What Every Person Needs to Survive in a Rapidly Changing World.* Santa Rosa, Calif.: Foundation for Critical Thinking, 1992.

Perry, W.G. *Forms of Intellectual and Ethical Development in the College Years: A Scheme.* New York: Holt, 1968.

Peters, T.J., and Waterman, R.H. *In Search of Excellence.* New York: Warner Books, 1982.

Popham, W.J., and Baker, E.L. *Establishing Instructional Goals.* Englewood Cliffs, N.J.: Prentice-Hall, 1970.

Reich, R. *The Work of Nations.* New York: Vintage Books, 1992.

Roueche, J.E., and Baker, G.A. *Access & Excellence: The Open Door College.* Washington, D.C.: The Community College Press, 1987.

Roueche, J.E., Baker, G.A., III, and Rose, R.R. *Shared Vision: Transformational Leadership in American Community Colleges.* Washington, D.C.: The Community College Press, 1989.

Schmoker, M.J., and Wilson, R.B. *Total Quality Education: Profiles of Schools that Demonstrate the Power of Deming's Management Principles.* Bloomington, Ind.: Phi Delta Kappa Educational Foundation, 1993.

Schroeder, C.C. "New Students—New Learning Styles." *Change*, October 1993, 21–26.

Schwab, J.J. "The Practical 3: Translation into Curriculum." *School Review*, 1973, *81* (4), 501–522.

Senge, P. *The Fifth Discipline: The Art and Practice of the Learning Organization.* New York: Doubleday, 1990.

Slavin, R.E. *Student Team Learning: An Overview and Practical Guide.* Washington, D.C.: National Education Association, 1988.

Stark, J.S., Lowther, M.A., and Smith, S. *Designing the Learning Plan: A Review of Research and Theory Related to College Curricula.* Ann Arbor, Mich.: The University of Michigan, 1986.

Vaughan, G. *The Community College Presidency.* New York: American Council on Education/Macmillan, 1986.

Ventimiglia, L.M. "Cooperative Learning at the College Level." *Thought & Action*, 1994, *9* (2), 5–30.

Yukl, G. *Leadership in Organizations.* Englewood Cliffs, N.J.: Prentice-Hall, 1994.

ABOUT THE AUTHORS

Sandra Acebo is in her sixth year as vice president for instruction at DeAnza College, California. A graduate of the Community College Leadership Program at the University of Texas, she has been a faculty member in Language Arts, a courseware developer for interactive media instruction, and a starting member of the basketball team in her Virginia high school.

George Baker was named to the Joseph D. Moore Endowed Chair in Community College Leadership at North Carolina State University in 1992. Previously, he served since 1978 as professor of higher and community college education at the University of Texas at Austin. Baker received the 1994 American Association of Community Colleges Leadership Award and the 1993 Distinguished Service Award from the Council of Universities and Colleges of the AACC. He is the editor of *A Handbook on the Community College in America*, published in 1994, and the author of *Cultural Leadership: Inside America's Community Colleges*, published in 1992.

George Boggs is superintendent/president of Palomar College in San Marcos, California. Under his leadership, Palomar College has grown from 15,500 students in 1985 to 24,000 students now served on the San Marcos campus and at nine educational centers throughout the district. Boggs has served on the boards of directors of the California Association of Community Colleges, the Community College League of California, and the American Association of Community Colleges, serving as board chair in 1993–94.

Helen Burnstad is serving her seventh year as director of staff development at Johnson County Community College in Overland Park, Kansas, and is a past president of the National Council for Staff, Program, and Organizational Development. She earned an Ed.D. in higher education administration from the University of Arkansas at Fayetteville. In addition to her roles as adjunct instructor in speech communication, consultant, and trainer, she is a coauthor of a monograph for new practitioners of staff development.

213

Kathleen Burson is division dean of child development and education, a member of the California Community Colleges Chancellor's Advisory Committee on Child Development, and a member of at least fifteen other teams.

Marguerite Culp is dean of student services at Seminole Community College, Florida. Coauthor of spring 1995 Jossey-Bass release *In the Service of Student Success: Student Affairs in the Community College,* Culp currently serves as chair of Commission XI (Student Development in the Two-Year College) of the American College Personnel Association.

Ann Doty is a research assistant in the Department of Adult and Community College Education at North Carolina State University and is director of research for the National Initiative for Leadership and Institutional Effectiveness (NILIE). Doty is currently conducting her dissertation research on the presidential selection process in community colleges and received a Joseph D. Moore Fellowship Award. She earned her master's degree in higher and adult continuing education at the University of Michigan and was a member of the institutional research and grants office at Schoolcraft College, Livonia, Michigan.

Amy Fugate is in her ninth year as an instructor in speech communication and is director of the debate and forensics program at Johnson County Community College. She holds a master's degree in communication studies from the University of Michigan and is currently a doctoral candidate in higher education at the University of Kansas.

Rosemary Gillett-Karam is an associate professor of community college leadership at North Carolina State University. She is coauthoring, with Carolyn Desjardins and Barbara Keener, *Women in the Community College: Theory and Practice,* and is working with Robin Spaid on *Environmental Equity.* Gillett-Karam is past director of the Fellows Program, ACCLAIM, which brought two cohorts of students from Maryland, North Carolina, South Carolina, and Virginia to pursue the doctoral degree at NCSU in community college leadership and community-based programming.

Cyril "Cy" Gulassa, an English instructor from DeAnza College, has been president of the Foothill-De Anza faculty association for 14 years. Gulassa was co-founder of both the California Community Colleges Independents (CCCI) and the Bay Faculty Association. Past president of the Faculty Association of California Community Colleges, he currently serves on the association's board of directors.

Constance Haire is the director of resource and community development at Southwestern Community College, North Carolina. She is responsible for college resource development, institutional research and planning, grant writing, and local fund raising with the college foundation. Because training is an important component in the quality improvement efforts at Southwestern, she coordinates professional development and continuous-improvement activities at the college. An experienced facilitator, trainer, and coordinator, she is one of three members of the leadership team for the statewide community college quality implementation program, the Carolina Quality Consortium, and coordinator for a regional three-college collaborative consortium. She is currently a doctoral student in the Adult and Community College Education Leadership Program at North Carolina State University.

Jeff Hockaday is the chancellor of Pima County Community College District (PCCD), Arizona, a five-campus community college serving 30,000 credit students. Before accepting the PCC position in 1990, Hockaday was chancellor of the State of Virginia Community College System, and earlier, a community college president and a school system superintendent.

Sharon Miller is a graduate of the Center for the Study of Higher Education at the University of Arizona. She has taught classes from Head Start to the university level and from Virginia to California, including her most memorable experience on the Navajo, Hopi, and Supai reservations. The Supai people, who reside at the bottom of the Grand Canyon, had the opportunity to attend college class through her efforts.

Lester Reed has more than 40 years' professional experience leading and managing complex organizations. Out of this experience, he has evolved a philosophy of leadership and management that balances participation and control. In the last 15 years, he has refined his leadership approach based on the needs of community colleges as senior vice president of Midlands Technical College, South Carolina, and at Oregon State University, where he serves as the associate director of the Western Center for Community College Development.

Barry Russell assumed the presidency at Southwestern Community College, North Carolina, on May 1, 1991. Russell is active in state and community organizations and currently serves on the executive committee of the North Carolina Community Colleges Presidents' Association, the board of the North Carolina Association of Colleges and Universities, the Jackson County Economic Development Commission, and on the local hospital and bank boards. He regularly serves on accreditation teams for the Southern Association of Colleges and Schools. He earned his baccalaureate, master's, and doctoral degrees from Clemson University.

Philip Silvers is senior assistant to the chancellor for research and planning at Pima County Community College District. Before his career as a university and community college administrator, Silvers was an executive management consultant in Washington, D.C., and San Francisco.

Chris Storer teaches philosophy and critical thinking at DeAnza College part-time. He is the executive secretary of the academic senate, editor of the senate newsletter, and a representative to the executive council of the faculty association. He earned his master of arts degree in philosophy at the University of Florida, taught philosophy full-time at Santa Fe Community College, Florida, and has worked as a consultant to industry in problem-solving effectiveness.

Vaughn Upshaw is a research assistant in the Department of Adult and Community College Education at North Carolina State University. Her area of interest is developing effective governance in health-care organizations. She was the executive director of the Association of North Carolina Boards of Health from 1986 to 1993, which serves more than 1,100 local health board members. The National Association of Local Boards of Health awarded Upshaw the first President's Award for her work on behalf of local health boards.